A FRENCH

REFERENCE

GRAMMAR

A FRENCH
REFERENCE
GRAMMAR

BY

H. FERRAR

HEAD OF MODERN LANGUAGES
RADLEY COLLEGE

SECOND EDITION

OXFORD UNIVERSITY PRESS

Oxford University Press, Walton Street, Oxford OX2 6DP

Oxford New York Toronto
Delhi Bombay Calcutta Madras Karachi
Petaling Jaya Singapore Hong Kong Tokyo
Nairobi Dar es Salaam Cape Town
Melbourne Auckland

and associated companies in
Beirut Berlin Ibadan Nicosia

Oxford is a trademark of Oxford University Press

First Edition 1955
Second Edition 1967
Reprinted (with corrections) 1970, 1973, 1974, 1975,
1976, 1978, 1980, 1981, 1982, 1983, 1984, 1985,
1988

Printed in Hong Kong

PREFACE TO
SECOND EDITION

The first edition of the REFERENCE GRAMMAR set out to provide, on a fairly comprehensive scale, all that could reasonably be required for O Level. It was found in practice that it was only in a comparatively small number of points that it failed to cover the ground for A Level as well. The Grammar has in fact been fairly widely used by students at this level and, in some cases, as a handbook at university subsidiary level.

The existence of this rather wider public indicated a duty to make up the deficiency in scope and at the same time to get rid of most of the obscurities and errors of the first edition. The present edition endeavours to do both of these. Additional material has been incorporated without, fortunately, changing the Section numbers, with which many users have become familiar, and a number of emendations have been made to the original text. Many of these are the result of very helpful suggestions received from a variety of sources, and their use is gratefully acknowledged.

It was also felt that the time had come to produce a new set of Exercises. These have been provided and are to be found at the end of the Grammar.

H.F.

WORCESTER
1967

3

PREFACE

This Grammar was called into existence to meet the need for a genuine Reference Grammar to which both pupil and teacher can refer with some confidence that they will find the information required. Such a Grammar is particularly in demand where Courses have been laid aside or completed.

At the front of the book is a very comprehensive index, in which the headings consist not only of grammatical terms but also of the principal French and English words involved. A special feature of this index is that, wherever applicable, the entry is clarified by a miniature example to assist the pupil in finding the right reference. The system is further explained in the note which precedes the index.

No great originality is claimed for the actual exposition of the Grammar. It remains strictly grammatical; and the kind of simplifications which involve some suppression of the truth have either been rejected or have been frankly admitted as such. However, every effort has been made to present matters sensibly and without fuss, and to ensure that the numerous problems that trouble the pupil, even if they do not trouble the grammarian, are not left unanswered.

Rather over half the examples in the Grammar are taken from modern French authors, though the shorter and simpler of these have been left unacknowledged.

The Grammar could be taken into use after a two-year introductory Course, and would suffice for at least the next three years of French. Its scope is approximately that required for the Ordinary Level of the G.C.E., but when in doubt more rather than less has been included. In particular no claim is made that this is the 'irreducible minimum'. Nor is it a graded Course; the teacher may select and expand, as desired.

An exercise section is available, which it is hoped will give some assistance in applying the more important points of grammar, in a creative way, to the writing of French.

This book owes an especial debt to Professor Johnston of

St. Andrews University, who took an active part in the inception of the work, and whose advice and help have been most generously available to the author at every stage, including the detailed revision of the manuscript.

Thanks are also due to M. Hibon of the Maison Française in Oxford, who kindly checked the vocabulary and syntax of the manuscript, and whose helpful emendations have been incorporated.

H.F.

WORCESTER
1954

CONTENTS

CONTENTS

THE INDEX

This Index is specially designed to make it possible to find one's way to the particular piece of information required.

There are three kinds of entry, which show:

1. Where to find various grammatical points, e.g. demonstratives, personal pronouns, agreement of participles.

2. Where to find the various uses of the main French words involved, e.g. *ce, celui, dont, il, on, quoi*.

3. Where to find information about how to deal with difficult English words, such as *it, should, some, what, &c.*

In addition, wherever appropriate, a small example is given with the entry, to assist in deciding which is the particular use or meaning required.

For instance, under *that*, there are examples to distinguish between the various kinds of *that* as in *that dog*; *I know that he is there*; *the house that I saw*, &c. Similarly, under *ce*, the examples distinguish between the *ce* in *ce chien*, and the *ce* in *c'est le chat*.

The numbers refer to sections
In the index headings **French** words are in **bold type**,
   English words in *italics*
n. after a section number refers to a footnote or N.B.
ff.= and following sections

a, *an*—indefinite article (*a* dog), 76, 78 ff.
   body, with parts of (he has *a* hooked nose), 73 (*c*) (i).
   in exclamations (what *a* nuisance! *a* difficult question!), 85.
   frequency (three times *a* week), 72 (*a*) (iii), (*b*).
   in negative sentences (I have not *a* dog; this is not *a* dog), 78.
   price (50 francs *a* pound, dozen, &c.), 72 (*a*) (i).
   rate (50 grammes *a* head), 72 (*b*).
   speed (50 miles *an* hour), 72 (*a*) (ii).
   after *without* (without *a* hat), see **sans** in Appendix B.
à—meanings, Appendix B.
   forming dative (je parle **à** l'homme; je vous présente **à** elle), 51–53, 167.
   distance, in expressions of (**à** 20 km. d'ici), 151 (*a*).
   with fractions, 139 (*d*).
   with infinitive, 28, 31.
   with object of verb (il obéit **à** ses parents; je pense **à** eux), 55.
   possession (ce livre est **à** moi), 181 (*b*).
   repetition, 237 (*c*).
à ce que, 45 (*f*).
à moins que, 239.
à peine . . . que, 239.
   inversion with, 115 (*f*) n. 1.
able, to be, see **pouvoir** 66 and **savoir**, 67 (*b*), (*c*).
about, see Appendix C.
above, see Appendix C.
abstract nouns, articles with, 80.
accents, Introduction II.
adjectives (see also headings DEMONSTRATIVE, FEMININE, INDEFINITE, POSSESSIVE,
   PLURAL):
   agreement, 109 ff.
      used as adverbs (ils sentent bon), 112, 116.
      with **je, tu, nous, vous**, &c. (je suis content(e)), 109.
      2 nouns, 1 adjective (la musique et la littérature françaises), 110.
   with additional masculine form (beau: bel), 95 (*d*) (i).
   position, 104 ff.
      after **comme** (comme il est beau!), 121 (*b*), 4.
      with complex noun (une grande maison de campagne; un homme
         d'affaires moderne), 107.

latter, 172 (*b*).

le—definite article (**le** livre), 70 ff.
>pronoun:
>>impersonal (elle est morte, je **le** sais), 158.
>>personal (voilà un homme, je **le** connais), 157.

lequel:
>interrogative (**lequel** (de ces chapeaux), est le vôtre?), 212–13.
>relative: form, 185.
>>after preposition (avec **lequel**), 193 (*b*).
>>to avoid ambiguity (un ami de mon père, **lequel** est ici), 198.

les—definite article (**les** livres), 70 ff.
>personal pronoun (je **les** vois), 157.

less, least, **moins,** 119.
>in comparison, 127, 129, 131–3.
>qualifying numerals (two litres *less*), 131 (*b*).

let:
>= *allow* (he *let* him go), 27 (*g*).
>imperative (*let* them be off!), 49 (*a*).

leur—possessive adjective (**leur** maison; **leurs** livres), 178 ff.
>possessive pronoun (le **leur**, la **leur**, les **leurs**), 179–81.
>personal pronoun (il **leur** parle), 154 ff., 167.

liaison (un‿homme; après‿elle), Introduction III, 70, 76, 135 (*i*) (*v*).
>of plural -s, -x, 103 (*a*) (*b*).

like, see Appendix C.

little, a little:
>adjective (*a little* boy) **petit,** 104 (*d*).
>adverb (he does *little*; *a little* bread), 119 (*d*).

lorsque, 239.

l'un, 135 (*g*).

l'un . . . l'autre, les uns . . . les autres, 222.

lui: conjunctive—*to him, to her* (il **lui** parle), 154 ff., 167.
>disjunctive= *him* (avec **lui**), 164 ff.

mal, 120, 129 (*b*).

manger, conjugation of verbs like, 9.

manquer—construction, 58.

many, much **beaucoup,** 119, sometimes **bien,** 120 (*b*) 4.
>*as many, as much* **autant,** 119, 133 (*b*).
>*how many, how much* **combien,** 119, 214 (*a*).
>*so many, so much* **tant,** 119, 133 (*b*).
>*too many, too much* **trop,** 119.

may, might:
>expressing possibility or permission (he *may* (*have*) come; he *might* (*have*) come; you *may* go now; I said he *might* go), see **pouvoir,** 66.
>subjunctive (I fear he *may* come), 45 (*b*), 48.

ne without negative force:

   with **à moins que, de peur (crainte) que,** 239, n. 1.

   in **que** clause in comparison (plus vite **que** vous **ne** pensez), 133 (*a*) (*b*), n.

   after verb of fearing (je crains qu'il **ne** vienne = I fear he will (may) come), 45 (*b*), n.

ne . . . guère, 249 (*a*).

ne . . . pas, see **pas.**

ne . . . plus, 249 (*a*) ff.

   position, 250 (*a*)–(*d*).

ne . . . point, 249 (*a*) ff.

ne . . . que, 249 (*b*), 250 (*f*).

   indefinite and partitive articles with, 78 (*d*).

near—preposition (*near* the station) **près de,** Appendix B.

nearly:

   of time or number (*nearly* 2 o'clock; *nearly* 100) **près de,** Appendix B.

   of degree (*nearly* dead) **presque.**

negation, 248 ff.

negative expressions (ne . . . pas, ne . . . jamais, ne . . . personne, &c.), 249 ff.

   double negatives (he never sees anybody), 251.

   order, 251.

   position, 250.

   subjunctive in clauses qualifying (pas un soldat qui ne mourût), 47 (*b*).

neither:

   conjunction (*neither* the man nor the boy came), 250 (*g*).

   pronoun (*neither* has done it), 222 (*b*).

neuf—pronunciation, 135 (*i*) (ii).

never, 249 ff., 252 (*a*).

new = *fresh* or *different* (a *new* effort; a *new* method) **nouveau,** 108.

   = *brand-new* (bright as a *new* pin) **neuf.**

ni . . . ni, 250 (*g*), 251, 252 (*b*) (ii).

   indefinite and partitive articles with, 78 (*c*).

n'importe lequel/quel, see *any.*

n'importe qui, see *anybody.*

n'importe quoi, see *anything.*

no:

   adjective = *not a, not any* (I have *no* pen, *no* eggs, *no* meat) usually **ne . . . pas de,** 78; if emphatic (I have *no* patience with him) **aucun, nul, pas un** in singular, 249 (*b*) ff.

   answer *no!*, 247.

no longer, no more, 249 (*a*) ff.

nobody, no one, 249 (*b*) ff., 252 (*a*).

non:

   = answer *no!*, 247.

   negativing nouns, adjectives, &c. (je parlais, **non** des livres, mais des journaux), 248 (*b*).

profession, article with nouns denoting (he is a doctor, the author), 83.

pronouns, see under separate headings, e.g. PERSONAL, DEMONSTRATIVE, REFLEXIVE.

pronunciation, see Introduction.
  of feminines, 97.
  of numerals, 135.
  of plurals, 103.

proper names, definite article with, 74.

punctuation, Introduction VII.

quand, 239.
  = *even if* with conditional, 239 n. 2.

quand même, 239 n. 2.

que:
  adverb:
    in exclamations (**que** je suis heureux! **que** d'argent!), 214 (*a*).
    = *than*, 132 (*a*), 133.
  conjunction (je sais **qu'**il est là):
    indicative or subjunctive, 44, 45.
    forming imperative or wish (**qu'**il meure!), 49.
    repeating subordinating conjunction (quand la voiture arriva et **que** nous fûmes prêts), 240.
  interrogative pronoun (**que** faites-vous?), 201–2, 206, 207 (*b*).
  relative adverb (un jour **qu'**ils sont venus), 195.
  relative pronoun (l'homme **que** je vois), 190–1.
    elision, 185 n. 1, 201 n. 2.

qu'est-ce que?, 201–2, 206, 207 (*b*).

qu'est-ce que c'est que?, 207 (*d*).

qu'est-ce qui?, 201–2, 204.

quel—in exclamation (**quelle** idée!), 214 (*c*).
  omission of article with, 85.
  interrogative adjective (**quelle** maison avez-vous achetée? **quel** est son nom?), 200.

quel que (**quel qu'**il soit; **quelles que** soient les raisons que), see WHATEVER and WHOEVER in Appendix C.

quelque:
  = *however, whatever* (**quelque** habile qu'il soit; **quelques** raisons que vous ayez), see HOWEVER and WHATEVER in Appendix C.
  = *some, a few* (il y a **quelque** difficulté; **quelque** deux cent mètres; j'ai **quelques** pommiers), 227.

quelque chose, 228.

quelqu'un, quelques-un(e)s, 229.

questions:
  order of words in, 242 ff.
  polite interest ('He is a doctor.' '*Is he?*'), 246 (*b*).

INDEX

36

as object (*what* did you do? I wonder *what* he did), 206.

after preposition (with *what* did you do it? *what* did you do it with?), 209.

sole word ('I know something good' '*What?*' '*What?* I can't hear you'), 211 (*a*).

as subject (*what* makes him angry? I wonder *what* makes him angry), 204.

relative = the/a thing which (*what* I don't like is his hat; this is *what* he said; after *what* he has said; *what* he likes most is raw meat), 196–7.

what ever? (*what ever* is that?), 207 (*d*).

whatever, see Appendix C.

when:

conjunction (*when* the day dawned) **quand, lorsque,** 239.

relative adverb (the day *when* he came) **où,** 194; **que,** 195.

after *scarcely* (*scarcely* had he done it *when* . . .) **à peine . . . que . . .,** 239.

whether **si** 244.

which:

interrogative:

adjective (*which* house? *which* is the house? I know *which* the house is), 200.

pronoun (*which* do you want? *which* of these is yours? I wonder *which* of these books is best), 212–13.

relative:

as complement (the rogue *which* he is), 191.

as object (the dog *which* he killed), 190.

of which, 192.

after other prepositions (by, with, in *which*, &c.), 193 (*b*), 194–5.

referring to fact or idea (he is deaf, *which* worries him), 196.

after preposition (to *which* he replied), 197 (*a*).

as subject (the apple *which* is ripe), 189.

while, 35 (*a*) (i), (*b*), 241 (*c*).

who:

interrogative:

as complement (*who* is there? *who* is that man?) usually **qui,** 207 (*a*), sometimes **quel,** 200 (*b*).

as subject (*who* did it? I wonder *who* did it), 203.

who of? (*who of* you will do it?), 213 (*b*).

relative (the man *who* is there), 189.

who ever? (*who ever* is that man?), 207 (*d*).

whoever, see Appendix C.

whole (he has eaten the *whole* (of the) cake; this reveals a *whole* story), 231 (*a*).

whom:

interrogative:

as object (*whom* did you see? I wonder *whom* you saw), 205.

after preposition (with *whom* did you go? *whom* did you go with?), 208.

INTRODUCTION
SPELLING & PRONUNCIATION

I. THE PHONETIC ALPHABET

French spelling, like English, has developed in such a way that the spelling of a word is not necessarily an accurate guide to its pronunciation, or vice versa.

No attempt is made in this book to teach the pronunciation of individual words, except when this arises from a point of grammar or syntax. In such cases use is made of the Alphabet of the International Phonetic Association. This alphabet enables the sounds of the spoken word to be indicated accurately on paper, and its relevant portions are given below.

Phonetic symbols are conventionally written in square brackets. Below, the phonetic symbol representing the sound is given on the left, and a phonetic transcription of the whole word is given after the word.

The letter or letters which represent the sound in the specimen written word are in bold type.

The sign [:] after a vowel symbol denotes that it is long.

[i]	ni, vive [ni, vi:v]		[ɥ]	lui, muet [lɥi, mɥɛ]
[e]	été, aller [ete, ale]		[p]	pas, obtenir [pa, ɔptəni:r]
[ɛ]	près, paire [prɛ, pɛ:r]		[b]	beau, robe [bo, rɔb]
[a]	patte, part [pat, pa:r]		[m]	mot, dame [mo, dam]
[ɑ]	pas, passe [pɑ, pɑ:s]		[f]	fort, phrase [fɔ:r, frɑ:z]
[ɔ]	note, fort [nɔt, fɔ:r]		[v]	vin, cave [vɛ̃, ka:v]
[o]	sot, saule [so, so:l]		[t]	tas, patte [tɑ, pat]
[u]	tout, tour [tu, tu:r]		[d]	dame, sud [dam, syd]
[y]	pu, mur [py, my:r]		[n]	nez, automne [ne, otɔn]
[ø]	creux, creuse [krø, krø:z]		[s]	si, soixante [si, swasɑ̃:t]
[œ]	neuf, neuve [nœf, nœ:v]		[z]	zone, rose [zo:n, ro:z]
[ə]	le [lə]		[l]	long, seul [lɔ̃, sœl]
[ɛ̃]	vain, prince [vɛ̃, prɛ̃:s]		[ʃ]	chou, lâche [ʃu, la:ʃ]
[ɑ̃]	temps, tante [tɑ̃, tɑ̃:t]		[ʒ]	je, rouge [ʒə, ru:ʒ]
[ɔ̃]	rond, ronde [rɔ̃, rɔ̃:d]		[k]	qui, roc [ki, rɔk]
[œ̃]	un, humble [œ̃, œ̃:bl]		[g]	gant, second [gɑ̃, səgɔ̃]
[j]	pied, viande [pje, vjɑ̃:d]		[ɲ]	agneau, digne [aɲo, diɲ]
[w]	oui, noir [wi, nwa:r]		[r]	rose, tour [ro:z, tu:r]

N.B. In correct usage **h** is never sounded: **homme** [ɔm], **herse** [ɛrs], **cahot** [kao].

In a few words **h** between vowels is equivalent to a tréma (see II (*c*) below): **cahier** [kaje].

The initial **h** of some words, such as **homme**, is classified **h-mute** (*h muette*), and of others, such as **herse, h-aspirate** (*h aspirée*). But in neither case is the **h** sounded [h], the distinction between mute and aspirate relating only to liaison (see III below) and elision (see IV below).

II. Accents, &c.

(*a*) In the written form accents are found on certain vowels either as an indication of pronunciation or as a distinguishing mark.

(i) An **acute accent** (´) (*accent aigu*) placed over an **e** denotes that it is sounded [e], e.g.:

été [ete]; **précisément** [presizemã]

(ii) A **grave accent** (`) (*accent grave*) placed over an **e** denotes that it is sounded [ɛ], e.g.:

père [pɛ:r]; **nègre** [nɛ:gr]; **près** [prɛ].

When placed over a final **a** or **u** it is simply a distinguishing mark and does not affect the pronunciation, e.g.:

à [a]; **là** [la]; **çà** [sa]; **où** (= *where*) [u].

cf.   **il a** [a]; **la** [la] **femme**;   **ça** (= *cela*) [sa]; **ou** (= *or*) [u].

(iii) A **circumflex accent** (ˆ) (*accent circonflexe*) may be found placed over any vowel, or over the second letter of the groups **ai, ei, eu, oi, ou.** Thus e.g. **âne, crête, île, pôle, flûte, maître, goût;** but note **bâiller.**

Ê is sounded [ɛ] and **ô**[o]:**bête** [bɛt], **hôte** [o:t]. Otherwise the circumflex accent does not in itself indicate the pronunciation of the vowel over which it is placed, nor does it necessarily indicate length.

In a number of cases it denotes the disappearance of an **s** or some other contraction from an earlier spelling.

It may also serve purely as a distinguishing mark in the spelling of otherwise identical words, e.g.:

je croîs, crû, from **croître,** cf. **je crois, cru,** from **croire.**
dû, from **devoir,** cf. **du** (= *de le*).
mûr (= *ripe*), cf. **mur** (= *wall*).

N.B. A circumflex accent over an **i** replaces the dot. Accents are frequently omitted over initial capital letters, though the acute accent is usually present over initial **E**.

(*b*) A **cedilla** (,) (*cédille*) placed under a **c** before **a, o, u** denotes that the **c** is sounded [s]:

	lança [lãsa];	**leçon** [ləsɔ̃];	**reçu** [rəsy].
cf.	**cave** [ka:v];	**conte** [kɔ̃:t];	**curé** [kyre].

(*c*) A **diaeresis** (¨) (*tréma*) denotes that the vowel on which it is placed is separated in pronunciation from the vowel preceding it, e.g.:

	haïr [ai:r];	**Noël** [nɔɛl];	**Moïse** [mɔi:z].
cf.	**je hais** [ɛ];	**poêle** [pwɑ:l];	**toise** [twa:z].

N.B. Over **i** the diaeresis replaces the dot.

In the feminine form of adjectives in **-gu,** the diaeresis denotes that the final **u** has its full value, e.g.:

contiguë [kɔ̃tigy], cf. **intrigue** [ɛ̃trig].

III. LIAISON

(*a*) The majority of final consonants are not sounded, but in spoken French such consonants are regularly sounded before a word beginning with a vowel sound or h-mute, forming a syllable with the initial sound of the following word, this process being known in French as liaison:

il était‿allé [etɛ tale]; **très‿aimable** [trɛ zɛmabl].

(*b*) Note that in liaison:

s or **x** is sounded [z]: **les‿enfants** [le zãfã]; **deux‿hommes** (dø zɔm]·
d is sounded [t]: **quand‿il** [kã til]; **un grand‿arbre** [grã tarbr].
g is sounded [k]: **un long‿arrêt** [lɔ̃ karɛ].
A final nasal **n** produces, in liaison, the sound [n] at the beginning of the following word.

In general, the original nasal sound disappears:

un bon‿ami [bɔ nami]; **moyen‿âge** [mwajɛ nɑ:ʒ];
vain‿espoir [vɛ nɛspwa:r]; **plein‿air** [plɛ nɛ:r].
But the nasal sound is retained in **un, aucun, on, rien, bien, en, combien:**
un‿homme [œ̃ nɔm]; **on‿arrive** [ɔ̃ nariv]; **bien‿aimable** [bjɛ̃ nɛmabl].

(*c*) Liaison can only correctly take place between words which belong together in sense and which would normally be spoken together without any pause, however slight. In practice the commonest of such sense-groups, where liaison is correct usage, are:

(i) Article—Noun or Adjective; Adjective—Noun.

les ̮ ordres   un ̮ ancien ̮ élève.

(ii) Personal Pronoun or *On*—Verb or *Y* or *En*.

vous ̮ avez   on ̮ allait   ils ̮ y pensent.

(iii) Verb—Personal Pronoun or *On*.

vont-ils?   dit-on?

(iv) 3rd Person Auxiliary Verb—Past Participle or Infinitive.

il est ̮ allé   ils voulaient ̮ entrer.

(v) Verb—Adjective or Noun Complement.

nous sommes ̮ heureux   il est ̮ auteur.

(vi) Preposition—Word Governed.[1]

devant ̮ elle   sans ̮ arrêt   en ̮ Amérique.

(*d*) Liaison does not take place between words that are not closely linked together in sense and do not form part of the same sense-group, as do those in (*c*) above. There is therefore no liaison in, e.g.:

l'enfant arriva [lãfã ariva]; **sortez à l'instant;** [sɔrte a lɛ̃stã].
allons-nous aujourd'hui? [nu oʒurdμi].
il n'est pas, heureusement, [pɑ œrøzmã] **le coupable.**

(*e*) There is also no liaison, e.g.:

(i) of **et: lui et elle** [lμi e ɛl].
(ii) with words beginning with h-aspirate.

un héros [œ̃ ero]; **nous haïssons** [nu aisɔ̃].

(iii) with a number of special cases, notably **un** (= *number one*), **huit,**[2] **huitième, onze,**[3] **onzième,**[4] **oui, yacht:**

quatre-vingt-un [vɛ̃ œ̃]; **les huit** [le μi] **maisons; les yachts** [le jɔt].

IV. ELISION

(*a*) (i) **A** and **e** are elided (that is, they are not sounded in speech and are replaced by an apostrophe in writing, before a word beginning with a vowel sound or h-mute) in **le, la, je, me, te, se, ce** (*pronoun*), **de, ne, que:**

l'air; l'heure; j'ai; il s'habille; il n'a pas; c'est; d'après; qu'il meure! jusqu'ici; puisqu'il le sait.

---

[1] But there is no liaison of **à travers, hors, selon, (en)vers.**
[2] But **dix-huit (ième)** [di zμit]; **vingt-huit** [vɛ̃ thit] or [vɛ̃ μit].
[3] But **il est ̮ onze** [ɛtɔ̃:z] **heures.**
[4] **l'onzième** [lɔ̃zjɛm] is now fairly frequent.

(ii) The final **e** of **quelque** and **presque** is similarly elided before a vowel sound in pronunciation, but is not replaced by an apostrophe in spelling except in **quelqu'un** and **presqu'île**. Thus, e.g. **quelque honneur** [kɛlk ɔnœ:r], **presque inutile** [prɛsk inytil].

(iii) The **i** of **si** is elided only before **il(s)**: **s'il** [sil]; but, e.g. **si elle** [si ɛl.]

(*b*) There is no elision:

(i) of **je, ce, le, la** after a verb:
puis-je aller? est-ce en ordre? ferme-la après toi!

(ii) before h-aspirate, and such words as in III (*e*) (iii) above:
le héros; le huitième mois; le yacht.

V. THE FRENCH ALPHABET

The letters of the French Alphabet, together with pronunciation of their names, are as follows:

a	a [ɑ]	**h**	ache [ɑʃ]	**o**	o [o]	**v**	vé [ve]
b	bé [be]	**i**	i [i]	**p**	pé [pe]	**w**	double vé [dublə ve]
c	cé [se]	**j**	ji [ʒi]	**q**	qu [ky]	**x**	icse [iks]
d	dé [de]	**k**	ka [kɑ]	**r**	erre [ɛ:r]	**y**	i grec [i grɛk]
e	é [e] (or) [ə]	**l**	elle [ɛl]	**s**	esse [ɛs]	**z**	zède [zɛd]
f	effe [ɛf]	**m**	emme [ɛm]	**t**	té [te]		
g	gé [ʒe]	**n**	enne [ɛn]	**u**	u[y]		

Note also: e.g. **B majuscule** = *Capital B*; e.g. **deux p** = *double p*.

é (**è**) (**ê**) = é accent aigu (accent grave) (accent circonflexe). **Comment cela s'écrit-il?** = *How is it spelt?*

VI. CAPITAL LETTERS

In general capital letters (*lettres majuscules*) are used as in English, except that the following are not written with a capital unless they begin a sentence:

(*a*) Days of Week and Names of Months: **le lundi, 4 mars.**

(*b*) Adjectives of Nationality and Names of Languages: **un livre anglais** (*an English book*); **traduire en allemand** (*translate into German*). But **un Anglais** (*an Englishman*); **les Français** (*the French people*).

(*c*) *Je*: **puisque je l'ai vu.**

(*d*) Words denoting rank, profession, &c., accompanied by a proper name: **le général Leclerc; le docteur Mercier; avec monsieur (madame) Laroche.**[1]

---

[1] But the corresponding abbreviations have a capital: **avec M. (Mme.) Laroche.**

(*e*) Common Nouns which are geographical terms forming part of a proper name: **la mer Noire** (*the Black Sea*); **l'océan Atlantique** (*the Atlantic Ocean*).

(*f*) Also, such words as **rue, boulevard, place,** &c., forming part of the name of a street, &c.: **la rue du Bac; il demeure place Saint-Michel.**

VII. Punctuation

(*a*) The principal Punctuation Marks (*signes de ponctuation*) and their French names are:

. le point	- le trait (d'union)
, la virgule	— le tiret (de séparation)
: les deux points	... les points de suspension
; le point-virgule	( ) les parenthèses
? le point d'interrogation	" " ⎱ les guillemets
! le point d'exclamation	« » ⎰

Note also: **alinéa** = *new paragraph.*

(*b*) (i) **Inverted commas** are often omitted altogether, or are only present at the beginning and end of a dialogue. They are very frequently omitted when a verb of saying is interpolated in a speech.

A change of speaker in a dialogue is often represented by a dash.

—Moi, dit-il, j'ai eu des affaires. J'ai été malade.

—Gravement? s'écria-t-elle.

—Eh bien! fit Rodolphe en s'asseyant à ses côtés sur un tabouret, non! ... C'est que je n'ai pas voulu revenir.

—Pourquoi?

—Vous ne devinez pas?

Il la regarda encore une fois.

(Flaubert, *Madame Bovary*. Paris, Eugène Fasquelle, 1904.)

(ii) Inverted commas are sometimes shown as « ». This form is especially used to emphasize a special word or phrase:

C'est de la poésie « dramatique », ce n'est pas de la poésie « lyrique ».

(Brunetière, *Les Époques du théâtre français*. Paris, Hachette.)

N.B. The use of single inverted commas for emphasis, as in English, has only recently become acceptable in French.

(*c*) **Hyphens** are used notably:

    (i) to link the verb to a following personal pronoun, or **on**, or **ce** (pronoun): **allez-vous? dépêche-toi! arrive-t-il? donnez-le-moi! dit-on? est-ce?**

46

(ii) to join **ci** or **là** to the word they qualify: **celui-ci; cette femme-là; là-bas;**

(iii) to link a disjunctive pronoun and the following adjective **même** (= *self*): **moi-même; eux-mêmes;**

(iv) in compound numerals (see 135 (*b*));

(v) in numerous other compound parts of speech, e.g. **chou-fleur; Grande-Bretagne; quelques-uns; peut-être; au-dessus de.** As there is no clear logical rule governing the presence or absence of the hyphen in such words, this must be learnt as part of the spelling.

VIII. WORD-DIVISION

In writing, words are divided between one line and the next as follows:

(*a*) A single consonant within a word begins a syllable wherever possible, and the division is therefore made before it: **au-pa-ra-vant, po-li-ment, di-ri-ger, su-pé-ri-eur.**

(*b*) In general, where there are two consonants together the division is between them: **par-ler, hon-neur, prin-temps, vil-lage, bril-lant, cail-lou.**

(*c*) (i) No division is made in the groups **ch, ph, th, gn: cro-chet, gé-o-gra-phie, sym-pa-thie, té-moi-gnage.**

(ii) No division is made between two different consonants the second of which is **l** or **r** (except the groups **lr, rl, nr, nl, tl**). Thus: **dou-bler, ré-gler, ré-ci-proque, ou-vrage;** but **par-ler, den-rée, ban-lieue, at-las.**

(*d*) Where there are three or more consonants together, and the rule given in (*c*) above does not apply, division is made after the second consonant: **obs-tiné, pers-pi-cace,[1] ins-truire.[1]**

But: **en-trer, af-freux, com-plot.**

N.B. The above divisions are those which are made in writing. In speech the divisions are made between sounds, regardless of how they are spelt.

A single consonant sound begins a syllable: **fi nir** [fɪ niːr], **ho nneur** [ɔ nœr], **vi llage** [vi laʒ], **bri llant** [bri jɑ̃].

Two consonant sounds are separated, unless they are one of the groups in (*c*) above: **parler** [par le], **dis tant** [dis tɑ̃], **ex-xact** [eg zakt]. But **vien drai** [vjɛ̃ dre], **si ffler** [si fle].

---

[1] In such words, the more logical division between prefix and stem is also permitted: **per-spi-cace, in-struire.**

47

I. CONJUGATION OF VERBS

1. Regular and Irregular Verbs

(a) There are three principal types of regular conjugation of French verbs, corresponding to the three infinitive endings: **-er, -ir, -re**. They are regular in that they provide the patterns for conjugating large numbers of verbs which have one or other of these infinitive endings.

(b) Irregular Verbs are those which do not conform entirely to such patterns, and which must be studied separately or in separate groups.

2. Formation of Verbs

(a) It is a convenient simplification for learning purposes to consider the formation of each part of the verb as consisting of the addition of an ending to a basic part, or stem, e.g. **parl/er, finiss/ons, vendr/ai**, and notes on this basis are inserted at the head of each regular tense, &c., in the following section.

(b) In particular it is essential to know the stem and ending of the Present Infinitive and of the Present Participle. From these all parts of a regular verb may be built up.

3. The Regular Conjugations

	(1)	(2)	(3)
Present Infinitive	**parl/er**	**fin/ir**	**vend/re**
Present Participle	**parl/ant**	**finiss/ant**	**vend/ant**
Past Participle	Stem + **-é** parlé	Stem + **-i** fini	Stem + **-u** vendu
Present Indicative	Stem + **-e, -es, -e, -ons, -ez, -ent**	Stem + **-is, -is, it.** Stem of Pres. Part.+ **-ons, -ez, -ent**	Stem + **-s, -s, -, -ons, -ez, -ent**[1]

[1] **Rompre**, otherwise regular, has 3rd Person Singular **il rompt** [rɔ̃], **battre** has singular **je bats, tu bats, il bat**, but is otherwise regular.

Present Indicative (contd.)		
je parle	je finis	je vends
tu parles	tu finis	tu vends
il parle	il finit	il vend
nous parlons	nous finissons	nous vendons
vous parlez	vous finissez	vous vendez
ils parlent	ils finissent	ils vendent

Imperative

2nd Singular, 1st Plural, and 2nd Plural of Present Indicative, without subject pronouns (except that First Conjugation drops final **s** of 2nd Sing., except before *y* and *en*)

parle	finis	vends
parlons	finissons	vendons
parlez	finissez	vendez

The 3rd Person Imperative is supplied by the Present Subjunctive (see 49 (*a*))

Imperfect

Stem of Present Participle + **-ais, -ais, -ait, -ions, -iez, -aient**

je parlais	je finissais	je vendais
tu parlais	tu finissais	tu vendais
il parlait	il finissait	il vendait
nous parlions	nous finissions	nous vendions
vous parliez	vous finissiez	vous vendiez
ils parlaient	ils finissaient	ils vendaient

Past Historic

Stem + **-ai, -as, -a, -âmes, -âtes, -èrent**   Stem + **-is, -is, -it, -îmes, -îtes, -irent**

je parlai	je finis	je vendis
tu parlas	tu finis	tu vendis
il parla	il finit	il vendit
nous parlâmes	nous finîmes	nous vendîmes
vous parlâtes	vous finîtes	vous vendîtes
ils parlèrent	ils finirent	ils vendirent

Future

Infinitive + **ai, -as, -a, -ons, -ez, -ont** (Third Conjugation drops final **e** of Infinitive)

je parlerai	je finirai	je vendrai
tu parleras	tu finiras	tu vendras
il parlera	il finira	il vendra
nous parlerons	nous finirons	nous vendrons
vous parlerez	vous finirez	vous vendrez
ils parleront	ils finiront	ils vendront

Conditional	Infinitive + **-ais, -ais, -ait, -ions, -iez, -aient**		
	je parlerais	je finirais	je vendrais
	tu parlerais	tu finirais	tu vendrais
	il parlerait	il finirait	il vendrait
	nous parlerions	nous finirions	nous vendrions
	vous parleriez	vous finiriez	vous vendriez
	ils parleraient	ils finiraient	ils vendraient
Present Subjunctive	Stem of Present Participle + **-e, -es, -e, -ions, -iez, -ent**		
	je parle	je finisse	je vende
	tu parles	tu finisses	tu vendes
	il parle	il finisse	il vende
	nous parlions	nous finissions	nous vendions
	vous parliez	vous finissiez	vous vendiez
	ils parlent	ils finissent	ils vendent
Imperfect Subjunctive	Remove final **s** from 2nd Sing. Past Historic and add **-sse, -sses, -ᵗt, -ssions, -ssiez, -ssent**		
	(tu parla/s)	(tu fini/s)	(tu vendi/s)
	je parlasse	je finisse	je vendisse
	tu parlasses	tu finisses	tu vendisses
	il parlât	il finît	il vendît
	nous parlassions	nous finissions	nous vendissions
	vous parlassiez	vous finissiez	vous vendissiez
	ils parlassent	ils finissent	ils vendissent

COMPOUND TENSES

The Compound Tenses which follow are formed with a tense of **avoir** (see 8) and the Past Participle of the verb; for agreement see 40. Some verbs (see 4) are compounded with *être* instead of *avoir*.

Perfect Infinitive	*Perfect Participle*
Infinitive *avoir* + Past Participle	Present Participle of *avoir* + Past Participle
avoir parlé, fini, vendu	ayant parlé, fini, vendu

Perfect	*Pluperfect*	*Past Anterior*
Present Indicative of *avoir* + Past Participle	Imperfect of *avoir* + Past Participle	Past Historic of *avoir* + Past Participle
j'ai	j'avais	j'eus
tu as	tu avais	tu eus
il a ⎫ parlé	il avait ⎫ parlé	il eut ⎫ parlé
nous avons ⎬ fini	nous avions ⎬ fini	nous eûmes ⎬ fini
vous avez ⎭ vendu	vous aviez ⎭ vendu	vous eûtes ⎭ vendu
ils ont	ils avaient	ils eurent

Future Perfect   *Conditional Perfect*

Future of *avoir* + Past Participle   Conditional of *avoir* + Past Participle

j'aurai			j'aurais		
tu auras			tu aurais		
il aura	parlé		il aurait	parlé	
nous aurons	fini		nous aurions	fini	
vous aurez	vendu		vous auriez	vendu	
ils auront			ils auraient		

Perfect Subjunctive   *Pluperfect Subjunctive*

Present Subjunctive of *avoir* + Past Participle   Imperfect Subjunctive of *avoir* + Past Participle

j'aie			j'eusse		
tu aies			tu eusses		
il ait	parlé		il eût	parlé	
nous ayons	fini		nous eussions	fini	
vous ayez	vendu		vous eussiez	vendu	
ils aient			ils eussent		

4. Verbs Conjugated with *être* (for conjugation of *être* see 8)

The Compound Tenses of some verbs (see 59) are formed with **être** instead of **avoir**. Provided they are regular verbs, they conform otherwise to the above patterns, and their Compound Tenses, Infinitives, and Participles are then, e.g.:

Perfect Infinitive: être arrivé   *Perfect Participle*: étant arrivé

Perfect Indicative: je suis arrivé, &c.   *Pluperfect Indicative*: j'étais arrivé, &c.

Future Perfect: je serai arrivé, &c.   *Conditional Perfect*: je serais arrivé, &c.

Perfect Subjunctive: je sois arrivé, &c.   *Pluperfect Subjunctive*: je fusse arrivé, &c.

For the agreement of the Past Participle of verbs compounded with **être** see 42.

5. Passive Conjugation

The Passive Conjugation of a transitive verb consists of the appropriate tense of **être** (see 8) + Past Participle. Thus, e.g.:

Present Infinitive: être blessé   *Present Participle*: étant blessé

Past Participle: été blessé   *Present Indicative*: je suis blessé, &c.

Imperfect Indicative: j'étais blessé, &c.

Past Historic: je fus blessé, &c.

Future: je serai blessé, &c.

Conditional: je serais blessé, &c.

Perfect Infinitive: avoir été blessé, &c.

Perfect Participle: ayant été blessé, &c.

Perfect Indicative: j'ai été blessé, &c.

Pluperfect Indicative: j'avais été blessé, &c.

Present Subjunctive: je sois blessé, &c.

Imperfect Subjunctive: je fusse blessé, &c.

For the agreement of the Past Participle see 42.

6. Conjugation of Reflexive Verbs

(*a*) Reflexive Verbs are conjugated in the same way as an active verb, except that the Auxiliary in the Compound Tenses is always **être.**

(*b*) The Reflexive Object Pronouns **me, te, se, nous, vous** are present and agree in number and person with the subject:

je me lave; il se lave; nous nous lavons; elles se lavent

In the case of Infinitives and Participles the Reflexive Pronoun is of the number and person required by the sense:

Je dois me laver.
I must wash (myself).

Je lui ai dit de se laver.
I told him to wash.

Après t'être lavé, range tes affaires.
After you have washed, put your things tidy.

Entrez vous chauffer un peu (Daudet).
Come in and warm yourselves a little.

(*c*) The position and form of the Reflexive Object Pronouns is governed by the same rules as those for other Object Pronouns (see 154, 162), but the following table may be useful:

Present Infinitive	me te se nous vous }laver	*Present Participle*	me te se nous vous }lavant

Present
  Indicative
	je me lave
	tu te laves
	il se lave
	nous nous lavons
	vous vous lavez
	ils se lavent
		Imperative
		
		Imperative
		  Negative
			lave-toi
			lavons-nous
			lavez-vous
			ne te lave pas
			ne nous lavons pas
			ne vous lavez pas

Imperfect *Indicative*	je me lavais, &c.	*Past Historic*	je me lavai, &c.
Future	je me laverai, &c.	*Conditional*	je me laverais, &c.

Perfect
  Infinitive
	m'
	t'
	s' }être lavé(e)(s)
	nous
	vous
		Perfect
		  Participle
			m'
			t'
			s' }étant lavé(e)(s)
			nous
			vous

Perfect
  Indicative
	je me suis lavé(e)
	tu t'es lavé(e)
	il s'est lavé
	elle s'est lavée
	nous nous sommes
	  lavé(e)s
	vous vous êtes
	  lavé(e)(s)
	ils se sont lavés
	elles se sont lavées
		Pluperfect
		  Indicative
		Future
		  Perfect
		Conditional
		  Perfect
		Past Anterior
			je m'étais lavé(e), &c.
			
			je me serai lavé(e), &c.
			
			je me serais lavé(e),
			  &c.
			je me fus lavé(e), &c.

Present
  Subjunctive
	je me lave, &c.	*Imperfect*
		  Subjunctive
			je me lavasse, &c.

Perfect
  Subjunctive
	je me sois lavé(e),
	  &c.
		Pluperfect
		  Subjunctive
			je me fusse lavé(e),
			  &c.

	Present Indicative	*Perfect Indicative*
Interrogative Order	se lave-t-il?	s'est-il lavé?
Negative Order	il ne se lave pas	il ne s'est pas lavé
Negative-Interrogative Order	ne se lave-t-il pas?	ne s'est-il pas lavé?

N.B. For the agreement of the Past Participle of Reflexive Verbs see 41.

7. Conjugation of Impersonal Verbs

Impersonal Verbs (and other verbs when constructed impersonally) are conjugated only in the 3rd Person Singular, the subject being Impersonal **il** (see 176). Thus, e.g.:

Present Infinitive: y avoir

Present Indicative: il y a		*Imperfect Indicative*: il y avait
Future: il y aura, &c.		*Perfect Indicative*: il y a eu, &c.

	Present Indicative	*Perfect Indicative*
Interrogative Order	y a-t-il?	y a-t-il eu?
Negative Order	il n'y a pas	il n'y a pas eu
Interrogative-Negative Order	n'y a-t-il pas?	n'y a-t-il pas eu?

8. Conjugation of *avoir* and *être*

	Avoir (to have)	*Être* (to be)[1]
Present Participle	ayant	étant
Past Participle	eu [y]	été
Present Indicative	j'ai	je suis
	tu as	tu es
	il a	il est
	nous avons	nous sommes
	vous avez	vous êtes
	ils ont	ils sont
Imperative	aie, ayons, ayez	sois, soyons, soyez
Imperfect Indicative	j'avais	j'étais
	tu avais	tu étais
	il avait	il était
	nous avions	nous étions
	vous aviez	vous étiez
	ils avaient	ils étaient
Past Historic	j'eus [ʒy]	je fus
	tu eus	tu fus
	il eut	il fut
	nous eûmes	nous fûmes
	vous eûtes	vous fûtes
	ils eurent	ils furent

---

[1] When used as the auxiliary of an active verb, as in 4 above, *être* has the sense of the English *have*, e.g. je suis allé = I have gone.

Future	j'aurai	je serai
	tu auras	tu seras
	il aura	il sera
	nous aurons	nous serons
	vous aurez	vous serez
	ils auront	ils seront
Conditional	j'aurais	je serais
	tu aurais	tu serais
	il aurait	il serait
	nous aurions	nous serions
	vous auriez	vous seriez
	ils auraient	ils seraient
Perfect Infinitive	avoir eu	avoir été
Perfect Participle	ayant eu	ayant été
Present Subjunctive	j'aie	je sois
	tu aies	tu sois
	il ait	il soit
	nous ayons	nous soyons
	vous ayez	vous soyez
	ils aient	ils soient
Imperfect Subjunctive	j'eusse [ʒys]	je fusse
	tu eusses	tu fusses
	il eût	il fût
	nous eussions	nous fussions
	vous eussiez	vous fussiez
	ils eussent	ils fussent
Perfect Indicative	j'ai eu	j'ai été
	tu as eu	tu as été
	il a eu	il a été
	nous avons eu	nous avons été
	vous avez eu	vous avez été
	ils ont eu	ils ont été
Pluperfect Indicative	j'avais eu, &c.	j'avais été, &c.
Past Anterior	j'eus eu, &c.	j'eus été, &c.
Future Perfect	j'aurai eu, &c.	j'aurai été, &c.
Conditional Perfect	j'aurais eu, &c.	j'aurais été, &c.
Perfect Subjunctive	j'aie eu, &c.	j'aie été, &c.
Pluperfect Subjunctive	j'eusse eu, &c.	j'eusse été, &c.

9. Verbs in -*cer* and -*ger*

Verbs whose infinitive ends in **-cer,** in order to preserve the sound of the soft **c** [s], change **c** to **ç** before endings in **a** or **o**. Similarly verbs in **-ger,** in order to preserve the soft **g** [ʒ], add **e** after the **g** before endings in **a** or **o**:

	lancer	**manger**
Present Participle	lançant	mangeant
Present Indicative	je lance	je mange
	tu lances	tu manges
	il lance	il mange
	nous lançons	nous mangeons
	vous lancez	vous mangez
	ils lancent	ils mangent
Imperfect Indicative	je lançais	je mangeais
	tu lançais	tu mangeais
	il lançait	il mangeait
	nous lancions	nous mangions
	vous lanciez	vous mangiez
	ils lançaient	ils mangeaient
Past Historic	je lançai	je mangeai
	tu lanças	tu mangeas
	il lança	il mangea
	nous lançâmes	nous mangeâmes
	vous lançâtes	vous mangeâtes
	ils lancèrent	ils mangèrent
Imperfect Subjunctive	je lançasse, &c.	je mangeasse, &c.
	(ç throughout)	(ge throughout)

10. Verbs of Types *mener, espérer, jeter, appeler*

Verbs with the final vowel of the stem in **e** or **é** undergo a change of stem as follows before endings **-e, -es, -ent,** and in the Future and Conditional:

(*a*) Most verbs with final vowel of stem in **e** (e.g. **men/er, soulev/er**) change **e** to **è**.

(*b*) Verbs with final vowel of stem in **é** (e.g. **espér/er, préfér/er**) change **é** to **è** before endings **-e, -es, -ent,** but retain **é** in Future and Conditional.

(c) Most verbs whose infinitives end in **-eler** or **-eter** (e.g. **appeler, jeter**) double the **l** or **t**.[1]

	(a)	(b)	(c)	
Present	je mène	j'espère	je jette	j'appelle
Indicative	tu mènes	tu espères	tu jettes	tu appelles
	il mène	il espère	il jette	il appelle
	nous menons	nous espérons	nous jetons	nous appelons
	vous menez	vous espérez	vous jetez	vous appelez
	ils mènent	ils espèrent	ils jettent	ils appellent
Present	je mène	j'espère	je jette	j'appelle
Subjunctive	tu mènes	tu espères	tu jettes	tu appelles
	il mène	il espère	il jette	il appelle
	nous menions	nous espérions	nous jetions	nous appelions
	vous meniez	vous espériez	vous jetiez	vous appeliez
	ils mènent	ils espèrent	ils jettent	ils appellent
Future	je mènerai	j'espérerai	je jetterai	j'appellerai
	(è throughout)	(é throughout)	(tt throughout)	(ll throughout)
Conditional	je mènerais	j'espérerais	je jetterais	j'appellerais
	(è throughout)	(é throughout)	(tt throughout)	(ll throughout)

11. Verbs in *-yer*

Verbs whose infinitives end in **-oyer** or **-uyer** (e.g. **employer, appuyer**) change the **y** of the stem to **i** before endings **-e, -es, -ent**, and in the Future and Conditional.

In the case of verbs in **-ayer** (e.g. **payer**) the change of **y** to **i** is optional. Thus, e.g.:

j'emploie   j'appuie   je paie (paye)
(nous employons)   (nous appuyons)   (nous payons)
j'emploierai   j'appuierai   je paierai (payerai)

12. Conjugation of Irregular Verbs

The following is a table of the more common Irregular Verbs (excluding *avoir* and *être*).

[1] The following common verbs in **-eter** and **-eler** are conjugated like **mener** (i.e. change **e** to **è**), and not like *jeter* or *appeler*: acheter (il achète); celer (il cèle); étiqueter (il étiquète); geler (il gèle); modeler (il modèle); peler (il pèle).

(a) The parts of each verb are set out in the pattern:

Present Infinitive   Present Indic.   Present Subj.   Remarks
   (bold type)   (in full)   (in full)
Meaning (italics)
Present Participle
1st Sing. Perf. Indic.
1st Sing. Past Hist.
1st Sing. Fut.

(b) It may be assumed that all other parts of the verb are formed regularly (i.e. as shown in the regular conjugations in 3). In particular it should be noted that all the irregular verbs given below form the following tenses regularly:

1. Imperfect Indicative from the Present Participle (exception: **savoir**: Pres. Part. **sachant**; Imperfect **je savais**).
2. Imperfect Subjunctive from 2nd Sing. Past Historic.
3. Conditional from same stem as Future (e.g. **courir**: Fut. **je courrai**; Conditional **je courrais**).

(c) A past Historic in **-us** is conjugated, e.g. **je vécus, tu vécus, il vécut, nous vécûmes, vous vécûtes, ils vécurent.**

(d) Unless otherwise stated, compounds of irregular verbs are conjugated in the same way as the simple verb, e.g. **reconnaître** as **connaître**, **promettre** as **mettre**, **devenir** as **venir**, &c.

absoudre *absolve*, see **résoudre**.

acquérir	j'acquiers	j'acquière	*Also* conquérir
acquire	tu acquiers	tu acquières	
acquérant	il acquiert	il acquière	
j'ai acquis	nous acquérons	nous acquérions	
j'acquis	vous acquérez	vous acquériez	
j'acquerrai	ils acquièrent	ils acquièrent	
aller	je vais	j'aille	*Imperative*:
go	tu vas	tu ailles	va (vas before *y*
allant	il va	il aille	or *en*), allons,
je suis allé	nous allons	nous allions	allez
j'allai	vous allez	vous alliez	
j'irai	ils vont	ils aillent	

apercevoir *perceive*, see **recevoir**.

s'asseoir	je m'assieds (asje)	je m'asseye	Some tenses also
sit down	tu t'assieds	tu t'asseyes	have forms in **-o**,
s'asseyant	il s'assied	il s'asseye	e.g. *Pres. Indic.*
je me suis assis	nous nous asseyons	nous nous asseyions	j'assois, &c.;
je m'assis	vous vous asseyez	vous vous asseyiez	*Fut.* j'assoirai, &c.
je m'assiérai	ils s'asseyent	ils s'asseyent	

atteindre *reach*, see **feindre**.

battre *beat*, see 3 n. 1.

boire	je bois	je boive	
drink	tu bois	tu boives	
buvant	il boit	il boive	
j'ai bu	nous buvons	nous buvions	
je bus	vous buvez	vous buviez	
je boirai	ils boivent	ils boivent	

conclure	je conclus	je conclue	*Also:*
conclude	tu conclus	tu conclues	exclure
concluant	il conclut	il conclue	inclure
conclu	nous concluons	nous concluions	
je conclus	vous concluez	vous concluiez	
je conclurai	ils concluent	ils concluent	

conduire	je conduis	je conduise	*Also:*
lead	tu conduis	tu conduises	construire
conduisant	il conduit	il conduise	cuire détruire
j'ai conduit	nous conduisons	nous conduisions	instruire
je conduisis	vous conduisez	vous conduisiez	introduire
je conduirai	ils conduisent	ils conduisent	nuire (*Past. Part.*
			nui invariable)
			réduire
			traduire

connaître	je connais	je connaisse	Note **î** before **t**
know (see 67 (a) n.)	tu connais	tu connaisses	in *Pres. Indic.,*
connaissant	il connaît	il connaisse	*Fut., Condit.*
j'ai connu	nous connaissons	nous connaissions	*Also* paraître
je connus	vous connaissez	vous connaissiez	
je connaîtrai	ils connaissent	ils connaissent	

conquérir *conquer*, see **acquérir**.

construire *construct*, see **conduire**.

coudre	je couds	je couse	
sew	tu couds	tu couses	
cousant	il coud	ils couse	
j'ai cousu	nous cousons	nous cousions	

je cousis	vous cousez	vous cousiez	
je coudrai	ils cousent	ils cousent	

courir	je cours	je coure	
run	tu cours	tu coures	
courant	il court	il coure	
j'ai couru	nous courons	nous courions	
je courus	vous courez	vous couriez	
je courrai	ils courent	ils courent	

couvrir *cover*, see **ouvrir.**

craindre	je crains	je craigne	*Also* plaindre
fear	tu crains	tu craignes	
craignant	il craint	il craigne	
j'ai craint	nous craignons	nous craignions	
je craignis	vous craignez	vous craigniez	
je craindrai	ils craignent	ils craignent	

croire	je crois	je croie	
think, believe	tu crois	tu croies	
croyant	il croit	il croie	
j'ai cru	nous croyons	nous croyions	
je crus	vous croyez	vous croyiez	
je croirai	ils croient	ils croient	

croître	je croîs	je croisse	*Past Part.:* crû,
grow (intr.)	tu croîs	tu croisses	crue, crus,
croissant	il croît	il croisse	crues
crû	nous croissons	nous croissions	
je crûs	vous croissez	vous croissiez	
je croîtrai	ils croissent	ils croissent	

cueillir (kœji:r)	je cueille	je cueille	
pluck	tu cueilles	tu cueilles	
cueillant	il cueille	il cueille	
j'ai cueilli	nous cueillons	nous cueillions	
je cueillis	vous cueillez	vous cueilliez	
je cueillerai	ils cueillent	ils cueillent	

cuire *cook*, see **conduire.**

décrire *describe*, see **écrire.**

détruire *destroy*, see **conduire.**

devoir	je dois	je doive	*Past Part.:* dû,
owe, must (see 64)	tu dois	tu doives	due, dus, dues
devant	il doit	il doive	
j'ai dû	nous devons	nous devions	
je dus	vous devez	vous deviez	
je devrai	ils doivent	ils doivent	

60

dire	je dis	je dise	*Also:* suffire (but
say	tu dis	tu dises	*Pres. Indic.* vous
disant	il dit	il dise	suffisez; *Perfect*
j'ai dit	nous disons	nous disions	j'ai suffi)
je dis	vous dites	vous disiez	
je dirai	ils disent	ils disent	

dormir	je dors	je dorme	*Past Part.* in-
sleep	tu dors	tu dormes	variable
dormant	il dort	il dorme	
j'ai dormi	nous dormons	nous dormions	
je dormis	vous dormez	vous dormiez	
je dormirai	ils dorment	ils dorment	

écrire	j'écris	j'écrive	*Also:*
write	tu écris	tu écrives	décrire
écrivant	il écrit	il écrive	inscrire
j'ai écrit	nous écrivons	nous écrivions	
j'écrivis	vous écrivez	vous écriviez	
j'écrirai	ils écrivent	ils écrivent	

émouvoir *move* (emotion), as **mouvoir** but *Past Part.*: ému.

envoyer	j'envoie	j'envoie	
send	tu envoies	tu envoies	
envoyant	il envoie	il envoie	
j'ai envoyé	nous envoyons	nous envoyions	
j'envoyai	vous envoyez	vous envoyiez	
j'enverrai	ils envoient	ils envoient	

éteindre *extinguish*, see **feindre.**

exclure *exclude*, see **conclure.**

faire	je fais	je fasse	
make, do	tu fais	tu fasses	
faisant [fəzã]	il fait	il fasse	
j'ai fait	nous faisons	nous fassions	
je fis	vous faites	vous fassiez	
je ferai	ils font	ils fassent	

falloir	il faut	il faille	3rd Sing. only
be necessary (see 65)			*Imperfect Indic.*:
il a fallu			il fallait
il fallut			*Past Part.* in-
il faudra			variable

feindre	je feins	je feigne	*Also:*
pretend	tu feins	tu feignes	atteindre
feignant	il feint	il feigne	éteindre
j'ai feint	nous feignons	nous feignions	peindre

61

| je feignis | vous feignez | vous feigniez |
| je feindrai | ils feignent | ils feignent |

fuir	je fuis	je fuie
flee	tu fuis	tu fuies
fuyant	il fuit	il fuie
j'ai fui	nous fuyons	nous fuyions
je fuis	vous fuyez	vous fuyiez
je fuirai	ils fuient	ils fuient

haïr [aːir]	je hais [ɛ]	je haïsse	Note tréma (¨)
hate	tu hais	tu haïsses	over **i** through-
haïssant	il hait	il haïsse	out except in
j'ai haï	nous haïssons	nous haïssions	*Sing.* of *Pres.*
je haïs	vous haïssez	vous haïssiez	*Indic.*
je haïrai	ils haïssent	ils haïssent	

inclure *include*, see **conclure.**

inscrire *inscribe*, see **écrire.**

instruire *instruct*, see **conduire.**

introduire *introduce*, see **conduire.**

joindre	je joins	je joigne
join	tu joins	tu joignes
joignant	il joint	il joigne
j'ai joint	nous joignons	nous joignions
je joignis	vous joignez	vous joigniez
je joindrai	ils joignent	ils joignent

lire	je lis	je lise
read	tu lis	tu lises
lisant	il lit	il lise
j'ai lu	nous lisons	nous lisions
je lus	vous lisez	vous lisiez
je lirai	ils lisent	ils lisent

luire *shine*, as **conduire,** but *Past Part.*: lui (invariable) and no *Past Hist.*

mentir *tell a lie*, see **sentir.**

mettre	je mets (mɛ)	je mette
put	tu mets	tu mettes
mettant	il met	il mette
j'ai mis	nous mettons	nous mettions
je mis	vous mettez	vous mettiez
je mettrai	ils mettent	ils mettent

mourir	je meurs	je meure
die	tu meurs	tu meures
mourant	il meurt	il meure

je suis mort	nous mourons	nous mourions	
il mourut	vous mourez	vous mouriez	
je mourrai	ils meurent	ils meurent	

mouvoir	je meus	je meuve	*Past Part.*: mû,
move	tu meus	tu meuves	mue, mus, mues.
mouvant	il meut	il meuve	*Also*:
mû	nous mouvons	nous mouvions	émouvoir,
je mus	vous mouvez	vous mouviez	*Past Part.*: ému
je mouvrai	ils meuvent	ils meuvent	

naître	je nais	je naisse	Note **î** before **t**
be born	tu nais	tu naisses	throughout
naissant	il naît	il naisse	
je suis né	nous naissons	nous naissions	
je naquis	vous naissez	vous naissiez	
je naîtrai	ils naissent	ils naissent	

nuire *harm*, see **conduire**.

ouvrir	j'ouvre	j'ouvre	*Also*:
open	tu ouvres	tu ouvres	couvrir
ouvrant	il ouvre	il ouvre	offrir
j'ai ouvert	nous ouvrons	nous ouvrions	souffrir
j'ouvris	vous ouvrez	vous ouvriez	
j'ouvrirai	ils ouvrent	ils ouvrent	

paraître *appear*, see **connaître**.

partir	je pars	je parte	
depart	tu pars	tu partes	
partant	il part	il parte	
je suis parti	nous partons	nous partions	
je partis	vous partez	vous partiez	
je partirai	ils partent	ils partent	

peindre *paint*, see **feindre**.

plaindre *pity*, see **craindre**.

plaire	je plais	je plaise	*Past Part.* in-
please	tu plais	tu plaises	variable
plaisant	il plaît	il plaise	*Also* se taire (but
j'ai plu	nous plaisons	nous plaisions	*Pres. Indic.* il tait
je plus	vous plaisez	vous plaisiez	—no circum-
je plairai	ils plaisent	ils plaisent	flex—and *Past*
			Part. tu, tue)

pleuvoir	il pleut	il pleuve	3rd Sing. only
rain			*Past Part.* in-
pleuvant			variable
il a plu			

il plut
il pleuvra

pourvoir *provide*, see **voir.**

pouvoir	je peux (puis)	je puisse	*Past Part.* invariable
be able	tu peux	tu puisses	
pouvant	il peut	il puisse	
j'ai pu	nous pouvons	nous puissions	
je pus	vous pouvez	vous puissiez	
je pourrai	ils peuvent	ils puissent	
prendre	je prends	je prenne	
take	tu prends	tu prennes	
prenant	il prend	il prenne	
j'ai pris	nous prenons	nous prenions	
je pris	vous prenez	vous preniez	
je prendrai	ils prennent	ils prennent	

produire *produce*, see **conduire.**

recevoir	je reçois	je reçoive	Note **ç** before **o** or **u** throughout
receive	tu reçois	tu reçoives	
recevant	il reçoit	il reçoive	
j'ai reçu	nous recevons	nous recevions	*Also:*
je reçus	vous recevez	vous receviez	apercevoir
je recevrai	ils reçoivent	ils reçoivent	concevoir
			décevoir

réduire *reduce*, see **conduire.**

se repentir *repent*, see **sentir.**

résoudre	je résous	je résolve	*Also:* absoudre, but *Past Part.*: absous, absoute
resolve	tu résous	tu résolves	
résolvant	il résout	il résolve	
j'ai résolu	nous résolvons	nous résolvions	
je résolus	vous résolvez	vous résolviez	
je résoudrai	il résolvent	ils résolvent	
rire	je ris	je rie	*Past Part.* invariable
laugh	tu ris	tu ries	
riant	il rit	il rie	
j'ai ri	nous rions	nous riions	
je ris	vous riez	vous riiez	
je rirai	ils rient	ils rient	

rompre *break*, see 3 n. 1.

savoir	je sais	je sache	*Imperfect Indic.*: je savais
know (see 67 (*a*))	tu sais	tu saches	
sachant	il sait	il sache	*Imperative*: sache, sachons, sachez
j'ai su	nous savons	nous sachions	

je sus	vous savez	vous sachiez	
je saurai	ils savent	ils sachent	
sentir	je sens	je sente	*Also:*
feel	tu sens	tu sentes	mentir
sentant	il sent	il sente	se repentir
j'ai senti	nous sentons	nous sentions	
je sentis	vous sentez	vous sentiez	
je sentirai	ils sentent	ils sentent	
servir	je sers	je serve	
serve	tu sers	tu serves	
servant	il sert	il serve	
j'ai servi	nous servons	nous servions	
je servis	vous servez	vous serviez	
je servirai	ils servent	ils servent	
sortir	je sors	je sorte	
go out	tu sors	tu sortes	
sortant	il sort	ils sorte	
je suis sorti	nous sortons	nous sortions	
je sortis	vous sortez	vous sortiez	
je sortirai	ils sortent	ils sortent	

souffrir *suffer,* see **ouvrir.**

suivre	je suis	je suive	
follow	tu suis	tu suives	
suivant	il suit	il suive	
j'ai suivi	nous suivons	nous suivions	
je suivis	vous suivez	vous suiviez	
je suivrai	ils suivent	ils suivent	

se taire *be silent,* see **plaire.**

tenir *hold,* as **venir,** but compounded with *avoir.*

traduire *translate,* see **conduire.**

vaincre	je vaincs [vɛ̃]	je vainque	*Also:*
conquer	tu vaincs	tu vainques	convaincre
vainquant	il vainc	il vainque	
j'ai vaincu	nous vainquons	nous vainquions	
je vainquis	vous vainquez	vous vainquiez	
je vaincrai	ils vainquent	ils vainquent	
valoir	je vaux	je vaille	
be worth (see 68)	tu vaux	tu vailles	
valant	il vaut	il vaille	
j'ai valu	nous valons	nous valions	
je valus	vous valez	nous valiez	
je vaudrai	ils valent	ils vaillent	

venir *come* venant je suis venu je vins je viendrai	je viens tu viens il vient nous venons vous venez ils viennent	je vienne tu viennes il vienne nous venions vous veniez ils viennent	*Past Hist.*: je vins, tu vins, il vint, nous vînmes (vɛ̃:m), vous vîntes (vɛ̃:t), ils vinrent (vɛ̃:r). *Impf. Subjunc.*: 3rd Sing.: il vînt
vêtir *clothe* vêtant vêtu je vêtis je vêtirai	je vêts tu vêts il vêt nous vêtons vous vêtez ils vêtent	je vêtisse tu vêtisses il vêtisse nous vêtissions vous vêtissiez ils vêtissent	*Also:* revêtir
vivre *live* vivant j'ai vécu je vécus je vivrai	je vis tu vis il vit nous vivons vous vivez ils vivent	je vive tu vives il vive nous vivions vous viviez ils vivent	
voir *see* voyant j'ai vu je vis je verrai	je vois tu vois il voit nous voyons vous voyez ils voient	je voie tu voies il voie nous voyions vous voyiez ils voient	*Also:* pourvoir, but *Past Hist.*: pourvus, *Fut.*: pourvoirai
vouloir *wish, want* (see 69) voulant j'ai voulu je voulus je voudrai	je veux tu veux il veut nous voulons vous voulez ils veulent	je veuille tu veuilles il veuille nous voulions vous vouliez ils veuillent	*Imperative* either regular or: veuille, veuillons, veuillez

II. USE OF TENSES

French tenses have, for the most part, the same range of uses as the tense of the same name in English. Such parallel uses (which must, of course, be grasped in English grammar before they can be understood in French) are not repeated here. The notes in the following sections refer only to the more frequent points where French usage differs from English, or where the choice of tense presents special difficulties.

The use and meanings of the Subjunctive are dealt with in Chapter IV.

13. English Equivalents of French Tenses

(*a*) It should be noted in particular that many English tenses have more than one form, while the corresponding French tense has only one. Thus, for example, the French Present **je parle** may have for its English equivalent *I speak*, *I am speaking*, or *I do speak*:

Elle sait toutes mes affaires.   C'est ce que je demande.
She knows all my business.   *It is what I am asking.*
Le moteur ne marche pas.
The engine is not working.
Croyez-vous que j'ignore ce qui se passe? (Stendhal)
Do you think that I do not know what is going on?

Similarly, e.g.:

Past Historic: je parlai   *I spoke, I did speak.*
Future: je parlerai   *I shall speak, I shall be speaking.*
Pluperfect: j'avais parlé   *I had spoken, I had been speaking.*

(*b*) Where the English form such as *I am speaking*, *I do speak* is emphatic, this may be conveyed by various expressions in French, e.g.:

Il était en train de faire ses malles quand le taxi arriva.
He was (engaged in) packing his trunks when the taxi arrived.

67

Je lui ai bien dit de s'arrêter.
I did (indeed) tell him to stop.

NOTES ON PARTICULAR TENSES

14. Present

(*a*) The French Present is sometimes used, where English normally uses the Future, to express immediate likelihood:

En deux jours je suis à Besançon (Stendhal).
In two days I shall be at Besançon.

Allons, cache-moi, ou je te tue (Mérimée).
Come on, hide me, or I will kill you.

(*b*) The use of the Present Tense to describe a rapid series of past actions is more common in French than in English. For instance, such a passage as the following, describing a thunderstorm, might well have been related in past tenses in English:

Pendant que je considérais ce phénomène, soudain **se lèvent** des nuages épais et lourds.... En un instant ils **s'étendent** au loin, **cernent** l'horizon, **enveloppent** le ciel entier.... A une lumière éclatante **succède** une nuit sépulcrale. Dans la profondeur de ces ténèbres, **jaillissent** des éclairs sur les nuées ... puis **se perdent** dans l'obscurité (Xavier Marmier).

15. Imperfect

The Imperfect is the past tense which:

(*a*) Conveys that the action of the verb is part of the state of affairs prevailing at the time:

Il neigeait et les routes étaient dangereuses.
It was snowing and the roads were dangerous.
Pendant tout cela il regardait fixement le plafond.
During all this he stared at the ceiling.
Je lui demandai si elle connaissait M. Barbelenet (Romains).
I asked her if she knew Mr. Barbelenet.

(*b*) Is the equivalent of the English form of the Imperfect *was (were) doing*:

Les autres frottaient le parquet.
The others were polishing the floor.

Elle racontait toutes ses démarches quand un poids léger lui tomba sur l'épaule (Flaubert).
She was recounting all her movements when a light weight fell on her shoulder.

(c) Describes an habitual past action:

Elle faisait la cuisine et le ménage, cousait, lavait, repassait (Flaubert).
She used to do the cooking and the housework, sew, wash, and iron.

Quand on lui parlait, il souriait et montrait ses dents (Daudet).
When one spoke to him, he would smile and exhibit his teeth.

16. Past Historic

(a) The Past Historic is the past tense which, in books and formal speeches and letters, conveys that the action of the verb is being viewed as an event, as something which happened:

Il sauta dans le trou.
He jumped into the hole.

L'ancien bâtiment fut démoli.
The previous building was demolished.

Nous restâmes un moment silencieux (Romains).
We stopped for a moment in silence.

Il y eut une explosion de rires (Daudet).
There was a burst of laughter.

Je fus reçue par les deux sœurs (Romains).
I was received by the two sisters.

(b) It may sometimes be used when the sudden emergence of a new state of affairs amounts virtually to an action:

Soudain il sut qu'elle l'avait trompé.
Suddenly he knew that she had been deceiving him.

Il le disait si gaiement que je ne pus m'empêcher de rire (Romains).
He said it so gaily that I could not help laughing.

69

17. Perfect

(a) The French Perfect Tense is the equivalent of the English forms of the Perfect *have (has) done, have (has) been doing*:

> Le curé a refusé d'obéir; il s'est même enfermé dans l'église (Maupassant).
> *The vicar has refused to obey; he has actually shut himself in the church.*
> Drôle, tu as fumé! (A. Theuriet)
> *You scamp, you have been smoking!*

(b) The Perfect, as a general rule, replaces, in conversation and in ordinary letters, the Past Historic as the tense which describes past events (see 16):

> 'Quand il a fallu lui déclarer mes dettes, j'ai souffert le martyre; mais enfin j'ai trouvé le courage de les dire' (Balzac).
> *'When I had to tell him about my debts, I went through tortures; but in the end I found the courage to relate them.'*
> Je m'y suis promenée tout le soir; j'y ai trouvé toutes mes tristes pensées (Letter of Madame de Sévigné).
> *I walked there the whole evening; I found in it all my sad thoughts.*

18. Imperfect, Past Historic, and Perfect Compared

It will have been seen above that the French Imperfect, Past Historic, and Perfect may all in turn be the equivalent of the English past tense *I did, I was*, &c. The following passage gives examples of all three so used, the type of use being indicated by numbers in brackets in the translation, as shown:

On **remonta** sur le pont après le dîner. Devant nous, la Méditerranée n'**avait** pas un frisson sur toute sa surface, qu'une grande lune calme **moirait**. Le vaste bateau **glissait** . . . et, derrière nous, l'eau toute blanche . . . **moussait, semblait** se tordre. . . .

We *went up*(1) on deck again after dinner. In front of us the Mediterranean *had*(2) not a ripple on its whole surface, on which a big peaceful moon *poured*(2) a shimmering light. The mighty ship *glided*(2) on . . . and behind us the water, all white . . . *foamed*(2), *seemed*(2) to writhe.

Nous **étions** là, six ou huit, silencieux, admirant, l'œil tourné vers l'Afrique lointaine où nous **allions.** Le commandant, qui **fumait** un cigare au milieu de nous, **reprit** soudain la conversation du dîner.

— Oui, j'**ai eu** peur ce jour-là. Mon navire **est resté** six heures avec ce rocher dans le ventre, battu par la mer. Heureusement que nous **avons été recueillis,** vers le soir, par un charbonnier anglais (Maupassant).

There *were*(2) six or eight of us there, silent, in admiration, our eyes turned towards distant Africa, whither we *were going*(2). The captain, who *was smoking*(2) a cigar in our midst, suddenly *resumed*(1) the conversation from dinner.

'Yes, I *felt*(3) fear that day. My ship *remained*(3) six hours with this rock in its belly, pounded by the sea. It happened fortunately that we *were picked up*(3), towards evening, by an English collier.'

(1) Past Historic recounting an event.
(2) Imperfect recounting a state of affairs.
(3) Perfect used, in conversation, to recount an event.

19. Pluperfect and Past Anterior

The French Pluperfect (**j'avais fait**) is the normal equivalent of the English Pluperfect forms *I had done, I had been doing,* but the French Past Anterior (**j'eus fait**) replaces the Pluperfect in Time Clauses (introduced by, e.g. *quand, après que, aussitôt que, dès que*) in sentences where the verb of the main clause is Past Historic:

Quand ils eurent dîné, ils approchèrent leurs chaises du feu.
When they had dined they drew their chairs up to the fire.
Dès qu'il eut pensé à lui, il se crut sauvé (Daudet).
As soon as he had thought of him, he felt he was saved.

The Past Anterior is also used, with Adverbs of Time, in a main clause to convey rapid completion of an event:

Il eut bientôt démonté l'antenne.
He had soon dismantled the aerial.

20. The Future and Conditional in Subordinate Clauses

(a) In subordinate clauses, principally those of Time, the Future and Future Perfect are used where the implication is that the action of the verb has not yet been performed. The English normally here uses the Present and Perfect respectively:

71

Ils entreront quand ils voudront (Daudet).
They will come in when they like.
Vous pouvez sortir dès que vous l'aurez fini.
You can go out as soon as you have finished it.

(*b*) The French Conditional and Conditional Perfect are similarly used when the sequence is historic:

Il leur dit de monter quand ils seraient prêts.
He told them to come up when they were ready.
Il devait partir dès qu'il l'aurait fini.
He was to leave as soon as he had finished it.

21. Will, Shall, Would, Should

(*a*) The English *I shall* (*will*) *go* may be a genuine Future Tense (i.e. it states that something will happen), and is then rendered by the French Future:

J'irai demain.   Il n'y sera pas.
I shall go tomorrow.   *He will not be there.*

Similarly *I should* (*would*) *go* may be a genuine Conditional Tense (i.e. it implies that something would happen if something else did). The equivalent is then the French Conditional:

En ce cas il le trouverait facilement.
In that case he would easily find it.

(*b*) But where *shall, will, should, would* have other senses, they must be rendered otherwise, e.g.:

(i) *shall, should*, meaning duty or obligation (*you shall stay at home; I should write it now*) usually by a tense of **devoir** (see 64);

(ii) *will, would*, expressing willingness (*will you help me; he would not answer*) or determination (*I will not put up with it; in spite of it he would go out*) usually by a tense of **vouloir** (see 69);

(iii) *would* expressing habit (*on Sundays he would work in the garden*) by the Imperfect of the verb concerned (see 15 (*c*)).

22. Tenses after *si* = if

The choice of tenses in the **si**-clause depends mainly on the tense present in the other half of the Conditional Sentence, the half which states what the result is or would be.

(*a*) If the tense in the 'result half' is Conditional or Conditional Perfect, **si** is normally followed by the Imperfect or Pluperfect Indicative, as appropriate:

Il ne dînerait pas chez vous, si vous l'invitiez (Maurois).
He would not dine with you if you invited him.
Si j'avais eu des parents tout cela ne serait peut-être pas arrivé (Balzac).
If I had had any family all this would perhaps not have happened.

(*b*) Elsewhere the tense after **si** may be any one that is appropriate to the meaning, except that the English Future becomes the Present in French. Thus, e.g.:

Si tu parles, nous serons fusillés (Daudet).
If you speak, we shall be shot.
S'il est avec vous, il n'y aura aucune difficulté.
If he will be with you, there will be no difficulty.
Si je me suis trompé, je le regrette infiniment.
If I have made a mistake, I am extremely sorry.

N.B. 1. Neither the Future nor the Conditional is ever present in the **si-** clause itself.

2. The English *should* and *would* do not always represent the Conditional Tense (see 21). Similarly *could* may = *would be able*, and is then Conditional,[1] or may = *was able*, and is then a past tense (see use of **pouvoir** in 66).

3. In a certain type of sentence, a **si-** clause may be present without a result clause, **si** then having the sense of *supposing*:

Si on ne le trouvait pas ! s'il n'allait pas venir ! (Daudet)
Supposing we did not find him! supposing he did not come!
Si nous allions au cinéma ?
What if we went to the cinema ?

        1 Unless it is in the **si**-clause (see N.B. (1) above).

23. Tenses with *venir de*

The Present and Imperfect Tenses of **venir de** express the ideas of *have just* and *had just* (*done something*) respectively:

> Il vient de m'annoncer la nouvelle.
> *He has just announced the news to me.*
> Le coup qu'il venait de recevoir (Balzac).
> *The blow which he had just received.*

24. Tenses with *depuis*, &c.

With **depuis, depuis que, il y a . . . que, voilà . . . que:**

(*a*) Where the action is considered as still going on at the time, the French Present and Imperfect represent the English Perfect and Pluperfect respectively:

> J'habite depuis[1] quarante ans la même maison (France).
> *I have been living for[2] forty years in the same house.*
> Il était absent depuis[1] quelques heures (Mérimée).
> *He had been absent for[2] some hours.*
> Depuis que je suis ici je n'ai vu personne.
> *Since I have been here I have not seen anyone.*
> Voilà six mois que je m'applique (Pailleron).
> *For six months I have been concentrating.*
> Il y avait une heure que je ne mangeais plus (Mérimée).
> *I had not been eating any more for the last hour.*

(*b*) Where the action is already completed, the tense with **depuis,** &c. is the same as in English:

> Depuis que nous avons débarqué nous avons été volées par tout le monde (About).
> *Since we came off the ship we have been robbed by everyone.*
> Le temps s'était gâté depuis[1] la veille.
> *The weather had got worse since the day before.*

(*c*) Where a negative is involved or implied, as in *I have not seen him for two years,* or *it is two years since I saw him,* either the Present or the Perfect may be used. (See examples in 253 (*c*)).

---

[1] Note that, as used in (*a*), the English equivalent of **depuis** is *for*; in (*b*) it is *since.*
[2] See also 'FOR' in Appendix C.

III. INFINITIVE

25. Nature of the Infinitive

(a) The Infinitive is the noun form of the verb. It is constructed like a noun in that it may stand as subject, complement, or object of another verb, or may be governed by a preposition:

Attendre serait inutile.
To wait would be pointless.
Cela s'appelle voler.
That is called stealing.
Il veut sortir (cf. Il veut du pain).
He wants to go out (cf. *He wants some bread*).
Sans parler; avant d'entrer; pour réussir.
Without speaking; before going in; in order to succeed.

(b) A few infinitives are also used as true nouns (all masculine). They may be preceded by the article, and some of them may be used in the plural, e.g.:

le devoir;   le rire;   le déjeuner, dîner, &c.
duty, homework;   laugh, laughter;   lunch, dinner, &c.
                un lever de soleil;   des vivres.
                a sunrise;   provisions.

(c) The Infinitive is sometimes used for the Imperative in official notices, etc.:

Ne pas se pencher au dehors.   S'adresser au concierge.
Do not lean out.   *Apply to the porter.*

(d) It may have a deliberative force in such forms of expression as:

Que faire?   Comment le demander?
What is to be done?   *How should one ask for it?*
Il se demandait quel chemin prendre (Maupassant).
He wondered which road to take.

75

(*e*) Or express an exclamation:

> L'attacher! Quelle drôle d'idée! (Saint-Exupéry)
> *Tie it up! What a funny idea!*

26. The Infinitive Governed by a Verb

The Infinitive is the form of the verb which is required when it is governed by another verb,[1] but with the distinction that some governing verbs require a plain infinitive, and some an infinitive with the preposition **à,** and some with the preposition **de;**

> Il veut le faire.   Il réussit à le faire.
> *He wants to do it.*   *He succeeds in doing it.*
> Il essaya de le faire.
> *He tried to do it.*

A few examples of such verbs are listed in the following sections, and some attempt has been made to classify them, but this is only a rough guide, and real familiarity can only come from learning.

A consolidated list of the commoner infinitive constructions is given in Appendix A.

27. Verb + Plain Infinitive

The following are the commoner groups of verbs which govern a plain infinitive:

(*a*) Verbs of Wishing, &c., e.g. **désirer, souhaiter, vouloir** *wish* to; **espérer** *hope to*; **préférer** *prefer to*:

> Je souhaite parler à M. Derville (Balzac).   Il préfère rester.
> *I wish to speak to M. Derville.*   *He prefers to stay.*

N.B. The infinitive construction is only possible with verbs of wishing when they and the infinitive both have the same subject. When there is a change of subject, **que** and a subjunctive clause must be used (cf. 45 (*a*)):

> Je veux qu'il s'en aille.   *I want him to go away.*

---

[1] This does not apply when **avoir** or **être** are used as auxiliaries in, for example, the Perfect Tense.

(b) Verbs of Motion, e.g. **aller, courir, descendre, monter, rentrer, retourner, revenir, venir** (see also 30), and also **envoyer**:

Il irait prendre des informations (Flaubert).
He would go and get some information.

Ils sont descendus voir la cascade.
They got out to see the waterfall.

Venez m'aider.
Come and help me.

Il envoya chercher un médecin.
He sent for a doctor.

Where the idea of purpose is emphatic, this may be conveyed by **pour** before the infinitive:

Je ne suis pas venu pour écouter des injures.
I have not come to listen to insults.

(c) Modal Verbs in **-oir**, e.g. **devoir, falloir, pouvoir, savoir, valoir** (for further examples of use and meaning see 64 ff.):

J'ai dû revenir.
I have had to return.

Il sait le faire.
He knows how to do it.

Il vaut mieux les garder.
It is better to keep them.

(d) Verbs taking a complement, e.g. **être** (but see also 32 (c)), **paraître, sembler,** and such expressions as **être jugé, être supposé, s'appeler**:

C'est gaspiller son argent.
It is wasting one's money.

Il semblait l'ignorer.
He seemed to be ignorant of it.

Elle est supposée être espagnole.
She is supposed to be Spanish.

(e) Verbs of Saying or Thinking, e.g. **affirmer** *declare*; **croire** *think*; **dire** (see also 30) *say*; **prétendre** *claim*:

Si quelqu'un dit être le colonel, ce n'est qu'un intrigant (Balzac).
If anyone says he is the colonel, he is only an impostor.

Elle crut distinguer une chose verte (Flaubert).
She thought she made out a green object.

N.B. 1. The above construction is only possible where the

77

subject of the infinitive is the same as that of the verb which governs it. Where the subject is different, **que** and a clause must be used, cf.:

Je crois être malade.   Je crois qu'il est malade.
I think I am ill.   *I think he is ill.*

For use of subjunctive with verbs of saying or thinking, see 45 (*d*).

2. Even where the subjects are the same, the infinitive construction is often replaced by the construction with **que** and a clause, e.g. **Je crois que je me suis enrhumé** *I think I have caught a cold.* The infinitive construction is the mark of careful writing, and is only used in rather precise speech.

(*f*) Verbs of Seeing, Hearing, Feeling, &c., e.g. **apercevoir** *perceive*; **écouter** *listen to*; **entendre** *hear* (see also (*g*) (ii)); **regarder** *watch*; **sentir** *feel, perceive, smell*; **voir** *see*:

On les entendait jouer du piano (Daudet).
One heard them playing the piano.
On voyait paraître un vieux paysan (Flaubert).
An old peasant was seen to appear.
Il regardait les mobiles faire l'exercice (Daudet).
He watched the militia drilling.
Il se sentit toucher le bras (Verne).
He felt his arm touched.

N.B. 1. In general the infinitive stands directly after the verb of seeing, &c., which governs it. The purpose of this is to produce a better balance of the sentence, and to avoid finishing with an unconvincing sound. Thus:

On voyait paraître un vieux paysan.
not   (*On voyait un vieux paysan paraître.*)
Il se sentit toucher le bras.
not   (*Il se sentit le bras toucher.*)

But where a better balance is preserved by postponing the infinitive, this is done. Thus:

Il regardait les mobiles faire l'exercice.
not   (*Il regardait faire l'exercice les mobiles.*)

2. The infinitive construction is not obligatory after verbs of seeing, &c. A relative clause or occasionally a present participle may be used instead (see 37 (*d*)).

3. Note that, in such sentences as **Il se sentit toucher le bras,** the French Infinitive has a sense equivalent to that of an English Passive (He felt his arm *touched*).

(*g*) **faire** and **laisser**

(i) In an *active* sense: **faire** = *make someone do something*; **laisser** = *let someone do something*.

Il me fit attendre en bas.
He made me wait downstairs.
Le soleil faisait luire la rivière (Flaubert).
The sun made the river glisten.
Laissez-moi dormir.
Let me sleep.

(ii) In a *passive* sense (the infinitive remaining *active* in French): **faire** = *have something done*; **laisser** = *let something be done*. (**Entendre** and **voir** may similarly be used with the infinitive having a passive sense, see examples in 54 (*d*)):

Elle fit appeler un prêtre (Flaubert).
She had a priest called.
Il se laissait tromper comme un enfant (Daudet).
He let himself be taken in like a child.

N.B. For the order of words in the above examples see the observations in Note 1 to (*f*) above (p. 78), which apply equally here.

28. Verb + Infinitive with *à*

(For verbs taking **à** with object see 51–53, 55)

In general the preposition **à** conveys an idea of:

(*a*) intention, purpose, end in view, as in e.g. **aider à** *help to*; **apprendre à** *learn* (*teach*) *to*; **commencer à** *begin to*; **condamner à** *condemn to*; **se décider à** *make up one's mind to*; **se préparer à** *make ready to*; **servir à** *be useful for*.

(*b*) the form the activity is taking (English *in* (*by*) *doing something*), as in e.g. **consister à** *consist in*; **exceller à** *excel in*; **s'occuper à** *occupy oneself in* (*by*); **persister à** *persist in*; **réussir à** *succeed in*; and expressions with similar force, as **passer** (**perdre**) **son temps à** *spend* (*waste*) *one's time in*; **prendre plaisir à** *take pleasure in*.

Il les aida à porter les valises.
He helped them to carry the bags.
Je ne peux pas me décider à les sacrifier (Duhamel).
I cannot make up my mind to sacrifice them.
Le travail consiste à tenir les comptes.
The work consists in keeping the accounts.

29. Verb + Infinitive with *de*
(For verbs taking **de** with object see 56)

This group, including as it does all relevant verbs that are not constructed with a plain infinitive or an infinitive with **à**, is too large to be easily classified. It may, however, be said that the following types are among those most likely to take an infinitive with **de**:

(*a*) Verbs whose English equivalent is followed by the word *of* or *from*, e.g. **accuser de** *accuse of*; **avoir peur de** *be afraid of*; **décourager de** *discourage from*; **empêcher de** *prevent* (*from*); **soupçonner de** *suspect of*.

(*b*) Verbs introducing an idea of ceasing, avoiding, refusing, e.g. **cesser de** *cease*; **éviter de** *avoid*; **omettre de** *omit*; **refuser de** *refuse*.

(*c*) Verbs expressing an emotion or opinion about an action, e.g. **blâmer de** *blame for*; **s'étonner de** *be astonished at*; **pardonner de** *forgive for*; **remercier de** *thank for*; **reprocher de** *reproach for*; and expressions having a similar force, e.g. **être content, dégoûté, de** *be pleased, disgusted, at*. (Perf. Infin. frequent after such verbs.)

(*d*) Verbs of Ordering, Requesting, Persuading, Permitting, Forbidding, &c., e.g. **commander** (**ordonner**) **de** *order to*; **défendre de** *forbid to*; **permettre de** *allow to*; **persuader de** *persuade to*. (Most of these also take a Dative of the Person, see sections 52, 53.)

(e) Most Impersonal Verbs and Expressions, e.g. **il s'agit de** *it is a question of*; **il importe de** *it is important to*; **il est temps de** *it is time to*; **il est prudent de** *it is wise to*.

> Il avait peur de se confier au radeau.
> *He was afraid to entrust himself to the raft.*
> Il a évité de les contrarier.
> *He avoided upsetting them.*
> Je regrette de vous avoir dérangé.
> *I am sorry to have disturbed you.*
> Je leur ai défendu de vous importuner (Balzac).
> *I have forbidden them to trouble you.*
> Il me remercia de l'avoir dit.
> *He thanked me for saying so.*

30. Verbs Taking More Than One Infinitive Construction

The following are the very commonest cases, involving a definite distinction of meaning or use:

AIMER

1. Plain Infin. when in Conditional or followed by *mieux* or *autant*	J'aimerais aller au spectacle	I would like to go to the play
	Il aime mieux rester à la maison	He prefers to stay at home
2. Otherwise (in strict usage only) **à**	J'aime (à) voir un spectacle	I like to see a play

DEMANDER (see also 45 (g))

1. *Ask to do something oneself*—**à**	Il demanda à sortir	He asked to go out
2. *Ask someone to do something*—**de**	Il demanda à l'enfant de l'aider	He asked the child to help him

DIRE

1. = *say*—Plain Infin. (but see also note to 27 (e))	Il dit être le chef	He says he is the leader
2. = *tell* (= *order*)—**de**	Il lui dit de s'en aller	He told him to go away

VENIR

1. Verb of Motion— Il vint me voir   *He came to see me*
   Plain Infin.
2. = *happen to*—**à**   Il vint à passer   *He happened to pass*
3. = *have just*—**de**   Je viens (venais) de le   *I have (had) just seen him*
                    voir

Note also:

commencer à (de) faire	*begin to do*
commencer par faire	*begin by doing*
décider à faire	*induce to do*
être décidé à faire	*be resolved to do*
décider de faire	*decide to do*
se décider à faire	*make up one's mind to do*
finir de faire	*finish doing*
finir par faire	*end up by doing*
s'occuper à faire	*occupy oneself (in) doing*
s'occuper de faire	*see to doing, take an interest in doing*
penser faire	*intend to do*
penser à faire	*think of doing (idea occurs)*
prendre garde à faire	*take care to do*
prendre garde de faire	*take care not to do, beware of doing*
tarder à faire	*be long (in) doing*
il me tarde de le faire	*I long to do it*

31. Other Uses of *à* with Infinitive

(*a*) Forming an adjectival phrase with a sense of purpose, suitability, &c.:

(i) with an *active* sense in English:

une salle à manger.   une machine à coudre.
a dining-room.   *a sewing-machine.*
quelque chose à faire.
something to do.
une bonne à tout faire.
a maid of all work.

Nous sommes des gens à vous suivre jusqu'au bout (Verne).
We are men to follow you to the end.

(ii) with a *passive* sense in English:

> Un homme à redouter.   Vous êtes à plaindre.
> *A man to be feared.*   *You are to be pitied.*
> La maison était à vendre.
> *The house was for sale.*
> Le chemin à suivre.
> *The course to be pursued.*

(b) Forming adverbial phrases expressing a degree of intensity:

> Je m'ennuie à mourir.   Elle est laide à faire peur.
> *I am bored to death.*   *She is frightfully ugly.*
> Une tape à tuer un rhinocéros (Balzac).
> *A blow that would have killed a rhinoceros.*

(c) For the use of **à** in such forms of expression as **long à venir** see under **à** in Appendix B, and as in **c'est difficile à faire** see 174 (b).

32. Other Uses of *de* with Infinitive

(a) After numerous nouns, particularly where *of* is present or implied in English:

> le besoin de le faire.   l'honneur de le recevoir.
> *the need to do (of doing) it.*   *the honour of receiving him.*
> le plaisir de vous voir.
> *the pleasure of seeing you.*

Note also, e.g.:

> Ayez la bonté de m'aider.   Je n'ai pas le temps de le faire.
> *Be so kind as to help me.*   *I have not time to do it.*
> Il combattait son envie de rire.
> *He was struggling with his desire to laugh.*

(b) After numerous adjectives, notably:

(i) those where *of* is present in the English version, e.g. **incapable de** *incapable of*; **certain, sûr de** *certain of, to*; **digne de** *worthy of*.

(ii) adjectives of emotion, e.g. **curieux de** *curious to*; **étonné de** *astonished at*; **fâché de** *annoyed at*; **fier de** *proud of*; **heureux de** *happy to*.

(c) Where the Infinitive stands as Complement:

Son premier geste fut d'ouvrir son panier (Flaubert).
Her first move was to open her basket.
Le plus important c'est d'obtenir des renseignements.
The most important thing is to get some information.

But **de** is omitted where the Subject is also an Infinitive; or where
the sole subject is a neuter pronoun, such as **ce, cela**:

Voir, c'est croire.   C'est perdre son temps.
Seeing is believing.   *It is wasting one's time.*

(d) In such forms of expression as:

De penser à cela le sang lui sauta à la tête (Daudet).
At the thought of that the blood rushed to his head.

(e) For the use of **de** with the Infinitive after *c'est* and *il est* (as in
c'est une folie de faire cela and **il est difficile de faire cela**)
see 174 (b).

(f) For the use of **de** with the Infinitive in the second part of a
Comparative Sentence (as in **Il vaut mieux rester que de partir**)
see 133 (c).

IV. PARTICIPLES

PRESENT PARTICIPLE

33. As an Adjective

Where the Present Participle describes a quality or state, it ranks as an adjective. It then agrees in Gender and Number with the noun or pronoun it qualifies or refers to:

Une femme charmante.	La semaine suivante
A charming woman.	*The following week.*
Elle est bien portante.	Les enfants sont très obéissants.
She is in good health.	*The children are very obedient.*

34. As Participle of the Verb

Where the Present Participle describes an action being performed, it is a pure participle and is invariable:

> Des troupes arrivaient, se massant derrière les murs (Daudet).
> *Troops were arriving, assembling behind the walls.*

> Trois cents femmes, toutes criant, hurlant, gesticulant (Mérimée).
> *Three hundred women all, shouting, shrieking, gesticulating.*

The Present Participle is also invariable when used in forming the Perfect Participle, e.g. **étant sorties.**

35. As Gerund, with *en*

(*a*) The Present Participle form also supplies that of the Gerund (invariable), which is almost always preceded by the Preposition **en.**[1] **En** and the Gerund convey:

(i) the senses of *while, in, on, by doing something,* &c.;

> En passant sous le pont elle entendit un bruit sourd.
> *While passing under the bridge she heard a dull noise.*

[1] **En** is absent in a few set expressions, such as: **ce disant** *saying this*; **chemin faisant** *while on the way*.

Il l'amusait en lui racontant des histoires (Flaubert).
He amused her by telling her stories.
En le voyant le Prussien se mit à rire (Daudet).
On seeing him the Prussian started laughing.
Son père s'était tué en tombant d'un échafaudage (Flaubert).
Her father had been killed in falling from a scaffolding.

Note the use of **en** + Gerund to describe manner of motion:

Il sortit (descendit) en courant. Je traversai la route en rampant.
He ran out (down).   *I crawled across the road.*

(ii) that the action they express is going on at the same time as
    that of the main verb:

Elle répondit en hésitant: 'Je ne sais pas' (Maupassant).
She replied hesitatingly: 'I don't know.'
'Couche-toi!' fit le grand, en se jetant par terre (Daudet).
'Lie down!' said the big fellow, throwing himself on the ground.

    Cf. the Present Participle (without *en*), which may be used
to express an action which precedes that of the main verb:

Descendant de son auto, il entra dans un café.
Getting out of his car, he went into a cafe.

(iii) that the action they express is being performed by the
    subject of the main verb:

J'ai vu mon frère en sortant de l'école.
I saw my brother as I came out of school.

    Cf. the Present Participle (without *en*) which may be used to
express an action by someone else than the subject:

J'ai vu mon frère sortant tristement de l'école.
I saw my brother coming sadly out of school.

(*b*) The addition of the Adverb **tout** (invariable) before **en**
emphasizes the fact that the action is simultaneous with that of the
main verb, or it may have a concessive sense:

Tout en mangeant, l'ancien soldat regardait son fusil (Daudet).
(All the time) while eating, the old soldier was looking at his rifle.
Tout en admettant vos raisons, je ne suis pas convaincu.
While admitting your arguments, I am not convinced.

36. As a Noun

The Present Participle may also be used as a noun, in which case it has normal feminine and plural forms:

Les vivants et les mourants.
The living and the dying.
Je ne suis pas une simple passante (Romains).
I am not a mere passer-by.

37. The Translation of English Verb Forms in -ing

The French form in **-ant** does not always correspond to the English form in *-ing*. Note that:

(*a*) Where the latter forms part of a tense, it must be rendered by the appropriate tense in French (see 13):

il parle	he is speaking	il a parlé	he has been speaking
il parlait	he was speaking	il avait parlé	he had been speaking
il parlera	he will be speaking	il aurait parlé	he would have been speaking

But see also Note to 38 (*b*).

(*b*) When governed by a Preposition the French form will be the Infinitive (or Gerund after **en**):

sans parler.   avant d'entrer.   en tombant.
without speaking.   *before entering.*   *in falling.*

(*c*) When governed by another Verb the French form will be the Infinitive (with or without a preposition, as the construction of that verb requires—see 26 ff.):

J'aime mieux patiner.   Elle s'occupait à coudre.
I prefer skating.   *She busied herself sewing.*
Il évita de tomber.
He avoided falling.

(*d*) Where a form in *-ing* is governed by a verb of seeing, hearing, &c., various constructions are possible in French:

(i) the Infinitive, as above:

On entendait chanter des poules (Flaubert).
One heard hens clucking.

(ii) a Relative Clause:

Je l'entendis qui demandait à voir son fils (Daudet).
I heard her asking to see her son.

(iii) occasionally a Present Participle:

On entendait la pluie tombant sur les mosaïques des cours
(Daudet).
One heard the rain falling on the mosaics of the courtyards.

(e) When standing as subject or complement the French form is
the Infinitive (see also 25 (a), 32 (c)):

Voir, c'est croire.   *Seeing is believing.*

Past Participle

38. As an Adjective

(a) The Past Participle may describe a quality or state. It then
ranks as an adjective, and agrees in gender and number with the
noun or pronoun it qualifies or refers to:

La semaine passée.	Une comédienne bien connue.
Last (the past) week.	*A well-known actress.*
Ils sont très fâchés.	*They are very annoyed.*

(b) It may thus be considered as an adjective in such expressions as:

Maman est sortie.	Les autres étaient morts.
Mother is out.	*The others were dead.*
L'hiver est passé.	Elle était assise derrière moi.
Winter is past.	*She was sitting behind me.*

In the above expression the participle expresses a *state, position,* &c.
Compare the following examples, where the participle forms part
of a tense describing an *action*:

Maman est sortie à dix heures.
Mother went out at ten o'clock.
Les autres étaient morts de soif.
The others had died of thirst.

L'hiver a passé vite.	Elle s'était assise derrière moi.
The winter has passed quickly.	*She had sat down behind me.*

N.B. In the case of some participles, used as adjectives, which express an attitude of the body, &c. (e.g. **assis.** = *sitting*, above), French uses the Past Participle where the English form is the Present Participle. Similarly: **appuyé, penché** *leaning*; **agenouillé** *kneeling*; **couché, étendu** *lying*; **(sus)pendu** *hanging*.

Il le voyait étendu là-bas dans la neige (Daudet).
He saw him lying out there in the snow.
Son fusil pendu à la muraille (Daudet).
His rifle hanging on the wall.

39. As Participle Alone

The Past Participle may stand as the verb in a clause, without *avoir* or *être*, in such sentences as follow. It agrees with the noun or pronoun it refers to:

La partie finie, il l'emmena dans un coin (Flaubert).
When the game was finished, he took him into a corner.
Une impression agréable quoique mêlée d'inquiétude (Romains).
A pleasant impression, though mingled with anxiety.

40. Past Participle with *avoir*

The Past Participle is used with **avoir** to form the compound tenses, perfect infinitives and participles of most verbs. When used with **avoir**:

(a) It agrees in Gender and Number with the *Direct (Accusative)* Object of the verb, provided that this Direct Object precedes it:

Je les ai tous rendus fous.
I have made them all wild.
Les lettres que vous avez reçues.
The letters which you received.
Nous a-t-elle entendues?
Did she hear us?
Quelle raison a-t-il donnée?
What reason did he give?

(b) Where these conditions are not fulfilled, the Participle remains unchanged. There is therefore no agreement:

(i) if there is no Direct Object, or if the Direct Object does not precede the verb:

Ils ont parlé trop vite.   Elle a trouvé les souliers.
They spoke too fast.   *She found the shoes.*

(ii) if the preceding object is not Direct but *Indirect* (*Dative*):

Vous nous avez donné une vraie fête (Romains).
You have given us a real treat.

(c) The Past Participle of Impersonal Verbs, and of **faire** when governing another verb, are invariable:

Les précautions qu'il a fallu.
The precautions which have been necessary.
Il nous a fait asseoir.
He made us sit down.

41. The Past Participle of Reflexive Verbs

The Past Participle of Reflexive Verbs, although they are compounded with **être**, follows the rule for agreement as with **avoir**.

(a) In most cases the Reflexive Pronoun is in fact the preceding Direct Object, and there is therefore agreement:

Elle s'était levée à cinq heures.
She had got up at five.
Ils se sont aidés entre eux.
They helped one another.

(b) However, in some cases the Reflexive Pronoun is dative, and the Participle cannot agree with it:

Elles se sont dit adieu.
They said goodbye to one another.
Elle s'est coupé le doigt.
She has cut her finger (the finger to herself).

(c) It should be remembered that the Reflexive Pronouns **me, te, nous, vous** may be masculine or feminine, according to whom they are referring to. If they are Direct Object, the Participle must agree as appropriate:

'Nous nous sommes déjà levées', répondirent-elles.
'Je me suis blessée', dit-elle.

Similarly **vous** may be either singular or plural:

'Vous êtes-vous levée?' demanda-t-elle à la bonne.
'Vous êtes-vous levés?' leur demanda-t-elle.

42. Past Participle with *être*

The Past Participle is used with **être** to form the compound tenses, perfect infinitives and participles of certain other verbs (see 59), and also the passive voice (see 5.) It then agrees in Gender and Number with the Subject of the verb:

Ils étaient venus si vite.
They had come so quickly.
Marie, qui était arrivée deux minutes plus tôt (Romains).
Mary, who had arrived two minutes earlier.
Vous serez bientôt libérées, mesdames.
You will soon be freed, ladies.
Ils se cachèrent, de crainte d'être aperçus.
They hid for fear of being seen.

43. As a Noun

The Past Participle may be used as a noun, in which case it has regular feminine and plural forms:

un mort.	la défunte.
a dead man.	*the deceased (woman).*
la prévenue	des évadés.
the accused (woman).	*escaped prisoners.*

V. SUBJUNCTIVE

44. Subjunctive and Indicative Compared

In general, the distinction between Indicative and Subjunctive as used in a subordinate clause lies in the way in which the action or the verb is thought of. If it is thought of simply as an action, that is to say that the main idea is that something happens, has happened, is going to happen, then the Indicative is appropriate.

The presence of the Subjunctive suggests that what happens is being viewed in the light of some sort of emotion, e.g. one wants it to happen, one fears it may have happened, one is glad it happened, one is not quite sure whether it is so, &c. Compare:

> Je sais qu'il est mort. (The emphasis is on his being dead.)
> *I know that he is dead.*
>
> Je regrette qu'il soit mort. (His death is viewed as being some-
> *I am sorry he is dead.*   thing that I am sorry about.)

The above distinction is given purely as a general guide, which will throw some light on what follows. In practice it will be found much simpler if the Subjunctive is considered as being required in certain set constructions and circumstances, the commonest of which are given below.

45. Verbs which Introduce a Subjunctive Clause

(*a*) Verbs of Wishing, &c., e.g. **désirer que** *desire that*; **préférer que** *prefer that*; **vouloir que** *wish that*:

> Je veux que tu le saches.
> *I wish you to know it.*
> Il désirait que la vie fût un splendide roman d'aventures (Maurois).
> *He wished that life were a splendid adventure story.*

But the Infinitive is normally used where there is no change of subject (cf. 27 (*a*)):

> Je veux le savoir.
> *I want to know it.*

(b) Verbs of Fearing, e.g. **avoir peur que, craindre que**:

Je crains qu'il n'aille trop vite.
I fear he may go too fast.
Sa mère craignait qu'il n'y fût malheureux (Maurois).
His mother was afraid that he might be unhappy there.
Il ne craignait pas qu'on le vît.
He was not afraid of being seen.
Craignez-vous qu'il le lui dise?
Are you afraid that he will tell it her?
Tu avais peur qu'il ne revînt pas (Pailleron).
You were afraid he would not come back.

N.B. After Verbs of Fearing the Subjunctive is preceded by **ne** (without negative force) if, as in the first two examples, both the Verb of Fearing and the Subjunctive are in the Affirmative.

But the Infinitive is normally used when there is no change of subject (cf. 29 (a)):

Il avait peur de tomber.
He was afraid of falling.

(c) Other Verbs of Emotion, e.g. **avoir honte que** *be ashamed that*; **s'étonner (être étonné) que** *be astonished that*; **être content que** *be glad that*; **se fâcher (être fâché) que** *be annoyed that*; **regretter que** *regret that*:

Je suis bien content que vous soyez là (Romains).
I am very glad that you are there.

But the Infinitive is normally used where there is no change of subject (cf. 29 (c)):

Je suis content d'être ici.
I am glad to be here.

(d) Verbs of Saying, Thinking, and Knowing, e.g. **croire que, penser que** *think, believe that*; **dire que** *say that*; **se douter que** *suspect that*; **être sûr que** *be certain that*; **savoir que** *know that*; **voir que** *see that*, and also **espérer que** *hope that*.

(i) Such verbs require the *Subjunctive* when they imply *uncertainty*.

This occurs principally when a verb such as the above is itself in the negative or interrogative, or if its meaning is negative or interrogative in nature (e.g. **nier que** *deny that*; **douter que** *doubt that*; **ignorer que** *be ignorant that*):

> Je ne dis pas que sa vie soit menacée (Pagnol).
> *I do not say that his life is in danger.*
> Je nie que la confusion soit possible (Pailleron).
> *I deny that the confusion is possible.*
> Pourquoi pensez-vous qu'il soit venu? (Bazin).
> *Why do you think he has come?*
> Elle ne se doutait pas qu'elle eût rien fait d'héroïque (Flaubert).
> *She did not suspect that she had done anything heroic.*

and after impersonal expressions that similarly imply uncertainty or denial, either by their meaning or through being in the negative or interrogative, e.g. **il est possible que** *it is possible that*; **il se peut que** *it may be that*; **il semble que** *it seems that*; **il n'est pas certain que** *it is not certain that*; **est-il vrai que?** *is it true that?*:

> Il se peut qu'il soit déjà revenu.
> *It may be that he has already come back.*
> Il n'est pas impossible que j'aie vu cette dame (France).
> *It is not impossible that I have seen this lady.*
> Est-il vrai que tu fasses corriger tes devoirs par Topaze? (Pagnol):
> *Is it true that you get your homework corrected by Topaze?*

(ii) But these verbs are followed by the *Indicative* where *certainty* is implied. This is usually, but not necessarily, when the Verb of Saying, &c., is in the affirmative:

> Ils savaient que nous étions leurs amis (About).
> *They knew that we were their friends.*
> J'espère que vous êtes content (Pagnol).
> *I hope that you are satisfied.*
> Il ne sait pas que je l'ai caché.
> *He does not know that I have hidden it.*

and after impersonal expressions that similarly imply certainty, e.g. **il est certain que** *it is certain that*; **il est évident que** *it is clear* *that*; **il est probable que** *it is probable that*; **il est vrai que** *it is true that*:

> Il était évident que la pierre avait rebondi (Mérimée).
> *It was clear that the stone had bounced back.*
> Il est probable qu'elle continua (Romains).
> *It is probable that she went on.*

(iii) Where there is no change of subject the Verb of Saying, &c., even when negative, is constructed with the Indicative, or sometimes the Infinitive (see 27 (*e*)):

> Je ne dis pas que je réussirai (Pagnol).
> *I do not say that I shall succeed.*
> Il ne doutait pas d'y réussir (Maurois).
> *He did not doubt that he would be successful in it.*

(*e*) Verbs Expressing a Judgement on the action involved, e.g. whether it is good, bad, fitting, notable, necessary, &c., e.g. **approuver que** *approve that*; **il faut que** *it is necessary that*; **mériter que** *deserve*; **il vaut mieux que** *it is better that*; **il est étonnant (fâcheux, heureux, &c.) que** *it is astonishing (annoying, fortunate, etc.) that*; **il est nécessaire (important) que** *it is necessary (important) that*; **il est temps que** *it is time that*; **c'est dommage que** *it is a pity that*:

> J'approuve que vous ayez parlé ainsi.
> *I approve your having spoken thus.*
> Il est important que tu le fasses tout de suite.
> *It is important that you do it at once.*
> Est-il nécessaire que vous l'essayiez? (Daudet)
> *Is it necessary for you to try it?*
> Il faut que je fasse quelques achats (Romains).
> *I have got to make a few purchases.*

But in some cases, where there is no subject other than Impersonal **il,** the infinitive construction may be possible:

> Il est nécessaire de faire cela.   Il faut partir.
> *It is necessary to do that.*   *One must go.*

(*f*) Verbs containing an idea of Purpose or Aim (some of these require **à ce que**), e.g. **attendre que** *wait until*; **avoir soin que** *take care that*; **éviter que** *avoid*; **tenir à ce que** *be anxious that*; **tâcher que** *endeavour that*; **veiller à ce que** *watch that*:

Attendez qu'il vienne.   Évitez qu'on vous voie.
Wait until he comes.   *Avoid being seen.*

Le roi tenait à ce que son autorité fût respectée (Saint-Exupéry).
The king was anxious for his authority to be respected.

(*g*) Verbs of Ordering, Allowing, Forbidding, e.g. **commander que** *command that*; **demander que** *ask that* (see also 30); **défendre que** *forbid that*; **dire que** *say* (= *give instructions*) *that*; **ordonner que** *order that*; **permettre que** *allow that*:

Il ordonna qu'il fût arrêté sur-le-champ.
He ordered him to be arrested on the spot.
Ils demandent que les soldats partent demain.
They ask that the soldiers should leave tomorrow.
Je ne permets pas qu'on me tutoie.
I do not allow people to speak to me familiarly.

But where the person who is being told to perform the action is specified, the *demander à quelqu'un de faire quelque chose* construction (see 53) is usual:

Il leur ordonna de l'arrêter.
He ordered them to arrest him.
Ils demandent aux soldats de partir.
They ask the soldiers to leave.

46. Conjunctions which Introduce a Subjunctive Clause

A number of Conjunctions, which convey senses similar to those of the verbs in 45 above, introduce a clause with verb in the Subjunctive. For list see 239.

47. Subjunctive in Relative Clauses

The Subjunctive is present in a Relative Clause, when this has the effect of placing something in a certain class (rather than giving it an individual characteristic). This occurs in clauses which:

(*a*) qualify a superlative, or such words as *premier*, *dernier*, *seul*, &c.:

C'est le plus beau livre qu'il ait écrit.
It is the best book he has written (i.e. *of all those he has written*).
Cet enfant est le premier de sa race qui ait fait une trahison (Mérimée).
This child is the first of his stock to have committed an act of treachery.
C'est le seul qui ne me paraisse pas ridicule (Saint-Exupéry).
He is the only one who doesn't seem comic to me.

(*b*) qualify a negative expression:

Je ne connais personne qui fasse ce travail-là.
I do not know anyone who does that kind of work.
Pas un champ qui n'eût été ravagé.[1]
Not a field which had not been devastated.

(*c*) express type, purpose, suitability, &c.:

Je veux un mouton qui vive longtemps (Saint-Exupéry).
I want a sheep which will live long.

But where the Relative Clause does not place something in a class, but simply describes it as being so, or as taking place, the Indicative is used. Compare with the above:

Son plus beau livre, qu'il a écrit à Cannes.
His finest book, which he wrote at Cannes.
Il avait un mouton qui vivait dans le pré.
He had a sheep which lived in the meadow.

48. Tenses of the Subjunctive

The tense of the subjunctive, in a *que*-clause, is usually controlled by that of the main verb introducing it. The normal sequence is:

	Verb Introducing Subjunctive	*Subjunctive*
Primary Sequence	Present Imperative Future Perfect with 'have' Future Perfect	{Present {Perfect

[1] Note that *pas* is here omitted in the relative clause.

Historic Sequence	Imperfect Past Historic Perfect without 'have' Conditional (but see N.B. 3 below) Pluperfect Conditional Perfect	}	{Imperfect {Pluperfect

je crains **je craindrai** **j'ai craint**	*I am afraid* *I shall be afraid* *I have been afraid*	**qu'il ne vienne**	*that he comes, is coming, will come, will be coming, may come, may be coming*
		qu'il ne soit venu	*that he has come, has been coming, will have come, may have come*

je craignais **je craignis** **j'ai craint** **je craindrais** **j'avais craint**	*I was afraid* *I was afraid* *I was afraid* *I should be afraid* *I had been afraid*	**qu'il ne vînt**	*that he came, was coming, would come, would be coming, might come, might be coming*
		qu'il ne fût venu	*that he had come, had been coming, would have come, might have come*

N.B. 1. It will be seen above that there is an immense variety of English renderings of the Subjunctive. The selection of the French tense is made much easier by adhering to the above sequence.

Note in particular that Future and Conditional senses are normally expressed by the Present and Imperfect Subjunctive as above.

2. After some verbs, especially those of Saying or Thinking, the meaning may allow the Primary and Historic Sequences to be combined, e.g.:

Je n'affirme pas qu'il fût en bas.
I do not state that he was downstairs.
Je ne disais pas qu'il soit un fripon.
I did not say that he is a scoundrel.

3. Where the Conditional is used to express, in a hesitant or dubious way, what is really an equivalent of the Present, the sequence is Primary:

$$\left.\begin{array}{l}\text{(Je ne crois pas)}\\ \text{Je ne croirais pas}\\ \textit{(I do not think)}\\ \textit{I should not think}\end{array}\right\}\begin{array}{l}\text{qu'il vienne.}\\ \\ \textit{he is coming.}\end{array}$$

49. Other Uses of the Subjunctive

(*a*) The Present Subjunctive, preceded by **que**, provides the 3rd Person of the Imperative:

Qu'il prenne un emploi !   Qu'ils s'en aillent !
Let him get a job!   *Let them be off!*
Que chacun donne son opinion !
Let everybody give his opinion!

(*b*) The Subjunctive, with or without **que,** or inverted, may express a wish in the form of an exclamation:

Dieu vous bénisse !   Qu'il arrive à temps !
God bless you!   *May he arrive in time!*
Plût à Dieu !   Qu'il ne l'eût jamais vue !
Please God!   *Would that he had never seen her!*

The idea of *may* can also be expressed by the subjunctive of **pouvoir**:

Puisse-t-elle réussir !   Que cela puisse suffire !
May she succeed!   *May that be sufficient!*

(*c*) For the Concessive uses of the Subjunctive rendering English, e.g. *whoever you are, whatever he may say, however safe it may be,* see under HOWEVER, WHATEVER, WHOEVER in Appendix C.

VI. VERB CONSTRUCTIONS

CONSTRUCTIONS WITH OBJECT

(See Appendix A for consolidated list, p. 272)

50. Verbs Taking a Direct Object

(*a*) The majority of transitive verbs in French take a direct (accusative) object. (Nouns do not vary in form for the accusative, but many pronouns do):

Je lis le livre.	Je le lis.	Le livre que je lis.
I read the book.	*I read it.*	*The book which I read.*

(*b*) A number of French verbs take a direct object, while their English equivalents are constructed with a preposition, e.g. **attendre** *wait for*; **chercher** *look for*; **demander** (see also 58) *ask for*; **écouter** *listen to*; **espérer** *hope for*; **ignorer** *be ignorant of*; **payer** (see also 58) *pay for*; **regarder** *look at*; **reprocher** *reproach for*:

Le petit pourboire qui l'attendait (Daudet).
The little tip which was waiting for him.
Le passeur, qui les écoutait (Daudet).
The ferryman, who was listening to them.
Ils espéraient un homme d'affaires (Maurois).
They were hoping for a business man.

51. Verbs Taking an Indirect Object

(*a*) Many French intransitive verbs may take an indirect (dative) object, as in English. (The dative form of nouns and of some pronouns is obtained by prefixing **à**; other pronouns have special dative forms):

Il parle aux officiers.	*He speaks to the officers.*
Il leur parle.	*He speaks to them.*
A qui parlais-tu?	*Whom were you speaking to?*

(b) A number of French verbs require an indirect (dative) object, whose English equivalents take a direct (accusative) object, e.g.: **nuire à** *harm*; **(dés)obéir à** *(dis)obey*; **(dé)plaire à** *(dis)please*; **répondre à** *answer*; **résister à** *resist*; **ressembler à** *resemble*; **se fier à** *trust*:

> Peut-on résister à ce pouvoir? (Romains).
> *Can one resist this power?*
> Elle lui ressemblait.
> *She resembled him.*
> Répondez à la question!
> *Answer the question!*

52. Verbs Taking a Direct and Indirect Object

(a) Many French transitive verbs, which take a direct object, may take an indirect object in addition:

The majority of these are the French equivalents of English verbs that can also take this construction, e.g. **donner** *to give*:

Je donne le livre à mon frère.
{ *I give the book to my brother.*
{ *I give my brother the book.*
Il lui offrit un cadeau.
He offered him a present.
Il enseigne le français à ses enfants.[1]
{ *He teaches French to his children.*
{ *He teaches his children French.*

Je le lui donne.
{ *I give it (to) him.*
{ *I give him it.*
Montrez-le-leur.
Show it them.

N.B. It will be seen that it is possible to translate the above examples into English omitting the word *to* (which is the sign of the dative). Note that French does not do this, and that where there are two objects, as above, one of them is always dative.

(b) Some French verbs take a direct and indirect object, where the English equivalents have a different, or alternative, construction:

acheter quelque chose **à** quelqu'un.   *buy something from some-body.*

---

[1] Note that in French, where both objects are nouns, the accusative object precedes the dative, unless the balance of the sentence requires otherwise.

cacher qc. à qn.	hide sg. from so.
défendre qc. à qn.	forbid so. sg.
demander qc. à qn.	ask so. for sg., ask sg. of so.
emprunter qc à qn.	borrow sg. from so.
pardonner qc. à qn.	forgive so. sg.
payer qc. à qn.	pay sg. for so.
prendre qc. à qn.	take sg. from so.
présenter qc. à qn.	present so. with sg., present sg. to so.
promettre qc. à qn.	promise so. sg.
reprocher qc. à qn.	reproach so. with sg.
voler qc. à qn.	steal sg. from so.

Aller lui demander l'hospitalité (Daudet).
To go and ask him for hospitality.
Elle lui payait ses dettes (Flaubert).
She paid his debts for him.
Ils volèrent les fusils aux soldats.
They stole the rifles from the soldiers.

53. Verbs Taking an Indirect Object and *de* with Infinitive

A number of verbs of ordering, permitting, &c. (including some of those in 52 (*b*) above), take a dative of the person when used in the construction of *ordering someone to do something*, notably:

commander à quelqu'un de faire quelque chose.	command someone to do something.
conseiller à qn. de faire qc.	advise so. to do sg.
défendre à qn. de faire qc.	forbid so. to do sg.
demander à qn. de faire qc.	ask so. to do sg. (see also 58).
dire à qn. de faire qc.	tell so. to do sg.
ordonner à qn. de faire qc.	order so. to do sg.
permettre à qn. de faire qc.	allow so. to do sg.
promettre à qn. de faire qc.	promise so. to do sg.

Il dit aux femmes de rester en bas.
He told the women to remain below.
Je leur ai défendu de vous importuner (Balzac).
I have forbidden them to trouble you.

54. Faire, Entendre, Voir, Laisser

These verbs, when governing an infinitive, take the following
constructions with their object:

(*a*) When only one object is involved, the object is accusative:

On les fit causer (Daudet).
One made them chat.
Je l'ai entendu sortir.
I heard him go out.
Il fit parler le prisonnier.[1]
He made the prisoner talk.
On le laissa aller.
They let him go.

(*b*) When both **faire** and the infinitive it governs each have an
object, the object of **faire** becomes dative:

Je fais lire le livre à mon fils.[2]
I make my son read the book.
Je lui fais lire le livre.   Je le lui fais lire.[3]
I make him read the book.   *I make him read it.*

N.B. A *que*-clause ranks as an object, and the object of **faire**
will then also be dative:

Je lui ai fait avouer qu'il l'avait volé.
I made him admit that he had stolen it.

(*c*) With **entendre, voir,** and **laisser** the construction of (*b*)
above is frequent, but not obligatory, cf.:

Je lui ai entendu dire qu'il avait appris la flûte (Romains).
I heard him say that he had learnt the flute.
On le vit faire de grandes révérences (Daudet).
He was seen to make deep obeisances.
Pour lui laisser connaître la vérité (Daudet).
To let him become acquainted with the truth.

[1] For the position of the infinitive see observations in 27 (*f*), n. 1.
[2] See note to 52 (*a*).
[3] For the position of the object pronouns see 162 (*d*).

On le laissait emmener sa femme (M. Prévost).
He was allowed to take his wife.

(*d*) Where **faire** or **entendre** govern an infinitive which has a passive sense in English, the dative may convey the sense of *by*. Thus the French:

Il fit repasser sa chemise à sa femme could be in English:

either　*He made his wife iron his shirt.*

or　*He had his shirt ironed by his wife.*

But the English *by* in this context is more usually rendered by **par** in French.

Faites faire l'élixir par qui vous voudrez (Daudet).
Get the elixir made by whomever you like.

Je l'ai entendu dire par des gens qui le savaient (Augier et Sandeau).
I have heard it said by people who knew it.

55. Verbs Taking Object with *à* (not dative)
(For those taking **à** with infinitive see 28)

Many intransitive verbs may, if the sense permits, be constructed with the preposition **à**, where this does not represent the dative (as in 51, 52), but some other idea, such as motion to, direction of thoughts, &c. (The distinction between dative and non-dative affects the form of some pronouns, see 167.)
Thus:

(*a*) Verbs of Motion may be constructed with non-dative **à**:

Il va à l'église.　　　　L'enfant vint à moi.
He goes to the church.　*The child came to me.*
Elle y courut.
She ran to it.

But **à** with Verbs of Motion when used *figuratively* is dative:

L'idée leur vint.　　　Cela me convient.
The idea came to them.　*That suits me.*
Cette robe lui va.
That dress suits her.

(b) **à** is also not dative after, for example, **appeler à** *call to*; **comparer à** *compare to*; **être à** *belong to*; **faire attention à** *pay attention to*; **habituer à** *accustom to*.

> Il ne fait aucune attention à eux.   Ce livre est à moi.
> *He pays no attention to them.*   *This book belongs to me.*

(c) A number of other French verbs are constructed with non-dative **à**, whose English equivalents take a direct object, or some other preposition, e.g. **arriver à, parvenir à** *reach*; **croire à** (see also 58) *believe in*; **s'intéresser à** *be interested in*; **jouer à** (see also 58) *play* (a game); **manquer à** (see also 58) *fail in*; **penser à** (see also 58) *think of*; **prendre garde à** *beware of*; **mêler à** *mix with*; **songer à** *think of*; **renoncer à** *renounce*.

> Dès qu'il eut pensé à lui (Daudet).
> *As soon as he had thought of him.*
> Il faut renoncer à elle.
> *You must give her up.*

56. Verbs Taking Object with *de*

(For those taking **de** with infinitive see 29)

A number of French verbs are constructed with **de**:

(a) Whose English equivalents take a direct object, e.g. **s'apercevoir de** *perceive, notice*; **(s')approcher de** *approach*; **changer de** (see also 58) *change*; **se défier (méfier) de** *mistrust*; **douter de** *doubt*; **se douter de** *suspect*; **jouer de** (see also 58) *play* (an instrument); **jouir de** *enjoy*; **manquer de** (see also 58) *lack*; **se souvenir de** *remember*; **user de** (see also 58) *use*:

> Il s'approchait de la gare.   La ville changea d'aspect.
> *He was approaching the station.*   *The town changed its appearance.*
> C'est un homme qui ne manque de rien.
> *He is a man who lacks nothing.*
> Vous ne vous en étiez pas aperçus (Romains).
> *You had not noticed it.*

(b) Whose English equivalents are constructed with various other prepositions, e.g. **blâmer de** *blame for*; **dépendre de** *depend on*;

se fâcher (être fâché) de *be annoyed at, sorry about*; **féliciter de** *congratulate on*; **punir de** *punish for*; **remercier de** *thank for*; **rire de** *laugh at*; **vivre de** *live on*:

> Cela dépend de ta conduite.
> *That depends on your behaviour.*
> Je n'en étais pas fâché (Romains).
> *It didn't bother me.*

57. Verbs Taking Object with Other Prepositions

Note in particular:

(*a*) **consister en** *consist of*; **se diriger vers** *make one's way to*; **entrer dans** *enter*; **se fâcher (être fâché) contre** *be angry with*; **pénétrer dans** *penetrate*:

> Le lit du colonel consistait en quelques bottes de paille (Balzac).
> *The colonel's bed consisted of a few bundles of straw.*
> Ils entrèrent dans une maison abandonnée (Daudet).
> *They entered an abandoned house.*

(*b*) The constructions with **prendre, choisir, boire, manger, lire,** where English has *from, out of, off,* &c.:

> Prendre dans sa poche, sur le rayon, au mur.
> *Take out of one's pocket, off the shelf, from the wall.*
> Où avez-vous pris cela?
> *Where did you take that from?*
> Choisir dans la collection.   Lire dans un livre.
> *Choose from the collection.*   *Read from a book.*
> Manger dans une assiette.
> *Eat off a plate.*
> Boire dans un verre, à une bouteille.
> *Drink out of a glass, from a bottle.*

But where the verb itself contains the idea of taking out of or from **de** is used:

> tirer (sortir) de sa poche.   enlever du rayon.
> *pull (take) out of one's pocket.*   *remove from the shelf.*

58. Verbs Having More Than One Construction with their Object

There are a number of these, where the difference of construction involves a difference of meaning. The following are the most common:

changer
change (i.e. alter, convert, exchange for something different)

il a changé son plan
he has changed his plan
changer un billet
change a note
changer des gants pour une autre paire
exchange some gloves for another pair

changer de
change (i.e. substitute or exchange for another one of the same kind)

changer de couleur
change colour
changer de train
change trains
ils ont changé de chapeau(x)
they have exchanged hats

croire
believe (to be true or truthful)

je crois ce que vous dites
I believe what you say
je le crois
I believe him

croire à
believe in (existence or genuineness of)

je ne crois pas aux revenants
I don't believe in ghosts
je crois à sa fidélité
I believe in his loyalty

croire en
put one's trust in

je crois en lui, en Dieu
I trust in him, in God

demander
ask (for)

demander un pourboire;   demander la raison
ask for a tip;   *ask the reason*

demander à
ask (somebody for something)

je lui demandai le tableau
I asked him for the picture

jouer
play (card, tune, part, &c.)

jouer une carte, une sonate, une comédie, un rôle
play a card, a sonata, a comedy, a part

jouer à
play (a kind of) game[1]

jouer au football, aux cartes
play football, cards

jouer de
play (an instrument)

jouer du violon
play the violin

---

[1] To play a (*particular*) game of (i.e. *have a game of*) is usually **faire une partie de**: **Il fit une partie de billard avec l'hôtelier.** *He had a game of billiards with the hotel-keeper.*

manquer
miss, be missing, be lacking

il manqua le but, le train
he missed the target, the train
les œufs manquent
the eggs are missing

manquer à
fail in, be lacking to

il a manqué à son devoir
he has failed in his duty
les mots lui manquaient
he was at a loss for words

manquer de
lack, be lacking in
il manque de (impers.)
there is a lack of

il manque d'intelligence
he is lacking in intelligence
il manque de main-d'œuvre
there is a shortage of labour

payer
pay someone, something,
  pay for sg. (N.B. If only
  one object, accusative.)
payer à
pay (for something) for
  someone, pay someone (for
  something) (N.B. If two
  objects, person in dative.)

j'ai payé le propriétaire
I have paid the proprietor
j'ai payé mes dettes;   j'ai payé le dîner
I have paid my debts;   I have paid for the dinner
J'ai payé le dîner à mon frère
I have paid for the dinner for my brother
J'ai payé 800 frs. au propriétaire
I have paid the proprietor 800 frs.
Je le lui ai payé 1000 frs.
I have paid him 1000 frs. for it

penser
think (=consider)
think (=have in mind)

je le pense fou;   tout ce qu'il pense
I think him mad;   all he is thinking

penser à
think of (i.e. turn thoughts
  to)

je pense aux épreuves
I am thinking of the exams
il y pensait sans cesse
he was thinking of it all the time

penser de
think of (i.e. have an opinion
  of)

qu'est-ce que tu penses de cela?
what do you think of that?

servir
serve (trans. or intrans.)

il me sert très bien;   il sert dans l'armée
he serves me very well; he serves in the army

servir à
be useful for

cela ne sert à rien
that is no use

servir de
serve as

le sol servait de table
the ground served as a table

se servir de
use

il se servait d'une hache
he used an axe

user
wear out

il a usé ses souliers
he has worn his shoes out

user de
make use of

il a usé de son talent
he has made use of his talent

OTHER VERB CONSTRUCTIONS

59. Verbs Compounded with *être*

Être is used to form the compound tenses of Reflexive Verbs (see 6), and the Passive of Transitive Verbs (see 5).

(*a*) There are also a few intransitive verbs, mainly verbs of motion,[1] which form their compound tenses with **être**. The commonest are the following (some of which may conveniently be thought of in pairs):

aller *go*	**arriver** *arrive*	**entrer** *go (come) in*
venir *come*	**partir** *depart*	**sortir** *go (come) out*
	monter *go (come) up*	**naître** *be born*
	descendre *go (come) down*	**mourir** *die*

also

rester *remain*; **retourner** *go back*; **tomber** *fall*;

and compounds of the above, e.g. **revenir** *come back*; **devenir** *become*; **parvenir** *reach, succeed*; **repartir** *set off again*; **rentrer** *re-enter, return home*; **remonter** *go up again*; **redescendre** *go down again*, &c.

Il est arrivé, sorti, descendu, rentré à dix heures.
He arrived, went out, came down, came home at ten o'clock.

Elle est morte le 5 janvier.
She died on 5th January.

Les autres sont restés.   Des tuiles sont tombées.
The others have stayed.   *Some tiles have fallen.*

(For the agreement of the Past Participle see 42.)

(*b*) Some of the verbs in (*a*) above may be used in a sense where they can take an object, e.g. **sortir** *take (bring) out*; **monter** *take (bring) up*; **descendre** *take (bring) down*; **rentrer** *take (bring) in*. When so used they are compounded with **avoir**:

---

[1] The list given here of verbs of motion which take **être** is practically complete, and it should be noted that almost all other verbs of motion take **avoir**, e.g. **courir**, *run*; **marcher** *walk*; **nager** *swim*; **rouler** *roll*; **sauter** *jump*; **voler** *fly*; therefore: **il a couru, a marché**, &c.

Descendez les valises.	Ils ont rentré les chaises.
Bring the bags down.	*They have brought the chairs in.*

Monter and **descendre** also take **avoir** in such expressions as:

Ils ont monté l'escalier.	J'ai descendu la rue.
They have gone up the stairs.	*I went down the street.*

(c) As the Past Participle of many verbs can be used as an adjective (see 38), it may, in such a use, be preceded by *être*, as can any other adjective, cf. *il est bon, il est fatigué.*

In the case of a few past participles the English translation may make it seem that a verb which is normally compounded with *avoir* is being compounded with *être.* This occurs particularly with, for example, **changer** *change*; **demeurer** *stay, remain*; **grandir** *grow*; **passer** *pass*; **vieillir** *grow old.* Cf.:

Tense of Verb with *Avoir*, Expressing Action	Past Participle (as Adjective) Preceded by *Être*, Expressing State
Il a demeuré là pour soigner sa mère.	Il est demeuré insensible à nos prières.
He has remained there to look after his mother.	*He has remained insensible to our entreaties.*
Elle a beaucoup grandi à l'école.	Comme elle est grandie !
She has grown a lot at school.	*How tall she is!*
La journée avait passé tranquillement.	Le danger était passé.
The day had passed quietly.	*The danger had passed (was past).*

60. Meaning and Use of Reflexive Verbs

(For the agreement of the Past Participle of Reflexive Verbs see 41, and for the position and form of the Reflexive Pronouns see 6 (c), 162.)

Reflexive Verbs may:

(a) Express a true reflexive action, as in **je me suis blessé** *I have hurt myself*, where, in both French and English, it is simply a case of an ordinary transitive verb being used reflexively.

(b) Express an action which is really reflexive, but where the reflexive idea is frequently omitted in English. Cf.:

Elle lave la vaisselle.   Elle se lave au lavabo.
She washes the dishes.   *She washes at the wash-basin.*
Il arrête l'autobus.   Il s'arrête devant la mairie.
He stops the bus.   *He stops in front of the town hall.*

Elle a habillé la poupée.
She has dressed the doll.
Elle s'est habillée.
She has dressed (herself).

(c) Express numerous actions which are thought of as reflexive in French, but where the reflexive idea is absent in the English equivalents, e.g.:

s'adresser à	*address (= speak to)*	se fier à	*trust*
s'apercevoir de	*perceive, notice*	s'imaginer	*fancy*
s'approcher de	*approach*	se méfier de	*mistrust*
s'asseoir	*sit down*	se moquer de	*laugh at*
se baisser	*stoop*	se noyer	*drown* (intr.)
se coucher	*lie down, go to bed*	se plaindre	*complain*
se demander	*wonder*	se promener	*(go for a) walk*
se dépêcher} se hâter }	*make haste*	se rappeler} se souvenir de }	*remember*
se diriger vers	*make one's way to*	se reposer	*rest*
se douter de	*suspect*	se sentir	*feel* (intr.)
s'enfuir	*flee*	se servir de	*use*
s'enrhumer	*catch cold*	se rendre à	*go to, make for*
se fâcher	*be angry*	se taire	*be silent*

(d) Represent an action expressed in English by the Passive (see 61).

(e) Express a reciprocal action (i.e. *A* does it to *B*, and *B* does it to *A*):

Nous nous regardâmes consternés (Daudet).
We looked at one another in consternation.
Tous trois descendent sans se parler (Daudet).
All three go down without saying anything to each other.

61. Translation of the English Passive

(a) The English Passive may often be rendered by the French Passive, e.g. **la tente fut dressée** (Verne) *the tent was erected*. The French Passive is, however, less frequently used than the English, and one or other of the following constructions is very commonly used in preference:

(i) **On** + Active Verb:

On les accabla de questions (About).
They were overwhelmed with questions.
On a mis le couvert.
The table has been laid.
On alluma le poêle.
The stove was lit.

(ii) A Reflexive Verb:

Leur voyage se fit sans difficultés (Verne).
Their journey was accomplished without difficulties.
A la fin une fenêtre s'ouvrit (Daudet).
At length a window was opened.

(iii) Where the agent or instrument is mentioned in English, the whole action may be expressed in French by the active:

Deux soldats l'accompagnaient.
He was accompanied by two soldiers.
Cette réponse l'étonna.
He was astonished at this answer.

(iv) Some other form of expression is used, e.g.:

A cause de la destruction du pont.
Because the bridge had been destroyed.
Il passe pour un connaisseur.
He is considered a connoisseur.

(b) The use of the French Passive presents a particular problem with certain verbs whose Past Participle can describe a state, as well as an action done. Thus such a statement as **la porte est ouverte** is understood, in the absence of any evidence to the contrary, to be describing the position the door is in (*the state*), and not what is happening to the door (*the action*). If, in such contexts, it is desired to convey the idea that something is being done to the door, **on** or a reflexive must be used. Cf.:

State	Action
La porte est ouverte.	On ouvre la porte.⎫ La porte s'ouvre.⎭
The door is open.	*The door is (being) opened.*

Where the agent or instrument is mentioned, the problem does not arise, as it is then clear that an action is being performed. Cf.:

State	Action
Il remarqua que la porte était ouverte.	Le matin la porte était ouverte par le concierge.
He noticed that the door was open.	*In the mornings the door was opened by the porter.*

There is likewise no problem with a tense such as the Past Historic, which describes an action in any case:

> La porte fut ouverte sans bruit.
> *The door was opened noiselessly.*

(*c*) A verb can only be turned into the Passive if, in its active construction, it takes an *accusative* object (in French). If and when a verb takes a dative object[1] or a preposition in its active construction it cannot be turned into the passive:

	Active Construction	Passive or Passive Equivalent
Accusative Object	montrer quelque chose *show something*	le livre est montré *the book is shown*
Dative Object	montrer à quelqu'un *show someone*	on me montre le livre *I am shown the book* le libraire me montre le livre *I am shown the book by the bookseller*

---

[1] Exceptionally, the dative verbs (**dés)obéir** and **pardonner** may be used in the passive:

Il ne fut pas obéi.	Vous êtes pardonné.
He was not obeyed.	*You are pardoned.*

Preposition with Object   songer à quelque chose   on n'y songeait guère
                                                          it was hardly thought of
                              se servir de quelque   on s'en servait peu
                              chose   *it was little used*

(*d*) Neither **on** nor, in general, a reflexive can be used where the agent or instrument is mentioned:

Le livre fut vendu par le libraire. } Il fut frappé d'une idée. }
Le libraire vendit le livre.   } Une idée le frappa.   }
The book was sold by the bookseller.   *He was struck by an idea.*

(*e*) The Passive is retained in French where the passive idea, the idea of something being done (rather than of someone doing it) is the important one:

Vingt-trois habitants furent fusillés.
Twenty-three inhabitants were shot.

or where the use of **on** would be illogical:

La prairie a été inondée.
The meadow has been flooded.

62. Agreement of Verb and Subject

(*a*) A Verb agrees with its Subject in Number and Person:

Vous ne voyez rien.   Je le lui donnai.
Nous, qui avons tant souffert.
Les États-Unis n'étaient pas représentés.

(*b*) Some difficulty may occur with Collective Nouns (i.e. nouns such as *a company*, *a dozen*, whose meaning suggests a number of persons or things). The French usage is as follows:

(i) A singular collective noun (except as in (ii) below) requires a singular verb, whereas in English the verb may be singular or plural:

Le conseil a voté contre le projet.
The council has (have) voted against the proposal.
La famille se lève à six heures.
The family gets (get) up at six o'clock.

(ii) Where a singular collective noun is followed by *de* and another noun, the verb may be singular or plural (more usually the latter):

> Un bataillon d'Allemands défendait la ville.
> *A battalion of Germans was defending the town.*
> Une douzaine de candidats se présentèrent.
> *A dozen candidates offered themselves.*

(iii) **Beaucoup, peu, combien,** and **la plupart,** as subjects, require a plural verb, unless the sense is singular:

> Beaucoup (des soldats) ont péri.
> *Many (of the soldiers) have perished.*
> Peu (de gens) sont restés.
> *Few (people) stayed.*
> La plupart (des assistants) ne l'ont pas remarqué.
> *The majority (of those present) did not notice it.*

But

> Combien (du livre) reste à faire?
> *How much (of the book) remains to be done?*
> La plupart en a été reconstruite.
> *Most of it has been rebuilt.*

(*c*) Where the same verb has two or more subjects, it is normally plural:

> Lui et elle viennent aujourd'hui.
> *He and she are coming today.*

Where the subjects are of different persons, the agreement in Person is as follows:

(i) A combination containing a 1st Person subject takes a 1st Person Plural verb:

> Ni toi, ni moi, nous[1] n'avons reçu d'éducation (Balzac).
> *Neither you nor I have had any education.*
> Ni moi, ni lui, ni ses amis, ni ses ennemis ne l'oublierons (Balzac).
> *Neither I, nor he, nor his friends, nor his enemies, will forget it.*

---

[1] See note 1 on p. 116.

(ii) A combination of 2nd and 3rd Person subjects takes a 2nd Person Plural verb:

> Vous et lui, vous[1] feriez mieux de vous réconcilier.
> *You and he would do better to make it up.*

(*d*) For the agreement of verbs in Relative Clauses see 188, and for the use of **c'est** or **ce sont** see 174 (*a*), n. 1 on p. 216.

63. Inversion of Subject and Verb

(*a*) Inversion of Subject and Verb (i.e. the placing of the subject after the verb) always takes place:

  (i) in certain types of Direct Question (see 242–3);

 (ii) when a verb of saying follows direct speech:

> 'C'est à gauche', dit-il.
> *'It is on the left', he said.*
> 'Je ne le sais pas !' s'est-elle écriée.
> *'I don't know!' she exclaimed.*
> 'Vous le trouverez à côté de la maison', a répondu la femme.
> *'You will find it at the side of the house', the woman answered.*

(iii) in some forms of Wishes (see 49).

(*b*) Inversion of a *Noun* Subject and Verb frequently takes place elsewhere with the purpose of giving a better balance to the sentence, and to avoid finishing with an unconvincing sound. It occurs particularly:

  (i) in Relative Clauses:

> La chandelle que tenait sa fille (Bazin).
> *The candle which his daughter was holding.*
> L'endroit où se trouvaient les perce-neige.
> *The place where the snowdrops were.*
> Remarquez ce qu'a causé un tel acte de négligence.
> *Observe what such a careless act has caused.*

---

[1] Where subjects are of different persons they are frequently summed up by **nous** or **vous** before the verb, as appropriate.

(ii) after **c'est . . . que:**

C'est là que demeure mon parrain.
It is there that my godfather lives.

It also occurs in some types of Indirect Question (see 245), after certain adverbs (see 115 (*f*), n. 1), and in the *que*-clause of Comparative Sentences (see 133 (*a*), n. 1).

USE AND MEANING OF MODAL VERBS

64. Devoir

(*a*) When not governing an infinitive, **devoir** = *owe*:

Quand on doit, il faut payer (Daudet).
When one owes, one must pay.
Ils me doivent quatre termes (Daudet).
They owe me four months' rent.

(*b*) When governing an infinitive, **devoir** has one or other of the following senses:

(i) *obligation* to do something:

Je dois me reposer pendant quelques jours.
I must rest for a few days.
Il devait travailler le dimanche.
He had to work on Sundays.
Nous avons dû renvoyer le jardinier.
We have been obliged to sack the gardener.

(ii) (in Conditional) *ought to* (*should*) do something;

    (in Conditional Perfect) *ought to have* (*should have*) done something:

Vous devriez vous dépêcher.
You ought to hurry.
J'aurais dû ne pas l'écouter (Saint-Exupéry).
I ought not to have listened to him.[1]

---

[1] Note that the infinitive after **devoir** is always *present infinitive*. Therefore in such phrases as *I should not have listened, it must have been terrible*, the idea of *have* is expressed in the past tense of **devoir**, and not in the infinitive.

(iii) being *supposed to, destined* to do something:

Je dois parler le premier.
I am supposed to speak first.
Le mariage civil devait se faire à la mairie (Mérimée).
The civil marriage was to take place at the town hall.
Il lui apprit qu'il ne devait plus la revoir (Balzac).
He told her that he was never to see her again.

(iv) *supposition* (that something is so):

Vous devez connaître son nom, qu'on a vu dans les journaux (France).
You must be familiar with his name, which one has seen in the papers.
Debout il devait être très grand (Daudet).
Standing up he must have been very tall.[1]
La porte du fond devait ouvrir sur la cuisine (Romains).
The door at the back presumably opened into the kitchen.
La bataille a dû être terrible (Daudet).
The battle must have been terrible.[1]

65. Falloir

Falloir is always constructed impersonally, its subject being Impersonal **il** (see 176), and the personal object, if present, being in the dative.

(*a*) When not introducing another verb, **falloir** conveys the idea that something is needed or is lacking:

Il me faut un homme de confiance (Pagnol).
I need a man I can trust.
S'il vous faut de l'argent, comptez sur moi (Balzac).
If you need any money, rely on me.
Il fallut encore trois quarts d'heure (Flaubert).
It took another three quarters of an hour.

(*b*) When introducing another verb, **falloir** conveys the idea that the course of action is essential:

(i) It may govern an infinitive, and may then take a personal

---

[1] See note 1 to (*b*) (ii).

pronoun object (in the dative), though this is frequently understood:

> Des garçons qu'il me faut dominer (Maurois).
> *Boys whom I must dominate.*
> Une série de nœuds qu'il nous faut rompre (Romains).
> *A series of knots, which we must unravel.*
> Tu n'as pas fini? Il faut travailler plus vite.
> *You haven't finished? You must work faster.*

(ii) Or it may be constructed with *que* and the Subjunctive:

> Il faut que je parte.
> *I have got to go.*
> Il faut que je fasse quelques achats (Romains).
> *I must make a few purchases.*

66. Pouvoir

Pouvoir has one or other of the following senses:

(a) *Physical Ability* (cf. **savoir** 67 (b)):

> Je ne peux pas le supporter.
> *I cannot endure it.*
> Il pouvait marcher à l'aide d'une canne.
> *He could (was able to) walk with the help of a stick.*
> Il a pu faire des progrès.
> *He has been able to make some progress.*
> Je n'aurais pas pu y assister.
> *I could not have been (would not have been able to be) present.*[1]

(b) *Permission to*:

> Tu peux sortir cet après-midi.
> *You may go out this afternoon.*
> Les femmes ne peuvent pas entrer (Daudet).
> *Women are not allowed to enter.*
> Je ne pourrais pas rester sans autorisation.
> *I could not (would not be able to) stay without permission.*

---

[1] See note 1 to 64 (b) (ii), which also applies to **pouvoir**.

(c) *Possibility* (of something being so):

Il peut être là.
It may be there (= is possibly).
Un enfant qui pouvait avoir dix ans (Daudet).
A child who might have been ten (= was possibly).[1]
Cela a pu arriver.
That may have happened (= has possibly).[1]
Il pourra peut-être nous aider.
He may be able to help us (= will possibly).
Ils pourraient vous mettre à la porte.
They might throw you out (= would possibly).

(d) (In the Subjunctive), *A Wish* (see 49 (b) (ii)).

67. Savoir

(a) **Savoir,** with a noun or pronoun object, or introducing a clause, = *know*, in the sense of *being aware of, having learnt,* or *having been informed about.*[2]

Je sais la réponse.	Il savait sa leçon.
I know the answer.	*He knew his lesson.*
Savez-vous son nom?	Je sais comment le faire.
Do you know his name?	*I know how to do it.*
Je ne l'ai su que plus tard.	Savez-vous l'heure du train?
I only knew it later.	*Do you know the time of the train?*
Elle ne savait pas s'il viendrait.	
She did not know if he would come.	
On sait qu'il est parti pendant la nuit.	
It is known that he left in the night.	

---

[1] See note 1 to (a).
[2] Cf. **connaître,** which = *know,* in the sense of *be familiar with, have an understanding of*:

Je connais cet homme, cette ville, le chemin, le bonheur.
I know that man, this town, the way, happiness.
Il connaît le droit, l'espagnol.
He knows law, Spanish.

(*b*) **Savoir,** governing an infinitive, has the sense of *know how to.*
(As this is frequently rendered by the English *can,* it must be distinguished from *pouvoir* in 66 (*a*), which means *can,* in the sense of
physically able to.)

Elle ne sait pas lire.   Je sais conduire.
She cannot read.   *I can drive.*
Il savait très bien soigner les poulets.
He could look after the chickens very well.

(*c*) The conditional of **savoir,** in the negative, but without *pas,*
is sometimes used as an equivalent of the (negative) present tense of
pouvoir:

Je ne saurais l'expliquer.
I cannot account for it.

68. Valoir
(*a*) = *be worth.*

Le cadre valait 700 frs.   Cela ne vaut rien.
The frame was worth 700 frs.   *That is no good.*

(*b*) **Il vaut mieux** (Impersonal **il**) with infinitive conveys the
idea that a course of action is to be preferred:

Il vaut mieux le laisser ouvert.
Better leave it open.
Il vaudrait mieux se taire.
It would be better to say nothing.

69. Vouloir
Vouloir has one or other of the following senses:

(*a*) *Wishing* or *wanting.* (The conditional, particularly in the 1st
Person, is politer than the present):

Il veut partir tout de suite.   Je veux un silence complet.
He wants to leave at once.   *I want absolute silence.*
Elle voulait voir le médecin.
She wished to see the doctor.

Je voudrais les emporter cet après-midi.
I should like to take them this afternoon.
Il aurait voulu danser.
He would like to have danced (would have liked to dance).

(b) *Being willing.* (**Bien** conveys additional politeness):

Au besoin il voulait porter la valise lui-même.
If needs be he was prepared to carry the case himself.
Ils avaient voulu se passer de dîner.
They had been willing to go without dinner.
Voulez-vous (bien) attendre un instant?
Will you (kindly) wait for a moment?

The Imperative **veuillez** conveys a polite and formal request:

Veuillez vous asseoir.
Kindly take a seat.

(c) *Being determined:*

Je ne veux pas qu'on se moque de moi.
I will not be laughed at.
Il ne voulut rien entendre (Daudet).
He would not listen to anything.

(d) (Occasionally, as an indignant question) *Expect:*

Et comment voulez-vous que je le reprenne? (About)
And how do you expect me to get it back?

VII. THE ARTICLES

70. Forms of the Definite Article

	With Masc. Noun	With Fem. Noun	
Sing.	le mur	la salle	before a consonant, in- cluding h-aspirate
	le héros	la haie	
	l'ordre	l'encre	before a vowel or h-mute
	l'homme	l'heure	
Plur.	les murs	les salles	same form in writing be- fore all nouns, but note liaison in speech with nouns beginning with vowel sound, s being sounded [z]
	les héros	les haies	
	les_ordres	les_encres	
	les_hommes	les_heures	

When the prepositions **à** or **de** are used before the Definite Article
they combine with **le** to form **au** and **du** respectively. Similarly
they combine with **les** to form **aux** and **des**. They make no change
before **la** or **l'**.

| au client | à l'hôtel | à la ferme | aux spectateurs |
| du héros | de l'église | de la maison | des nouvelles |

71. Basic Uses of Definite Article

In modern French[1] the Definite Article:

(*a*) is the equivalent of the English *the*, making it clear that the
noun refers to a *particular* object or objects:

L'après-midi du même jour (France).
The afternoon of the same day.

---

[1] The Definite Article, derived from the Latin *ille*, retains a demonstrative force in
the expression **de la sorte** = in that way, of that kind. Cf. also **le plat du jour** = today's dish (lit. the dish of this day).

Les dernières miettes du pain (Mérimée).
The last crumbs of the loaf.

(*b*) shows that the noun is being used in a *general* sense, to mean the whole of its class or type (the English *the* is rarely used in this way):

Il faut taxer la farine (France).
Flour must be taxed.
L'homme aime mieux la paix que la guerre.
Mankind prefers peace to war.
Ils s'intéressent au commerce (Camus).
They are interested in trade.

72. The Definite Article Expressing Price, Rate, &c.

(*a*) The Definite Article is present as follows to express:

(i) Price per quantity:

Ces pommes se vendent à
$\begin{cases} 5 \text{ francs le kilo.} \\ 1 \text{ franc les 200 grammes.} \\ 8 \text{ francs la douzaine.} \end{cases}$

These apples are sold at
$\begin{cases} 5 \text{ francs a kilo.} \\ 1 \text{ franc for 200 grams.} \\ 8 \text{ francs a dozen.} \end{cases}$

Ce drap coute 23 francs le mètre.
This cloth costs 23 francs a metre.

(ii) Speed per hour, &c. (here preceded by Preposition **à**):
On roulait à 80 km. à l'heure.
They were doing 50 m.p.h.

(iii) Frequency during a period:

Trois fois la semaine elle recevait une lettre (Flaubert).
Three times a week she received a letter.

(*b*) The Definite Article is not present in expressions of the above or similar kinds when they are rendered by **par**:

Trois fois par semaine.	20 francs par personne et par jour.
Three times a week.	*20 francs per person per day.*

73. The Definite Article with Parts of the Body

(*a*) The Definite Article is frequently present with names of parts of the body where English has the Possessives *my*, *his*, &c.:

Elle ferma les yeux.
She closed her eyes.
Ouvre la bouche !
Open your mouth!
La plaie que j'avais à la tête (Balzac).
The wound I had on my head.

(*b*) With the Definite Article construction, the owner of the part of the body is frequently indicated by a Dative Personal Pronoun:

On lui cria à l'oreille (Flaubert).
They shouted in her ear.
La tête me tourne.
My head is spinning.
La vieille me saisit le bras (Mérimée).
The old woman seized my arm.
Il se grattait la tête (Camus).
He scratched his head.

(*c*) The Definite Article is not so used:

(i) if the part of the body is qualified by an adjective:

Avec sa grosse main (Barrès).
With his big hand.
Ses beaux yeux doux (Maurois).
His fine, gentle eyes.

But it is present after **avoir** in sentences of the following type, which describe someone as having a particular feature:

Il a le nez crochu *He has a hooked nose*;

(ii) where a Possessive is necessary to show whose head, &c., is meant, because there would otherwise be ambiguity, or because the action is unusual:

Ils exposèrent sa tête sur les murs.
They displayed his head on the walls.

125

(d) The Definite Article is usually present with parts of the body in sentences of the following types:

(i) (without a preposition) to convey a person's appearance or attitude on a particular occasion:

Il m'accueillit les bras ouverts (Mérimée).
He received me with open arms.

(ii) (with the preposition **à**) to convey a more or less permanent physical characteristic by which a living creature may be recognized:[1]

L'homme à la moustache noire.
The man with the black moustache.
Des oiseaux aux ailes cassées (Daudet).
Birds with broken wings.

74. The Definite Article with Proper Names and Titles

(a) The Definite Article actually forms part of a few Proper Names: e.g. **La Rochefoucauld, La Bruyère, Le Sage.**

Les Fables de La Fontaine   *La Fontaine's Fables.*

(b) The Definite Article is found with Proper Names when they are preceded:

(i) by a French title or rank:

La comtesse Ferraud, veuve du colonel Chabert (Balzac).
Countess Ferraud, widow of Colonel Chabert.

(ii) by the name of a profession, &c., used as title:[2]

Le docteur O'Grady.
Doctor O'Grady.
Le président de Gaulle.
President de Gaulle.

---

[1] This construction may also be used in reference to other visible characteristics by which persons or things may be recognized, e.g.:

     La dame aux camélias.   La maison aux volets verts.
     The lady with the camellias.   *The house with the green shutters.*

[2] Note also the ceremonious form of address, e.g. **Monsieur le président; madame la duchesse; messieurs les délégués.**

(iii) by a qualifying adjective:

Le petit Stenne se leva furieux (Daudet).
Little Stenne got up in a fury.

(*c*) The Definite Article is present with names of festivals, e.g.:

La Pentecôte.	La Toussaint.	Le vendredi saint.
Whitsun.	*All Saints' Day.*	*Good Friday.*

but not with **Pâques** (Easter); and **Noël** (Christmas) is more common than **La Noël.**

(*d*) The Definite Article is also present before Common Nouns when they are in fact the title of something individual, e.g. when referring to a particular numbered, or lettered, section, page, room, &c.:

Vous trouverez cela à la page 28.
You will find that on page 28.
La chambre 17 est libre.
Room 17 is free.

It is not present where such nouns stand as a heading, or on a notice:

Chapitre XII (*at head of chapter*).   Salle D (*over entrance*).

75. The Definite Article with Geographical Names

(*a*) The Definite Article is normally present with names of continents, countries, provinces, &c., mountains, seas, rivers, and lakes (but see also 84 (*a*)):

Parlez-moi de l'Europe, de la France (Verne).
Speak to me of Europe, of France.
La Bretagne et la Normandie font face à l'Angleterre.
Brittany and Normandy are opposite England.
La Moselle se jette dans le Rhin.
The Moselle flows into the Rhine.

(*b*) The ideas of *to, from, in* are in general expressed with continents, countries, provinces, &c., as follows:

(i) with *feminine singular* names by **en** (= *to* or *in*) and **de** (= *from*) with *no article*:

aller		en Afrique	*go to*		*Africa*
arriver	}...	en France	*arrive in*	}...	*France*
demeurer		en Provence	*live in*		*Provence*

		d'Amérique			*America*
revenir ...	{	de Russie	*return from* ...	{	*Russia*
		de Turquie			*Turkey*

(ii) with *masculine or plural* names, and with names qualified by a distinctive[1] adjective, by **à** (= *to* or *in*) and **de** (= *from*) *with article*:

aller		au Japon	*go to*		*Japan*
arriver	}...	au Mexique	*arrive in*	}...	*Mexico*
demeurer		aux États-Unis	*live in*		*the United States*

(*c*) The Definite Article is not present with names of towns, unless they are qualified by an adjective. *To* or *in* or *at* is expressed by **à**, and *from* by **de**:

Paris est la capitale de la France.
Paris is the capital of France.
De Toulon il retourna à Marseille.
From Toulon he returned to Marseille.
Le directeur est actuellement à Bruxelles.
The manager is at present in Brussels.
Je te retrouverai à Dieppe.
I will meet you at Dieppe.
Je contemplais le Paris moderne (Balzac).
I was beholding modern Paris.

But in a few cases the Article is part of the name:

Le Caire.   Aller à la Mecque.
Cairo.   Go to Mecca.
Les phares du Havre.
The lighthouses of Le Havre.

---

[1] Where the adjective really forms part of the name, usage varies, e.g.:

> à la Nouvelle-Zélande
> en Nouvelle-Zélande   } are all found
> dans la Nouvelle-Zélande

but in many cases, e.g. **en basse Bretagne,** a usage has been established and must be acquired by practice.

76. Forms and Meaning of Indefinite Article

(a)

	SINGULAR		PLURAL	
	Masc. Noun	*Fem. Noun*	*Masc. Noun*	*Fem. Noun*
	un livre	une maison	des livres	des maisons
	un accident	une étoile	des accidents	des étoiles
	un hôtel	une héroïne	des hôtels	des héroïnes
	un héros	une haie	des héros	des haies

Note liaisons in speech with nouns beginning with vowel sound, **un** then being pronounced [œ̃n] and **des** [dez].

(b) The meaning of the French Indefinite Article in the singular corresponds to the English *a*, meaning that the noun represents one of its particular species or type:

> Elle en sortit une petite assiette (Maupassant).
> *She took out of it a little plate.*
> Tu vivras comme un prince (Mérimée).
> *You will live like a prince.*

and in the plural to the English plural *some* or *any* (as in *there are some dogs; are there any eggs?*), meaning that the noun represents more than one of its species or type:

> On apporta une table et des chaises.
> *They brought a table and some chairs.*
> As-tu acheté des pommes?
> *Have you bought any apples?*
> Il y avait des tableaux aux murs.
> *There were pictures on the walls.*

N.B. *Some* is frequently omitted here in English: **des** is not so omitted in French.

77. Forms and Meaning of Partitive Article

(a)

	Masc. Sing. Noun	*Fem. Sing. Noun*
Before a consonant	du lait	de la crème
including h-aspirate	du houx	de la houille
Before a vowel and	de l'air	de l'eau
h-mute	de l'huile	de l'harmonie

(*b*) The meaning of the French Partitive Article corresponds to the English singular[1] *some* or *any* as in *I have some bread; have you any meat?*, meaning that what the noun describes is here present in an indefinite quantity:

> On me donne du fromage, du sel et de la moutarde.
> *I am given some cheese, salt, and mustard.*
> De la glace couvrait les fossés (Flaubert).
> *Ice covered the ditches.*
> Y a-t-il du la sauce?　　　*Is there any sauce?*

N.B. *Some* is frequently here omitted in English: **du,** &c., are not so omitted in French.

78. The Form *de*—In Negative Sentences

(*a*) The Indefinite Article **un, une, des,** and the Partitive **du, de l', de la** have a single negative form **de.** This is used in negative sentences when the noun is negative in *quantity* (i.e. when *no, not a, not any* means *no amount of, no number of*):

> Je n'ai pas de plume.
> *I have no (not a) pen* (i.e. *The number of pens I have is nil*).
> Il n'y avait pas de rats dans la maison (Camus).
> *There were no (not any) rats in the house.*
> Ne perdez pas de temps (Mérimée).　*Don't lose any time.*
> André n'avait guère fait de résistance (Bazin).
> *André had scarcely made any resistance.*

(*b*) **Un, une, du, de l', de la, des** remain unchanged in a negative sentence when the noun is negatived as to its *identity* (i.e. when the meaning is that it is not that kind of thing):

> Il ne prit pas une plume mais un crayon.
> *He did not take a pen but a pencil.*
> Je ne suis pas un révolutionnaire (Labiche et Martin).
> *I am not a revolutionary.*
> Ce n'est pas de la soie.　　　*It is not silk* (i.e. *it might be cotton*).

---

[1] **Des** (=plural *some*), which is the plural of the Indefinite Article, has not been included here. **Des fromages** = *some cheeses* is the plural of **un fromage** = *a cheese.* **Du fromage** = *some cheese* cannot be turned into the plural.

(c) The Indefinite and Partitive Articles are not present in any form after **ni . . . ni,** when the quantity is negatived:

> On ne trouve au marché, ni œufs, ni légumes, ni fromage (France).
> *One finds at the market neither eggs, nor vegetables, nor cheese.*

but are present when the identity is negatived as in (b) above:

> Ce n'est ni de la soie ni du coton.
> *It is neither silk nor cotton.*

(d) After **ne . . . que,** and **ne . . . pas que,** the Articles **un, une, du, de l', de la, des** remain unchanged, as *only* is not felt to be a negation of quantity.

Nous n'avons {qu'une vache / que des porcs / que du lait}   We have only {a cow / some pigs / milk}

> Il n'y avait pas qu'un manque d'argent.
> *There was not only a lack of money.*

(e) **Un, une,** when it represents the number *one*, or has the sense of *a single one*,[1] remains unchanged in the negative:

> Il n'invite pas un camarade mais deux.
> *He is not inviting one friend but two.*
> Il n'y avait pas un homme de moins de 60 ans.
> *There was not a man below 60.*
> Je ne pouvais faire un pas (Mérimée).
> *I could not move a step.*

(f) **Du, de l', de la, des** when they are not the Indefinite or Partitive Article, but are the Definite Article **le, la, les,** preceded by the Preposition **de,** remain unchanged in negative sentences:

> On ne disait rien du pain.
> *Nothing was said about the bread.*
> Je ne parle pas des rats dans la maison (Camus).
> *I am not talking of the rats in the house.*

---

[1] This latter meaning may be reinforced by **seul:**
Une seule visite aurait suffi.   *One visit would have been sufficient.*

79. The Form *de*—Before a Preceding Adjective

(*a*) In careful written French the Indefinite and Partitive Articles **du, de l', de la, des** are rendered **de** when an adjective precedes and qualifies the noun (**un** and **une** remain unchanged):

Il fallait prendre de grandes précautions (Daudet).
Great precautions had to be taken.

But they remain unchanged when the adjective and noun are commonly associated in that particular meaning:

e.g. des jeunes filles	des petits pains	des petits pâtés
girls	*rolls*	*pasties*
du bon sens	des petits pois	des bons mots
common sense	*green peas*	*witty remarks*

(*b*) As in 78 (*f*) above, **du, des,** &c., which are the Definite Article preceded by the Preposition **de,** remain unchanged:

Il s'étonnait des grandes précautions nécessaires.
He was astonished at the great precautions necessary.

80. Articles Before Abstract Nouns

(*a*) Where the sense does not require the Indefinite or Partitive Article, Abstract Nouns are in general preceded by the Definite Article:

Et vous appelez cela la justice! (Balzac)
And you call that justice!
Un effet curieux du hasard (Verne).
A curious effect of chance.

(*b*) The Definite Article is not present when the Abstract Noun stands alone after a preposition, forming an adverbial phrase:

Il accepta avec joie.	Sans hésitation.
He accepted joyfully.	*Without hesitation.*
Il le fit par amitié.	*He did it out of friendliness.*

(*c*) When the Abstract Noun is qualified by an adjective, it is preceded in the singular by **un** or **une,** and in the plural by **des**:

> Une voix d'une puissance étonnante (Maurois).
> *A voice of surprising power.*
> Il fait des progrès remarquables.
> *He is making remarkable progress.*

81. Articles Before Certain Concrete Nouns

(For the use of the Articles with *dates, days of the week, seasons, time of the day,* &c., see Chapter XIV.)

Where the sense does not require the Indefinite or Partitive Article, the Definite Article usually precedes:

(*a*) Names of languages (these are masculine and are not spelt with a capital letter):

> Le russe est une langue difficile.   Il comprend l'allemand.
> *Russian is a difficult language.*   *He understands German.*

but the Definite Article is frequently absent in simple statements with **parler**:

> parler (le) français.   il parle (l')espagnol.
> *speak French.*   *he speaks Spanish.*

(*b*) Names of meals and games:

> Le dîner est servi.   Pendant le souper.   Jouer au football.
> *Dinner is served.*   *During supper.*   *To play football.*

82. Articles Before Nouns in Apposition

(*a*) When a noun is inserted in explanation of a noun or phrase just used (i.e. *in apposition*) the Article is usually absent:

> M. Schuman, ministre des affaires étrangères, a prononcé un discours.
> *M. Schuman, the Foreign Minister, delivered a speech.*
> A Édimbourg, ville immense, il y avait 31 électeurs (Maurois).
> *In Edinburgh, an immense city, there were 31 electors.*

Virginie se sentit moins faible, résultat du changement d'air (Flaubert).
Virginia felt less weak, a result of the change of air.

(b) But when the noun in apposition is felt to provide the more important information the Article is usually present:

C'était Blériot, le célèbre aviateur.
It was Blériot, the famous airman.

L'hébreu, une langue incompréhensible qui s'écrivait à l'envers (Maurois).
Hebrew, an incomprehensible language which was written the wrong way round.

Un seul bruit lui arriva maintenant aux oreilles, la voix du perroquet (Flaubert).
Only one noise now reached her ears, the voice of the parrot.

83. Articles Before Complements of *être*, &c.

When a noun is the complement of a verb such as **être, devenir, paraître,** &c.:

(a) The Article is absent where the sense is that of placing the person or thing in a general class, profession, or type (except after **c'est,** see 155 (b)).

On dit qu'il était journaliste (Camus).
He was said to be a journalist.

Elle enrageait d'être née Juive (Maurois).
She was furious at having been born a Jewess.

Malgré ses efforts pour paraître gentilhomme (Flaubert).
In spite of his efforts to appear a gentleman.

(b) The Article is present where the sense gives the person or thing an individual characteristic, or where the complement is qualified by an adjective:

Le comte Ferraud était le fils d'un ancien conseiller (Balzac).
Count Ferraud was the son of a former councillor.

Il était devenu un mari désagréable (Maurois).
He had become a disagreeable husband.

84. Articles After the Preposition *de*

(*a*) No Article is present in a phrase, formed by **de** and a noun, which has the force of an adjective or an attribute:

Une maison de campagne.	Les vins de France.
A country house.	*The wines of France* (i.e. *French wines*).
Des troncs d'arbre.	Une cravate de soie noire.
Tree-trunks.	*A black silk tie.*
Un collier de perles.	Un homme de génie.
A pearl necklace.	*A man of genius.*

(*b*) The presence of the Preposition **de** dispenses with the Partitive Articles **du, de l'**, and **de la,** and the Indefinite Article **des.**

This particularly arises:

(i) in expressions of quantity,[1] or absence or lack:

Un peu de souper.	Tant de raisons.
A little supper.	*So many reasons.*
Des tranches de viande froide.	Un manque d'argent.
Some slices of cold meat.	*A shortage of money.*
L'absence de personnel spécialisé (Camus).	
The absence of specialist staff.	

(ii) and where **de** is the appropriate preposition after various verbs, nouns, and adjectives:

Je manque de tabac.
I am short of tobacco.
Vêtus de robes blanches.
Clad in white robes.

---

[1] But **bien** and **encore,** used as expressions of quantity, take **du, de la, des** before the noun:

Bien des années se passèrent.	Encore du vin, monsieur?
Many years passed.	*Some more wine, sir?*

and **la plupart** takes **de** and the Definite Article (whether or not the English has *the*):

La plupart des enfants n'avaient pas compris.
Most of the children had not understood.
La plupart des Norvégiens parlent un peu d'anglais.
The majority of Norwegians speak a little English.

Un panier chargé de provisions.
A basket loaded with provisions.
La terre était couverte de neige.
The ground was covered with snow.
J'ai besoin d'argent.
I need money.
Ils parlaient de roses.
They were talking about roses.
Leur sac était plein de pommes de terre (Daudet).
Their bag was full of potatoes.

(*c*) The Definite Article, in the sense where the English has *the*, is never omitted after **de**:

Un peu du souper qui restait.   J'ai besoin de l'argent.
A little of the supper which was left.   I need the money.
Leur sac était plein des pommes de terre ramassées la veille.
Their sack was full of the potatoes gathered the day before.

but, as can be seen from examples in (*b*) above, the Definite Article as used *in a general sense* (see 71 (*b*)), or as used with Abstract Nouns (see 80), is not normally present after Preposition **de,** except where the preceding noun is itself qualified by the Definite Article. Cf.:

Un désir de vengeance.   Les bienfaits de la médecine.
A desire for vengeance.   The blessings of medicine.

(For the use of the Article with the Prepositions **à, en, sans,** see under these prepositions in Appendix B.)

85. Omission of Articles in Exclamations

(*a*) The Article is not present after **quel** used in exclamations:

Quelle idée !   Quelle jolie maison !
What an idea!   What a pretty house!

(*b*) Nor is it usually present before nouns used in exclamatory phrases:

Erreur ! Une baleine n'est pas un poisson.
Wrong! A whale is not a fish.

Mauvaise rencontre ! me dis-je (Mérimée).
An evil encounter! I said to myself.

86. Omission of Articles in Set Expressions and Proverbs

(*a*) The Article is not present in many expressions in which the noun is closely linked in sense with the verb, e.g.:

mettre fin à	prendre plaisir à	avoir envie de
put an end to	*take pleasure in*	*have a desire to, want to*
tenir parole		
keep one's word		

or where used in a stock phrase with a preposition, e.g.:

à terre	par exemple	à travers champs
on (to) the ground	*for example*	*across country*
sans cause	en avion	à voix basse
without cause	*by air*	*in a low voice.*

(*b*) The Article is also absent in numerous proverbs:

Pauvreté n'est pas vice.	Possession vaut titre.
Poverty is not a sin.	*Possession is nine points of the law.*

87. Repetition of Articles

The Article is normally present before each noun to which it applies, including those in a series:

L'arrivée et le départ des trains.
The arrival and departure of the trains.

Il y avait une fois un roi et une reine.
Once upon a time there was a king and queen.

Des passagers, des paysans, des enfants qui vont à l'école (Flaubert).
Passers-by, peasants, children going to school.

VIII. GENDER OF NOUNS

88. The Idea of Gender

(*a*) All French Nouns, whether referring to living beings or not, are either masculine or feminine in gender.

The terms *masculine gender* and *feminine gender* are grammatical ones, and are not equivalent to the terms 'male' and 'female'.

The ideas may overlap in certain cases (e.g. **un homme** *a man* is masculine, and **une femme** *a woman* is feminine), but with the vast majority of nouns the masculine or feminine gender either has no connexion with sex (e.g. **un rat** = *a rat* (of either sex), and **une souris** = *a mouse* (of either sex)), or, in the case of inanimate objects, it is applied to nouns which cannot be considered as male or female (e.g. **un fauteuil** *an arm-chair*, **une chaise** *a chair*).

(*b*) It is possible to list, by meaning or spelling, certain classes of nouns as being likely to be masculine or feminine, and the largest of these classes are given in Sections 91 and 92.

It is also generally true that French nouns derived from Latin masculines and neuters are masculine, and those derived from Latin feminines are feminine.

However, the exceptions and complications are so numerous that the problem remains one of learning. In this connexion, much time will be saved if French nouns are invariably learnt with some accompanying word, such as the Article or an adjective, which shows their gender by its sound or spelling.

E.g. learn:

> *not* monde = *world, but* **le monde**
> *not* ferme = *farm, but* **une ferme**
> *not* habit = *attire, but* **des habits blancs**
> *not* eau = *water, but* **de l'eau froide.**

89. Gender of Human Beings

(a) Generally speaking, names of males are masculine and names of females feminine:

(i) a different word, or a different form of the word, may be used for the male and the female, e.g.:

Masc.		Fem.	
un homme	*man*	une femme	*woman, wife*
un roi	*king*	une reine	*queen*
un acteur	*actor*	une actrice	*actress*
un Allemand	*a German*	une Allemande	*a German woman*

For further examples see 96 (a).

(ii) Or, in a few cases, the same word may have either gender, as appropriate, e.g.:

Masc. (referring to a man or boy)	Fem. (referring to a woman or girl)	
un aide	une aide	*assistant*
un artiste	une artiste	*artist*
un camarade	une camarade	*friend, comrade*
un domestique	une domestique	*servant*
un élève	une élève	*pupil*
un enfant	une enfant	*child*
un malade	une malade	*patient*
un propriétaire	une propriétaire	*owner*

(b) But many words retain the one gender whether they refer to men or women, e.g.:

Masc. (especially many names of professions)		Fem.	
un auteur	*author*	une connaissance	*acquaintance*
un médecin	*doctor*	Sa Majesté	*His (Her) Majesty*
un professeur	*teacher*	une personne	*person*
un ange	*angel*	une recrue	*recruit*
un témoin	*witness*	une sentinelle	*sentry*
		une vedette	*scout (military), (stage or screen) star*
		une victime	*victim*

Madame Colette est un auteur célèbre.
Madame Colette is a well-known author(ess).
La victime était un homme de quarante ans.
The victim was a man of forty.

Where required, use may be made of such expressions as: **une femme professeur** *a lady teacher*; **un homme de ma connaissance** *a male acquaintance of mine*, &c.

90. Gender of Animals

(*a*) In general, names of animals have only one gender whatever their sex, e.g.:

Masc.		Fem.	
un animal	*animal*	une bête	*animal*
un éléphant	*elephant*	une girafe	*giraffe*
un rat	*rat*	une souris	*mouse*
un moineau	*sparrow*	une hirondelle	*swallow*
un saumon	*salmon*	une truite	*trout*
un papillon	*butterfly*	une abeille	*bee*

Where necessary, use may be made of such expressions as:

un éléphant femelle
une souris mâle, &c.

(*b*) In the case of some familiar or domestic animals, separate masculine and feminine words may exist to distinguish between males and females, while at the same time a single word (of one gender) may be used to describe the species as a whole, or where no distinction of sex is made, e.g.:

Masc. (male)		Fem. (female)		General term	
un lion	*lion*	une lionne	*lioness*	les lions (m.)	*lions*
un bélier	*ram*	une brebis	*ewe*	les moutons (m.)	*sheep*
un bouc	*he-goat*	une chèvre	*she-goat*	les chèvres (f.)	*goats*
un taureau	*bull*	une vache	*cow* ⎫	⎰ les vaches (f.)	*cows*
un bœuf	*bullock, ox*	une génisse	*heifer* ⎭	⎱ les bœufs (m.)	*cattle, oxen*
un chien	*dog*	une chienne	*bitch*	les chiens (m.)	*dogs*
un coq	*cock*	une poule	*hen*	les poulets (m.)	*chickens*

For further examples see list in Section 96 (*a*) (ii).

HINTS ON GENDER

The following is a rough guide to the most likely gender for certain types of nouns.

91. Gender by Meaning

Masc.		Fem.	
Trees and Shrubs, e.g.		*Flowers, Fruit, and Vegetables ending in* **-e**, e.g.	
un arbre	*tree*	une rose	*rose*
un chêne	*oak*	une marguerite	*daisy*
un orme	*elm*	une pomme	*apple*
un pommier	*apple-tree*	une poire	*pear*
un arbuste	*shrub*	une carotte	*carrot*
un laurier	*laurel*	une laitue	*lettuce*
Principal exceptions:			
une aubépine	*hawthorn*	un légume	*vegetable*
la bruyère	*heath, heather*		
la ronce	*bramble*		

Names of Countries and Rivers not ending in **-e**, e.g.		*Names of Countries and Rivers ending in* **-e**, e.g.	
le Danemark	*Denmark*	la France	*France*
le Canada	*Canada*	la Pologne	*Poland*
le Japon	*Japan*	la Chine	*China*
le Rhin	*the Rhine*	la Loire	*the Loire*
		Principal exceptions:	
		le Mexique	*Mexico*
		le Bengale	*Bengal*
		le Danube	*the Danube*
		le Rhône	*the Rhone*

Concrete Nouns in **-eur**:		*Abstracts in* **-eur**:	
le conducteur	*driver, leader*	la chaleur	*heat*
le travailleur	*worker*	la douceur	*sweetness, gentleness*
un aspirateur	*vacuum cleaner*	la largeur	*breadth*
le moteur	*engine*	la peur	*fear*
		Exceptions:	
		le bonheur	*happiness*
		la malheur	*unhappiness, ill fortune*
		un honneur	*honour*
		un déshonneur	*dishonour*

		Abstracts in **-té**:	
		la bonté	*kindness*
		la nouveauté	*newness, novelty*
		Principal exceptions:	
		le comité	*committee*
		le traité	*treaty*

Masc.		Fem.	
Languages:		*Arts, Trades, Sciences, School Subjects,* e.g.	
le français	*French*	la peinture	*painting*
le russe	*Russian*	la sculpture	*sculpture*
le suédois	*Swedish*	la menuiserie	*joinery*
le latin	*Latin*	la quincaillerie	*ironmongery*
		la chimie	*chemistry*
		la physique	*physics*
		la géométrie	*geometry*
		les mathématiques	*mathematics*

Principal exceptions:

le droit	*law*
le calcul	*arithmetic*
le dessin	*drawing*

Days, Months, Seasons:		*Festivals,* e.g.	
le dimanche	*Sunday*	la Pentecôte	*Whitsun*
le lundi	*Monday*	la Toussaint	*All Saints' Day*
le février	*February*	la Saint-Jean	*St. John's Day*
le décembre	*December*		
le printemps	*spring*		

Exception: Noël *Christmas* is masc. except when preceded by Definite Article: Joyeux Noël! *Happy Christmas!* but à la Noël *at Christmas.*

Metric Weights and Measures, Fractions, Compass Points

un gramme	*gramme*
un kilomètre	*kilometre*
un litre	*litre*
un hectare	*hectare*
un demi	*a half*
un tiers	*a third*
un quart	*a quarter*
un cinquième	*a fifth*
le sud	*the south*
l'orient	*the east*

Principal exceptions:

une livre	*pound* (500 grammes)
une tonne	*ton* (1,000 kilogrammes)
une moitié	*a half*

Metals

le fer	*iron*
le plomb	*lead*
le cuivre	*copper*
le platine	*platinum*

Principal exceptions:

la fonte	*cast iron*
la tôle	*sheet iron*

92. Gender by Ending

(a)	**Masculine**		*Feminine Exceptions*	
-acle	un miracle			
	un obstacle			
	un spectacle			
-age	le courage		la cage	la plage
	le ménage		une image	la rage
	le paysage		la nage	
	le village		la page (*page*	
	le voyage		of a book)	
-eau	le bateau	un oiseau	l'eau	
	le marteau	le rouleau	la peau	
-ème	le problème			
	le système			
-isme	le communisme			
	l'héroïsme			
	le réalisme			
-ment	le commencement		la jument (*mare*)	
	le rationnement			
	le dévouement			
	un ornement			
	le serment			

(b)	*Masculine Exceptions*			**Feminine**	
			-aison	la combinaison	la maison
					la raison
			-ance	la chance	la vengeance
			-anse	la danse	
	le silence		-ence	la patience	la prudence
			-ense	la défense	
	le lycée	le musée	-ée	une arrivée	la journée
				une épée	
			-sion	une invasion	
				la mission	
			-tion	la conservation	la nation
			-ude	la multitude	
			-ure	la nature	la mesure
			-xion	la connexion	la réflexion

93. Gender Showing Distinction of Meaning

A number of nouns have a different meaning according to whether they are masculine or feminine. The following are the most common:

Masc.		Fem.	
un aide	(male) assistant	une aide	(female) assistant, assistance
le crêpe	crape	la crêpe	pancake
le critique	critic	la critique	criticism
le livre	book	la livre	pound (weight)
le manche	handle	la manche	sleeve
		La Manche	English Channel
le mémoire	memorandum, memoir	la mémoire	memory
le merci	thanks	la merci	mercy
un office	office, service	une office	pantry
le page	page-boy	la page	page (in a book)
le pendule	pendulum	la pendule	clock
le poêle [pwa:l]	stove	la poêle	frying-pan
le poste	position (employment), post (military, police, etc.), station, (broadcasting), wireless set	la poste	post (mail), post-office
le somme	sleep, nap	la somme	sum, total
le tour	turn, tour, trick	la tour	tower
le vapeur	steamer	la vapeur	steam
le voile	veil	la voile	sail

IX. FEMININE OF NOUNS AND ADJECTIVES

A number of nouns describing living beings have masculine and feminine forms which are used when referring to males and females respectively (cf. 89).

Adjectives have masculine and feminine forms which are used when qualifying, or referring to, nouns or pronouns of the masculine and feminine genders respectively:

un grand jardin   il est petit   une grande maison   elle est petite

94. General Rule

(a) In general, the feminine form differs in writing from the masculine by the presence of a final **-e**:

un ami	une amie	brun	brune
un marquis	une marquise	gris	grise
un cousin	une cousine	fort	forte
un Français	une Française	français	française
un ours	une ourse	grand	grande
un mineur	une mineure[1]	meilleur	meilleure[1]

Principal exceptions (other than those dealt with in 95):

bas	basse	las	lasse	long	longue
épais	épaisse	frais	fraîche	bénin	bénigne
exprès	expresse	gentil	gentille	malin	maligne
gras	grasse	nul	nulle	un paysan	une paysanne
gros	grosse	sot	sotte		

N.B. 1. Adjectives whose masculine form ends in **-gu** require a diaeresis (¨) over the final e of the feminine: **aigu aiguë, exigu exiguë.**

2. In a few feminine compound nouns, formed with **grand,** the older feminine form **grand** (without an e) is retained,

---

[1] But see 95 (g).

and **grand** is joined to the noun by a hyphen or apostrophe, e.g. **grand-mère, grand-tante, grand-rue** (*main street*), **pas grand-chose** (*nothing much*), or **grand'mère,** &c.

(*b*) Nouns[1] and Adjectives whose masculine form ends in **-e** make no further change in the feminine:

un artiste	une artiste	aimable	aimable
un camarade	une camarade	énorme	énorme
un élève	une élève	riche	riche
un propriétaire	une propriétaire	solitaire	solitaire

95. Further Variations

In the following groups the feminine form differs from the masculine by further changes in addition to the final **-e**:

(*a*) *Masculine in* **-c**: *Feminine in* **-che**

blanc   blanche   franc   franche   *and* sec   sèche (*with grave accent*)

Principal exceptions: public publique, turc turque, grec grecque.

(*b*) *Masculine in* **-f**: *Feminine in* **-ve**

un Juif   une Juive   naïf   naïve
un veuf   une veuve   vif   vive *and* bref   brève (*with grave accent*)

(*c*) *Masculine in* **-x**: *Feminine in* **-se**

un époux   une épouse   heureux   heureuse   jaloux   jalouse

Principal exceptions: faux fausse, doux douce, roux rousse; *for* vieux *see* (*d*).

(*d*) {Masculine in **-eau** (**-el**): *Feminine in* **-elle**
    {Masculine in **-ou** (**-ol**): *Feminine in* **-olle**

(i) The following common adjectives, which have an additional masculine form in **-l** used when they precede a masculine singular noun beginning with a vowel or h-mute, form their feminine from this latter masculine form:

beau (bel)	belle	fou (fol)	folle
nouveau (nouvel)	nouvelle	mou (mol)	molle

Note also: vieux (vieil)   vieille.

---

[1] The number of nouns following this rule is comparatively small, being those of the type shown in 89 (*a*) (ii). Many nouns whose masculine ends in **-e** have special feminine forms (see 96).

N.B. The masc. form in **-l** is only used when the adjective immediately precedes the noun beginning with a vowel or h-mute:

un bel enfant   le nouvel élève

but

un beau et agile enfant   un homme fou

(ii) Similarly a few nouns in **-eau** have feminine in **-elle**:

un agneau   une agnelle   un jumeau[1]   une jumelle

(e) *Masculine in* **-el, -eil, –en, -et, -on**: *Feminine in* **-elle,
-eille, –enne, –ette, –onne**

un Italien	une Italienne	cruel	cruelle	bon	bonne
un chien	une chienne	pareil	pareille		
un baron	une baronne	ancien	ancienne		
un lion	une lionne	muet	muette		

Exceptions: a few adjectives in **-et** form feminines in **-ète**, e.g.:

(in)complet	(in)complète	inquiet	inquiète
(in)discret	(in)discrète	secret	secrète

(f) *Masculine in* **-er, -ier**: *Feminine in* **-ère, -ière**

un boulanger	une boulangère	léger	légère
un fermier	une fermière	premier	première

(g) *Masculine in* **-eur**: *Feminine in* **-euse**

Words in **-eur,** whose stem is also the stem of a present participle,
have feminines in **-euse**:

un danseur	une danseuse	flatteur	flatteuse	un vendeur une vendeuse
un pêcheur	une pêcheuse	menteur	menteuse	trompeur trompeuse
(*fisherman*)				

Principal exceptions: un enchanteur une enchanteresse, un pécheur (*sinner*)
une pécheresse.

N.B. 1. Words which are comparative in meaning form their
feminines regularly, e.g. un mineur (*minor*) une mineure,
meilleur (*better*) meilleure, supérieur (*higher, upper,
superior*) supérieure.

2. Many words in **-teur,** whose stem is not that of
a present participle, have feminine in **-trice,** e.g.
un directeur une directrice. For list see 96 (*c*).

[1] **Jumeau** may also be used as an adjective, but has no masculine form in **-l**.

3. Many other nouns in **-eur** have no feminine form, e.g. un professeur *a teacher (of either sex)* (cf. 89 (*b*)).

96. Special Groups

(*a*) Many nouns describing persons and animals have feminine equivalents which are a different word, or which are not formed regularly from the masculine. Those in common use are:

(i) Persons (a few of the following may be used as adjectives):

un compagnon	*companion*	une compagne
un empereur	*emperor*	une impératrice
un favori	*favourite*	une favorite
un fils	*son*	une fille
un beau-fils	*stepson*	une belle-fille
un frère	*brother*	une sœur
un garçon	*boy*	une fille
un gendre	*son-in-law*	une bru
un gouverneur	*governor, tutor*	une gouvernante
un héros	*hero*	une héroïne
un homme	*man*	une femme
un mâle	*male*	une femelle
un mari	*husband*	une femme
un monsieur	*gentleman*	une dame
monsieur	*Mr., sir*	madame
un neveu	*nephew*	une nièce
un oncle	*uncle*	une tante
papa	*father, daddy*	maman
un parrain	*godfather*	une marraine
un père	*father*	une mère
un beau-père	*father-in-law, stepfather*	une belle-mère
un roi	*king*	une reine
un serviteur	*servant*	une servante
un vieillard	*old man*	une vieille

(ii) Animals:

un bélier	*ram*	une brebis	*ewe*
un mouton	*sheep, wether*		
un bœuf	*ox, bullock*	une vache	*cow*
un taureau	*bull*	une génisse	*heifer*
un bouc	*he-goat*	une chèvre	*goat, she-goat*
un cerf	*stag*	une biche	*hind, doe*
un cheval	*horse*	une jument	*mare*
un étalon	*stallion*		

un canard	*drake, duck*	une cane	*female duck*
un chat	*cat* ⎱	une chatte	*female cat*
un matou	*tomcat* ⎰		
un cochon ⎱	*pig* ⎱	⎧ une truie ⎫	*sow*
un porc ⎰		⎨ une coche ⎬	
un verrat	*boar* ⎰	⎩ ⎭	
un coq	*cock*	une poule	*hen*
un dindon	*turkey-cock*	une dinde	*turkey-hen*
un jars	*gander*	une oie	*goose*
un lièvre	*hare*	une hase	*doe-hare*
un loup	*wolf*	une louve	*she-wolf*
un mulet	*(he-)mule*	une mule	*(she-)mule*
un poulain	*colt, foal*	une pouliche	*filly*
un singe	*monkey, male monkey*	une guenon	*female monkey*

(*b*) A number of nouns describing persons and animals have feminine in **-esse**, e.g. (a few of these may be used as adjectives):

un âne	*donkey*	une ânesse
un comte	*count*	une comtesse
un hôte	*host*	une hôtesse
un maître	*master*	une maîtresse
un prince	*prince*	une princesse
un Suisse	*a Swiss*	une Suissesse
un tigre	*tiger*	une tigresse
un traître	*traitor*	une traîtresse

Note also

un abbé	*clergyman, abbot*	une abbesse (*no accent*)
un dieu	*god*	une déesse
un duc	*duke*	une duchesse
un nègre	*negro*	une négresse (négresse *is not used as adjective*)

(*c*) Many words (mostly nouns describing living beings) in **-teur**, whose stem is not that of a present participle (cf. 95 (*g*)), have feminine in **-trice**, e.g.:

acteur	actrice	fondateur	fondatrice
aviateur	aviatrice	instituteur	institutrice
bienfaiteur	bienfaitrice	moteur	motrice
conducteur	conductrice	protecteur	protectrice
créateur	créatrice	rédacteur	rédactrice
destructeur	destructrice	spectateur	spectatrice
directeur	directrice	tuteur	tutrice

97. Note on Pronunciation

(*a*) In the majority of cases, the change of spelling in the feminine form does not involve a difference of pronunciation. Note in particular that:

(i) the final **-e** of the feminine is not sounded in normal speech:

ami [ami]   **amie** [ami]   **cruel** [kryɛl]   **cruelle** [kryɛl]
bon ami [bɔnami]   **bonne amie** [bɔnami]

(ii) the addition of final **-e** does not by itself make any difference to the pronunciation of a preceding vowel or sounded consonant:

joli [ʒɔli]	**jolie** [ʒɔli]	**aigu** [egy]	**aiguë** [egy]
meilleur [mɛjœːr]	**meilleure** [mɛjœːr]	**cher** [ʃɛːr]	**chère** [ʃɛːr]
grec [grɛk]	**grecque** [grɛk]	**ours** [urs]	**ourse** [urs]

(iii) the doubling of **-l** before the final **-e** makes no difference to the pro-nunciation or to the length of sound:[1]

mortel [mɔrtɛl]   **mortelle** [mɔrtɛl]   **pareil** [parɛːj]   **pareille** [parɛːj]
nul [nyl]   **nulle** [nyl]

(*b*) The addition of **-e** in the feminine does, however, involve a change of pronunciation in the following circumstances:

(i) a final consonant, not sounded in the masculine, is sounded before **e** in the feminine, or is replaced by a sounded consonant or consonants:

grand [grɑ̃]	**grande** [grɑ̃ːd]	**gris** [gri]	**grise** [griːz]
heureux [œrø]	**heureuse** [œrøːz]	**faux** [fo]	**fausse** [foːs]
muet [mɥɛ]	**muette** [mɥɛt]		

(ii) in addition to the above, a change may be produced in the vowel-sound of the preceding syllable:

sot [so]   **sotte** [sɔt]   **léger** [leʒe]   **légére** [leʒɛːr]

(iii) final **-n**, nasal in the masculine, becomes denasalized when doubled and followed by **-e** in the feminine:

paysan [peizɑ̃]   **paysanne** [peizan][2]   **importun** [ɛ̃pɔrtœ̃]   **importune** [ɛ̃pɔrtyn][2]

ancien [ɑ̃sjɛ̃]	**ancienne** [ɑ̃sjɛn]	**vain** [vɛ̃]	**vaine** [vɛn]
cousin [kuzɛ̃]	**cousine** [kuzin][2]	**plein** [plɛ̃]	**pleine** [plɛn]
bon [bɔ̃]	**bonne** [bɔn]		

---

[1] But **gentil** [ʒɑ̃ti], **gentille** [ʒɑ̃tiːj].
[2] Note that here the vowel-sound preceding the **-n** is also changed in the feminine.

X. PLURAL OF NOUNS AND ADJECTIVES

Almost all Nouns and Adjectives have plural forms.

Adjectives take the plural form when qualifying, or referring to, plural nouns or pronouns:

les grands arbres   elles sont petites

98. General Rule

In general, the plural of nouns and the plural of the masculine and feminine of adjectives are distinguished in writing from the singular by the addition of a final **-s**:

Sing.	Plur.	Sing.	Plur.	Sing.	Plur.
le jardin	les jardins	bon	bons	bonne	bonnes
la forêt	les forêts	petit	petits	petite	petites
le détail	les détails	pareil	pareils	pareille	pareilles
le cri	les cris	joli	jolis	jolie	jolies
la pluie	les pluies	aigu	aigus	aiguë	aiguës
le cou	les cous	fou	fous	folle	folles

Principal exceptions (other than those dealt with in 99):

le travail	les travaux	le ciel (*sky*)	es cieux
le vitrail	les vitraux	un œil	des yeux

and the following nouns in **-ou**, which take plural in **-x**: le bijou, le caillou, le chou, le genou, un hibou, le joujou, le pou. *Plurals*: les bijoux, les cailloux, &c.

99. Particular Rules

(a) *Singular in* **-s, -x, -z**: *Plural no change*

le bras	les bras	un mur gris	des murs gris
la noix	les noix	il est heureux	ils sont heureux
le gaz	les gaz		

(b) Singular in **-au, -eau, -eu**: *Plural in* **-aux, -eaux, -eux**

le tuyau	les tuyaux	beau	beaux
le moineau	les moineaux	nouveau	nouveaux
le feu (*fire*)	les feux		
le lieu	les lieux		

Principal exceptions:

le pneu	les pneus	bleu	bleus
		feu (*late, deceased*)	feus

(c) Singular in **-al**: *Plural in* **-aux**

le cheval	les chevaux	brutal	brutaux
le journal	les journaux	loyal	loyaux

Principal exceptions:

le bal	les bals	fatal	fatals
le carnaval	les carnavals	final	finals
le festival	les festivals	naval	navals

100. Plural of Compound Nouns

The formation of the plural of Compound Nouns is complicated and often illogical, and can only be fully mastered by learning. The only principles which apply with any frequency are that:

(a) Only such parts of a compound noun as are themselves nouns or adjectives can be turned into the plural; any element which is a verb, preposition, or adverb will not vary:

le chou-fleur	les choux-fleurs
le beau-père	les beaux-pères
le rouge-gorge	les rouges-gorges

but

la garde-robe	les garde-robes
le tire-bouchon	les tire-bouchons
le laissez-passer	les laissez-passer
un pis-aller	des pis-aller
la chambre-à-coucher	les chambres-à-coucher
une avant-garde	des avant-gardes
une arrière-pensée	des arrière-pensées
le passe-partout	les passe-partout

(*b*) Frequently, when the compound is formed of two nouns, the second noun remains singular in idea, and does not take the plural form, e.g.:

le chemin de fer	les chemins de fer
le timbre-poste	les timbres-poste
un arc-en-ciel	des arcs-en-ciel
le verre-à-vin	les verres-à-vin

(*c*) Compound Nouns which are written in one word without a hyphen take final **-s** only:

le gendarme	les gendarmes
le passeport	les passeports
le pourboire	les pourboires

and words of the *grand-mère* type (cf. 94 (*a*), N.B. 2) follow this rule:

la grand-mère (grand'mère)   les grand-mères (grand'mères)

but note the following special cases:

le monsieur	les messieurs
monsieur (M.)	messieurs (MM.)
madame (Mme)	mesdames (Mmes)
mademoiselle (Mlle)	mesdemoiselles (Mlles)
le bonhomme	les bonshommes
le gentilhomme	les gentilshommes

101. Invariable Words

(*a*) In general Family Names do not vary for the plural:

Les Lambert sont arrivés.   Les deux Corneille.
The Lamberts have arrived.   *The two Corneilles.*

(*b*) Other parts of speech (prepositions, adverbs, names of letters, &c.), when used as nouns, do not vary for the plural:

Les pour et les contre.
The pros and cons.
Les pourquoi et les comment.
The whys and wherefores.
Le mot *jette* s'écrit avec deux t.
The word jette *is spelt with two t's.*

102. Nouns Having a Special Meaning in the Plural

The following common nouns have a special additional sense in the plural:

une affaire	*affair*	des affaires	*affairs, business*
le blé	*wheat*	les blés	*wheats, cornfields*
un ciseau	*chisel*	des ciseaux	*chisels, scissors*
un gage	*pledge*	des gages	*pledges, wages*
la lettre	*letter*	les lettres	*letters, literature*
une lunette	*telescope, field-glass*	des lunettes	*telescopes, spectacles*
une vacance	*vacancy*	des vacances	*vacancies, holidays*

103. Note on Pronunciation

(*a*) The addition of final -s or -x makes no difference to the pronunciation of individual words:

sac [sak]   **sacs** [sak]   **beau** [bo]   **beaux** [bo]

but in connected speech -s and -x are sounded [z] in liaison. This occurs principally between plural adjective and noun:

de beaux enfants [də bo zɑ̃fɑ̃]   **de belles images** [də bɛl zima:ʒ]

(*b*) There is no liaison of the final -s of a noun forming the first part of a compound noun containing a hyphen:

des arcs-en-ciel [de zark ɑ̃ sjɛl]
des salles-à-manger [de sal a mɑ̃ʒe]

but

des bonshommes [de bɔ̃zɔm]
des gentilshommes [de ʒɑ̃tizɔm]

(*c*) In a few nouns there is a difference in pronunciation in the plural which is not related to any change of spelling, e.g.:

un bœuf [œ̃ bœf]   **des bœufs** [de bø]
un œuf [œ̃ nœf]   **des œufs** [de zø]
un os [œ nɔs]   **des os** [de zo]

XI. POSITION AND AGREEMENT OF ADJECTIVES

POSITION

The position of an adjective qualifying a noun is not fixed. In the writings of French authors its position is varied for considerations of style, emphasis, and rhythm in a way that can only come from a very real familiarity with the language. The beginner is well advised to accept for the time being the rules given below, learning to modify them as a feeling for the language increases.

104. Adjectives Which Usually Precede the Noun

(*a*) Possessive and Demonstrative Adjectives always precede:

    ma canne   leurs roses   cet homme   ces enfants

(*b*) Numeral Adjectives precede:

         les trois frères   le cinquième mois

unless they are used as a distinguishing title:

    Louis Quatorze.
    Louis the Fourteenth.
    A la page sept.
    On page seven.

(*c*) Most[1] Indefinite Adjectives precede:

    chaque jour
    plusieurs raisons
    dans quelques sillons (G. Sand).
    Il n'y a pas d'autre travail (G. Sand).

[1] But **certain, différent, divers, même, pareil** may follow the noun in certain uses. See under these headings in Chapter XX.

(*d*) The following common adjectives usually precede:

beau	jeune	pauvre (*see also* 108)
bon (meilleur)	joli	sot
court	long	vaste
grand (*see also* 108)	mauvais (pire)	vieux
gros	méchant	vilain
haut	petit (moindre)	

Les belles prairies.   Dans les grandes villes.
Dans les longues herbes.   De mauvais ouvriers.
Une vaste campagne.   Le vieux laboureur.
    (G. Sand: *La Mare au diable*.)

N.B. But such adjectives may be found following the noun if any of the rules given in 105 (*d*), 106 (*c*), 108 apply.

105. Adjectives Which Usually Follow the Noun

As a general guide to the writing of simple French other adjectives may be considered as having their position after the noun:

Le résultat général d'un travail excessif et d'une misère profonde (G. Sand).
Des choses rares tiraient les yeux (Flaubert).
Les influences extérieures (G. Sand).

In particular the following types of adjectives almost always follow the noun:

(*a*) Adjectives denoting a physical quality, especially colour:

Une table ronde.   L'oiseau bleu.
A round table.   *The blue bird.*
Un enfant maigre.   Des tapis verts.
A thin child.   *Green carpets.*

(*b*) Adjectives of nationality, religion, rank, &c.:

Un écrivain espagnol.   Une école catholique.
A Spanish author.   *A Catholic school.*
Des pays orientaux.   Le gouvernement socialiste.
Oriental countries.   *The socialist government.*
Un palais ducal.   *A ducal palace.*

(c) Participles used as adjectives:

>De l'eau courante.
>Une maison abandonnée (Daudet).
>A côté des chevaux effrayés (G. Sand).

(d) Adjectives which are modified by an adverb or phrase:

>Une position vraiment haute (Maurois).
>La domination nouvellement imposée (G. Sand).
>Un tabac doux comme le miel.
>Une rue longue de 500 m.

But adjectives which would normally precede the noun may do so when modified by the adverbs **très, bien, fort, plus, moins, assez, aussi, si**:

>Une très belle position.
>De si bonnes raisons (Daudet).
>Le plus petit bateau.
>Une assez courte distance (Camus).

(e) Adjectives which are noticeably longer than the noun they qualify:

>La vie rustique (G. Sand).
>Des pages historiques (G. Sand).
>Des œuvres immortelles (G. Sand).
>Un repas interminable.

106. Two Adjectives: One Noun

Where there are two adjectives qualifying a single noun, their position is mainly a matter of sound and emphasis. However, it may be said that:

(a) Two adjectives which normally precede the noun (see 104 (d)) may both do so:

>Deux belles petites lanternes (Daudet).

If either of them is modified it will follow the noun:

>Un gros homme assez vieux (France).

(*b*) If one adjective normally precedes and one normally follows the noun, they may both occupy their normal position:

> Un grand arbre mort (Flaubert).
> Les gros papillons blancs (Daudet).
> La plus haute puissance humaine (Balzac).

(*c*) Two adjectives following the noun are linked by **et** if they present two equal and separable characteristics, but not if both adjectives are necessary to complete the meaning:

> Une odeur forte et chaude.
> *A strong, warm smell.*
> Un conducteur jeune et inexperimenté.
> *A young and inexperienced driver.*
> L'Afrique Occidentale Française.
> *French West Africa.*
> Une revue mensuelle littéraire.
> *A monthly literary review.*

107. Complex Noun

An adjective qualifying a complex noun (composed of two nouns linked by **de** or **à**—e.g. **maison de campagne** = *country house*) may either be placed before the first noun or after the second noun, with due regard to the rules given in 105, 106:

> Une grande maison de campagne (Maurois).
> *A large country house.*
> De minces filets d'argent (G. Sand).
> *Slender silver nets.*
> Une tasse à thé ébréchée.
> *A chipped teacup.*
> Des maux de tête continus (Maurois).
> *Continual headaches.*

It is not usually placed after the second noun if there might be ambiguity as to which noun it agrees with:

> Une rude journée de travail (G. Sand).
> *A rough day's work.*

Une extraordinaire énergie d'expression (Maurois).
A remarkable vigour of expression.

108. Meaning Differing According to Position

A number of adjectives have a different sense according to
whether they are placed before or after the noun. The following
are the commonest and least ambiguous examples:

ancien	un ancien élève *a former pupil* un ancien combattant *an ex-serviceman*	une maison ancienne *an ancient house*
brave	un brave homme *a good fellow*	un homme brave *a brave man*
certain (see 219)		
cher	mon cher ami *my dear friend*	un repas cher *an expensive meal*
dernier	la dernière course *the last race (of several)*	la semaine dernière *last week (the one before this week)*
différent **divers** } (see 221)		
grand	un grand homme *a great man*	un homme grand *a tall man*
nouveau	un nouvel effort *a new (=fresh) effort*	un procédé nouveau *a new (=novel) procedure*
pauvre	mon pauvre enfant *my poor child*	des gens pauvres *poor people (no money)*
prochain	la prochaine fois *(the) next time* la prochaine réunion *the next meeting* le prochain village *the nearest (next) village*	le mois prochain l'année prochaine *next month/year (i.e. the one after this one)* une maison prochaine *a near-by house*
propre	sa propre maison *his own house*	une maison propre *a clean house*
seul	un seul candidat *a single (only one) candidate* la seule raison *the only reason*	les murs seuls restaient *the walls, alone (only the walls) remained* la force seule ne suffira pas *force alone will not be sufficient*
vrai	la vraie cause *the real cause* un vrai ami *a true (=genuine) friend*	une histoire vraie *a true (=not fictitious) story*

AGREEMENT

109. General Rule

Adjectives, and participles used as adjectives, agree with the noun they qualify, or refer to, in gender and number:

une jolie fleur	des histoires fausses
de grands événements	elle est française
des choses intéressantes	les vitres cassées
elle est intelligente	les provisions sont épuisées
je la trouve charmante	ils la croyaient morte

N.B. **Je (me), tu (te), nous, vous,** may be masculine or feminine according to whom they refer to:

'Je suis content', dit-il.
'Je suis contente', dit-elle.
'Ernest, je te crois paresseux!'
'Ernestine, je te crois paresseuse!'
Les hommes répondirent: 'Nous sommes prêts.'
Les femmes répondirent: 'Nous sommes prêtes.'

In addition, **vous** may be singular or plural (see 154 n. 1).

110. Two Nouns: One Adjective

Where one adjective qualifies two or more nouns, it is plural, and agrees in gender:

Le symbole de l'honnêteté et de la solidité anglaises (Maurois).
Un goût et des moyens particuliers (G. Sand).

If the nouns are of different genders the adjective is masculine:

Les vieillards et les femmes épouvantés.
'Heureusement, nous sommes seuls, madame', dit-il (Balzac).

111. Adjectives of Colour

(a) Some words describing colour, which are adjectives in English, remain nouns in French and do not agree, even when standing in an adjectival position:

160

Aux murs blancs et or (Maurois).
With white and gold walls.
Une longue redingote marron (Daudet).
A long maroon riding-coat.

(*b*) Compound adjectives of colour are also invariable:

Une pairè de petits yeux bleu clair (About).
A pair of little light blue eyes.

112. Adjectives Used as Adverbs

Adjectives, when used as adverbs in a few common expressions, do not agree:

Elles parlaient bas.
They spoke low.
Les roses sentent bon.
The roses smell sweet.

For further list see 116.

113. Note on Nouns Used as Adjectives

(*a*) French nouns used adjectivally (i.e. qualifying another noun) are usually preceded by a preposition. In general:

   (i) **de** is used where the second noun describes the species of the first noun, or states what it is made[1] or composed of:

Une maison de campagne.	Le trimestre d'été.
A country house.	*The summer term.*
Un pot de fer.	Des bottes de paille.
An iron pot.	*Bundles of straw.*

   (ii) **à** is used where the second noun expresses the intended use of the first noun, or how it works, or what it is fitted with:

Une tasse à café.	Une brosse à dents.
A coffee-cup.	*A tooth-brush.*
Un moteur à réaction.	Un roulement à billes.
A jet engine.	*A ball-bearing.*

[1] The sense of *made of* may also be rendered, more emphatically, by **en: un cendrier en cuivre** a copper ash-tray (an ash-tray made of copper).

(b) In cases where a noun may stand in an adjectival position (without an intervening preposition):

(i) in general there is no agreement:

Les fenêtres sud. Une industrie clef.
The south windows. *A key industry.*

See also 111 (a) above.

(ii) a few nouns which have feminine forms (see 96) are also adjectives, and agree:

Une branche maîtresse. Des amies actrices.
A main branch. *Actress friends.*

(iii) a few nouns, describing professions, &c., which have no feminine forms (see 89 (b)), may stand as adjectives and agree in the plural:

Des femmes professeurs. Des philosophes poètes.
Lady teachers. *Philosopher poets.*

XII. ADVERBS

114. Formation of Adverbs of Manner

(a) Regular Formation: **-ment** is added to the *feminine* form:

  (i) of adjectives that end in a consonant:

        pur: purement;   net: nettement;
        léger: légèrement;   doux: doucement

  (ii) of adjectives whose masculine and feminine forms both end in **-e**:

        simple: simplement;   sage: sagement

  (iii) of **beau, nouveau, mou, fou**:

        nouveau: nouvellement;   fou: follement

(b) **-ment** is added to the *masculine* form of other adjectives that end in a vowel:

      poli: poliment;   vrai: vraiment;   résolu: résolument

A few such adjectives take a circumflex accent on the final vowel when **-ment** is added, e.g.:

      gai: gaîment (*or more usually* gaiement);
      continu: continûment;   assidu: assidûment

(c) Adjectives in **-ant** and **-ent** form adverbs as follows:

      constant: constamment [kɔ̃stamã]
      prudent: prudemment [prydamã]

Exceptions: lent: lentement; présent: présentement

(d) Some adjectives change the final **e** of the feminine form to **é** when **-ment** is added, e.g.:

  commun: communément;   confus: confusément;
  précis: précisément;   profond: profondément

(*e*) A similar change is made by some adjectives whose masculine form ends in **-e,** e.g.:

> aveugle: aveuglément;   commode: commodément;
> énorme: énormément;   immense: immensément

(*f*) Among irregular forms note:

> gentil: gentiment   bref: brièvement
> impuni: impunément   grave: grièvement (*or* gravement)
> bon: bien   traître: traîtreusement
> mauvais: mal   prodigue: prodigalement

(*g*) There are some adjectives from which no adverb is formed. These include: **charmant, concis, content, crédule, fâché, hautain, possible.**

An adverbial sense is then conveyed by some other form of expression, e.g.:

> d'une façon charmante
> avec crédulité
> il est possible qu'il vienne.

115. Position of Adverbs

The usage as regards the position of adverbs is not fixed, and is frequently affected by considerations of emphasis or balance. Apart from these considerations, the rules given below generally apply.

(*a*) When qualifying a *verb* in a *simple tense*, the adverb (or adverbial expression) normally *follows* the verb:

> Je lui cède toujours.
> *I always give way to him.*
> Je donnerais gaiement une pinte de mon sang (Augier et Sandeau).
> *I would cheerfully give a pint of my blood.*
> Elle choisissait avec soin ses couleurs (Saint-Exupéry).
> *She chose her colours carefully.*

(b) When qualifying a *verb* in a *compound tense* or an *infinitive*:

(i) Adverbs of Place, and **tôt, tard, aussitôt, aujourd'hui, hier, demain** *follow* the Past Participle or Infinitive:

Tu l'as mise là.   Elle a dû chercher partout.
You put it there.   *She had to look everywhere.*
Il est parti hier.   Ils voulaient manger aussitôt.
He left yesterday.   *They wanted to eat straight away.*

(ii) Other short adverbs, and a few short adverbial expressions usually *precede* the Past Participle or Infinitive:

Il avait trop parlé (Maurois).   Je l'ai tout à fait oublié.
He had talked too much.   *I completely forgot it.*
Il aurait bien pu vous mieux loger (Balzac).
He could well have lodged you better.

(iii) Other long or heavy-sounding adverbs, and most adverbial expressions usually *follow* the Past Participle or Infinitive:

Cela ne peut pas durer longtemps (Augier et Sandeau).
That cannot last long.
Pour rompre irrévocablement avec les folies de mon passé (Augier et Sandeau).
To break irrevocably with my past follies.
Tu ne pouvais arriver plus à propos (Augier et Sandeau).
You could not arrive at a more opportune moment.

(c) Adverbs qualifying an *adjective, participle, adverb,* or *adverbial expression* normally *precede* them:

Elle est extrêmement belle.   Il court bien vite.
She is extremely beautiful.   *He runs very fast.*
Un homme bien vêtu.   Un chapeau très à la mode.
A well-dressed man.   *A very fashionable hat.*

(d) Adverbs and adverbial expressions which connect the sense of a sentence with what has preceded most commonly stand at the beginning:

Dedans on entendait des enfants qui toussaient (Daudet).
Inside one could hear children coughing.

En attendant il vaut mieux se taire.
Meanwhile it is better to say nothing.

(e) Other adverbs may also stand at the beginning for emphasis:

Tant son intelligence était bornée (Flaubert).
So limited was her understanding.
Tout à coup il dressa l'oreille.
All of a sudden he pricked up his ears.

(f) Adverbs which qualify not merely the verb, but the idea of
the sentence as a whole, may stand wherever the balance and sense
permit, though they are most commonly found at the beginning:[1]

Sérieusement, j'ai fait un mariage magnifique (Augier et
Sandeau).
Joking apart, I have made a wonderful marriage.
Dehors la neige tombait.
Outside the snow was falling.
C'était bon autrefois.
It was all right in the old days.
Elle est en réalité agrandie (Pagnol).
It is in reality increased.

(g) Adverbs which qualify Numeral or Indefinite Adjectives
stand after the relevant noun:

Trois ans plus tard.
Three years later.
Trois jours de suite.
Three days in succession.
Pour une nuit seulement.
For one night only.

---

[1] In careful writing and speech, Inversion (see 242) takes place in clauses begun by,
e.g. **à peine, au (du) moins, aussi** (= *therefore*), **peut-être, encore** (= *furthermore,
nevertheless*), **en vain (vainement), toujours** (= *nevertheless*):

A peine a-t-on le temps de marquer les points (Daudet).
One scarcely has time to score the points.
Peut-être l'as-tu caché (Mérimée).
Perhaps you have hidden it.
Peut-être les élèves auraient-ils été moins surpris (Maurois).
Perhaps the pupils would have been less surprised.

116. Adjectives Used as Adverbs

(*a*) Some adjectives are used adverbially in certain set expressions, e.g.:

parler haut (bas)	coûter (vendre, acheter) cher	voir clair
speak aloud (softly)	*cost (sell, buy) dear*	*see clearly*
s'arrêter court	sentir bon (mauvais)	aller droit
stop short	*smell good (bad)*	*go straight*

(*b*) Some other adjective forms are often used adverbially, e.g.:

bref	fort	même (see 223)
in short	*very, hard, loud, &c.*	*even*
juste	soudain	tout (see 234)
exactly, &c.	*suddenly*	*quite, very, &c.*

Notes on Certain Adverbs

1. For adverbs used interrogatively (**quand, combien,** &c.) see Chapter XXII.
2. For **même, quelque, tout** see Chapter XX.
3. For Negative Adverbs (**pas, jamais,** &c.) see 248 ff.
4. For **où** and **que** as Relative Adverbs (**Le moment où,** &c.) see 194–5.
5. For **y** and **en** see 159–60.

117. *Arrière, avant, derrière, dessous, dessus, devant*

(*a*) **Arrière** and **avant** may be used as adjectives (invariable):

     Une roue arrière (avant).   *A back (front) wheel.*

Derrière, dessous, dessus, devant may be constructed adjectivally with **de**:

Les pattes de devant.	Des vêtements de dessous.
The front feet.	*Under-garments.*

(*b*) All the above may also stand as nouns (masculine), e.g.:

l'arrière	le dessous	un avant	prendre le dessus
the rear	*the underneath*	*a forward*	*take the upper hand*
		(football)	

(c) **Arrière** and **avant** are preceded by **en** in the following senses:

Rester en arrière.	Aller en arrière.
Remain behind.	*Go back, backwards, astern, &c.*
Courir en avant.	Il s'est trouvé bien en avant.
Run forward.	*He found himself well to the front.*

La tête était légèrement inclinée en avant (Mérimée).
The head was leaning slightly forward.

118. *Assez* (see also 119)

1. Sufficiently	Il avait assez parlé.
	He had spoken enough.
	Si j'étais assez malheureux pour en conserver (Beaumarchais).
	If I was unfortunate enough to retain any.
2. (Qualifying	Ils l'ont bâti assez bien.
adj. or adv.	*They have built it quite well.*
only) *fairly,*	Une assez courte distance.
somewhat	*A fairly short distance.*

119. *Beaucoup, peu, trop, assez, tant, autant, combien, plus, moins*

(a) The above may also stand as pronouns:

Je crois que c'est beaucoup et peut-être trop (Stendhal).
I think that it is a lot and perhaps too much.

Combien a-t-il reçu?	Il a reçu plus que moi.
How much did he receive?	*He received more than I did.*
Je vous dois tant.	*I owe you so much.*

(b) When standing before a noun, to express a quantity, they are followed by **de** (but see also 84 (c)):

Tant de bon sens.	Si peu d'exigences.
So much common sense.	*So few demands.*
Trop de vivacité.	
Too much vivacity.	
Assez de place.	*Enough room.*

(c) **Beaucoup** (and **beaucoup de**) are not found qualified by any other adverb except the negative *pas*. Therefore, *très beaucoup*, &c., are not admissible, and when the idea of *very* in *very much* is emphatic, the sense is provided by some other expression, e.g. **un très grand nombre de**, &c.

(d) Distinguish: (i) **peu** = *little, few, not very*:

Il travaille peu.   Peu de gens sont restés.
He works little.   *Few people stayed.*
Les vitres laissaient passer peu de jour (Balzac).
The panes let little light through.
Une communauté peu nombreuse (Maurois).
A not very numerous community.

and (ii) **un peu** = *a little, rather*:

Attendez un peu.   Prenez un peu de beurre.
Wait a little.   *Take a little butter.*
Ton mari te traite un peu légèrement (Augier et Sandeau).
Your husband treats you rather light-heartedly.

(e) **Plus, moins, trop**[1] are constructed adjectivally with **de**:

Un kilogramme de plus, de moins, de trop.
A kilogram more, less, too much.
Il ne put rien dire de plus (Saint-Exupéry).
He could say nothing more.

120. *Bien, mal*

(a) These have an adjectival sense in certain, mainly colloquial uses, e.g.:

C'est bien !   Ce n'est pas mal.
All right!   *It's not bad.*
Nous sommes bien (mal) ici.
We are comfortable (uncomfortable) here.

[1] Note also the idiom: **(Ils sont) de trop** = (*They are*) *not wanted.*

(b) Note also adverbial senses of **bien**:

1. *Well*	Il travaille bien.	
	He works well.	
2. *Very*	Cela est bien difficile.	
	That is very difficult.	
3. *Indeed, really*	C'est bien la vérité.	
	It is indeed the truth.	
	Est-ce bien lui?	
	Is it really he?	
4. *Many* (fol-	Je l'ai vu bien des fois.	
lowed by	*I have seen him many times.*	
des)	Bien des honnêtes gens ont souffert.	
	Many decent people have suffered.	

121. *Combien, comme, comment*
(see also Chapter XXII)

(a) **Combien**

1. *To what extent*	Il avait compris combien il est difficile de juger (Maurois).	
	He had realized how difficult it is to judge.	

(b) **Comme**

1. *Like, in the same way as, in the role of*	Faites comme moi.	
	Do as I do.	
	Comme ça.	
	Like that.	
	Se conduire comme un fou.	
	To behave like a madman.	
	Il avait servi comme artilleur (Daudet).	
	He had served as a gunner.	
2. *To what extent* (= **combien**)	Tu sais comme il exagère.	
	You know how he exaggerates.	

3. *As if, as though* — Elle voyait la procession comme si elle l'eût suivie (Flaubert).
She saw the procession as though she had followed in it.

Comme pour la distraire.
As though to amuse her.

Comme par hasard.
As if by chance.

Comme foudroyé.
As though thunderstruck.

4. *How*, in exclamations — Comme Camille est jolie!
How pretty Camille is!

(c) Comment

1. *In what way* — On ne savait comment il prendrait l'absence de son frère (Bazin).
One did not know how he would take his brother's absence.

2. *What!* — Comment! tu l'as perdu?
What! have you lost it?

122. Davantage

Davantage cannot qualify an adjective or adverb, and is, in normal use, only found at the end of the clause or sentence:

Je m'intéressais à lui davantage (Gide).
I was more interested in him.

On n'en disait pas davantage (Flaubert).
No more was said about it.

123. Encore

1. *Still* (time or degree) — Est-ce qu'il parle encore?
Is he still speaking?

Cela est encore plus difficile.
That is still more difficult.

2. *Yet* (in negative contexts) — Il n'est pas encore arrivé.
He has not yet arrived.

Il n'y avait encore personne sur la plage
(Daudet).
There was nobody yet on the beach.

3. *Again*   Encore une fois.   Je l'ai vu encore à Paris.[1]
        Once again.   *I saw him again in Paris.*

4. Further   Encore une tasse.
   quantity   *Another cup.*
         Encore du vin.
         Some more wine.

124. *Ici, là, çà*

Ici (**ci-** as prefix) and **là** have a demonstrative force in such
expressions as:

ci-après	*hereafter*	là-haut	*up there, in heaven*
là-dedans	*in it, in there*	là-bas	*over there, down there*
là-dessous	*under it, under there*	par ici	*this way, along here*
		par là	*that way, along there*
là-dessus	*on it, over it, about it, thereupon*	jusqu'ici	*as far as this, up till now*
		jusque-là	*as far as that, up till then*

Çà appears in the expression **çà et là** = *here and there.*

125. *Si, aussi*

(*a*) **Si** and **aussi** (= *so* or *such*), may qualify an adjective or
adverb:[2]

De si bonnes raisons.
Such good reasons.
D'aussi parfaits modèles.
Such perfect models.
N'allez pas si vite.   Il y a si longtemps.
Don't go so fast.   *So long ago.*

---

[1] A more usual way of expressing this would be: Je l'ai revu à Paris.
[2] When qualifying a verb the sense of *so* or *so much* is conveyed by, for example,
tellement, tant:
     Elle pleura tellement que sa maîtresse lui dit . . . (Flaubert).
     She cried so much that her mistress said to her . . .

(b) **Aussi** (= *too, also*) follows the part of speech to which it particularly applies:

> Est-ce qu'il vient aussi?   Eux aussi (Les voisins aussi) l'ont dit.
> *Is he coming too?*   *They too (The neighbours too) said so.*

126. *Toujours*

1. *Always*   Il se repose toujours le dimanche.
   He always has a rest on Sundays.

2. Continuation   L'autre avançait toujours (Daudet).
   The other kept on advancing.

3. *Still*   Tarascon est toujours à la même place (Daudet).
   Tarascon is still in the same place.

4. *At any rate*   Ils n'auront toujours pas le mien (Daudet).
   At any rate they won't have mine.

XIII. COMPARISON

127. Comparative and Superlative Forms of Adjectives

(a) The Comparative is formed regularly by adding **plus** to the Positive, and the Superlative by adding **le, la,** or **les**, as required, to the Comparative:

	Positive	*Comparative*	*Superlative*
Masc. sing.	**long**	**plus long**	**le plus long**
	long	longer	the longest
Fem. sing.	**belle**	**plus belle**	**la plus belle**
	beautiful	more beautiful	the most beautiful
Masc. plur.	**grands**	**plus grands**	**les plus grands**
	large	larger	largest
Fem. plur.	**récentes**	**plus récentes**	**les plus récentes**
	recent	more recent	the most recent

(b) **Moins** (= *less*) is employed in the same way as **plus,** giving, for example, **moins long** *less long,* **les moins récentes** *the least recent.*

(c) These comparisons are irregular or partly irregular (the forms given make the normal changes for feminine and plural):

bon	**meilleur**	**le meilleur, &c.**
good	better	the best
mauvais	⎰**plus mauvais**	**le plus mauvais, &c.**
	⎱**pire**[1]	**le pire, &c.**
bad	worse	the worst
petit	⎰**plus petit**	**le plus petit, &c.**
	⎱**moindre**[2]	**le moindre, &c.**
small, little	smaller, lesser	the smallest, the least

---

[1] **Pire** generally has the sense of *morally worse,* cf.

Son frère est pire que lui.	Sa composition est la plus mauvaise.
His brother is worse than he.	*His essay is the worst.*

[2] **Moindre** generally has the sense of *less in importance,* and **plus petit** *less in size,* cf.

C'est là le moindre danger.	Les pains vont être plus petits.
That is the least danger.	*Loaves are going to be smaller.*

128. Constructions of Comparative and Superlative

(*a*) Comparative and Superlative forms may, like the Positive, stand before or after the noun, according as the usage or emphasis requires (see 104 ff.):

> Une plus grande pendule.
> *A larger clock.*
> Les plus vieux modèles.
> *The oldest models.*
> Des voitures plus élégantes.
> *Smarter carriages.*

(*b*) When a Superlative Adjective follows the noun, the Article is present both with the noun and with the adjective:

> Le livre le plus intéressant.
> *The most interesting book.*
> Les appartements les plus modestes.
> *The most modest flats.*
> Une des rues les plus animées.
> *One of the busiest streets.*

(*c*) When a Superlative Adjective is preceded by a Possessive Adjective, the Definite Article is omitted, unless the superlative stands after the noun:

> Mes meilleures fleurs.   Ses pensées les plus intimes.
> *My best flowers.*   *His most intimate thoughts.*

The Definite Article is also omitted after **de** in such expressions as (**tout**) **ce qu'il y a de**:

> Ce qu'il y a de plus intéressant.   Tout ce qu'il y a de meilleur.
> *What is most interesting.*   *All that is best.*

(*d*) The sense of *in* after a superlative is conveyed by **de**:

> Le plus grand avion du monde.
> *The largest aeroplane in the world.*

(e) Measure of difference with a comparative or superlative is expressed by **de**:

C'est plus élevé de quelques mètres.
It is several metres higher.
L'aîné de trois mois.
The elder by three months.
Il est de beaucoup le plus âgé.
He is by far the oldest.

But **de** is omitted before **beaucoup** with a comparative:

Il est beaucoup plus habile.
He is much cleverer.

129. Comparative and Superlative Forms of Adverbs

(a) The Comparative is formed regularly by adding **plus** (or **moins,** as required) to the Positive; and the Superlative by adding **le plus**:

Positive	Comparative	Superlative
vite	**plus vite**	**le plus vite**
fast, quickly	faster	(the) fastest
souvent	**moins souvent**	**le moins souvent**
often	less often	(the) least often

The **le** so added is invariable:

La fillette courait le plus vite.
The little girl ran the fastest.
Les vieilles venaient le moins souvent.
The old women came the least often.

(b) The following comparisons are irregular:

beaucoup	much	**plus**	more	**le plus**	most
bien	well	**mieux**	better	**le mieux**	best
mal	badly	**plus mal** / **pis**[1]	worse	**le plus mal** / **le pis**	worst
peu	little	**moins**	less	**le moins**	least

[1] Pis and le pis are usually only found in certain set expressions, e.g.
aller de mal en pis.   de pis en pis.   tant pis.
go from bad to worse.   *worse and worse.* *so much the worse.*
c'est le pis.   au pis.
this is the worst.   *at the worst.*

130. Repetition of Definite Article

The Definite Article is repeated with each Superlative Adjective and Adverb, including those in a series:

> Le garçon le plus fort et le plus solide.
> *The strongest and sturdiest boy.*
> Ceux qui parlent le plus vite et le plus distinctement.
> *Those who speak the quickest and most distinctly.*

131. More, Most, Less, Least

(*a*) Where **plus** conveys the idea of *more* or *most* before a noun (as in *more men*) it is followed by **de.** Similarly with **moins**:

> Il a plus (moins) d'adresse que les autres.
> *He has more (less) skill than the others.*
> C'est lui qui a fait le plus (moins) de travail.
> *It is he who has done the most (least) work.*

though frequently some other form of expression may be appropriate to the context:

> Il y a encore des pommes à la cuisine.
> *There are more apples in the kitchen.*
> Nous aurons besoin d'un plus grand nombre d'ouvriers.
> *We shall need more workers.*
> Ils ont la plus grande quantité d'or.
> *They have the most gold.*

For uses of **davantage** see 122.

(*b*) Note the constructions where *more* or *less* qualify a numeral:

> Deux secondes de plus.[1]
> *Two seconds more.*
> Une raison de plus.
> *One more reason.*

---

[1] **Encore** is a frequent equivalent here of **plus**:

> Il y a encore deux choses à faire.
> *There are two more things to do.*

Il a vingt livres de moins que moi.
He has twenty books less than I.

(c) Where *most* is the equivalent of *very*, the sense is conveyed in French by, for example, **très, fort, bien**:

Un homme très spirituel.
A most witty man.
Des idées fort dangereuses.
Most dangerous ideas.
Vous êtes bien aimable.
You are most kind.

Or by a number of other idioms, e.g.:

Un pays des plus primitifs.
A most primitive country.
Il est des plus opiniâtres.
He is most obstinate.
Sa tenue est tout ce qu'il y a de plus correct.
His dress is most correct.

132. More Than, Less Than

(a) Where *more than*, *less than* express a genuine comparison, *than* is rendered by **que**:

Il gagne plus que vous, moins que les trois autres.
He earns more than you, less than the other three.
Une maison beaucoup plus élégante que l'ancienne.
A much more elegant house than the old one.

(b) Where *more than* means *a quantity greater than*, **de** is used. Similarly with **moins**:

Les frais se monteront à plus de douze ou quinze mille francs (Balzac).
The costs will amount to more than twelve or fifteen thousand francs.
Il a moins de treize ans.
He is under thirteen.
Plus d'un candidat en sortit découragé.
More than one candidate came out discouraged.

133. Comparative Sentences

(a) *With* **plus** *and* **moins**

Il travaille plus (moins) que moi.
He works more (less) than I.
Il a plus (moins) de livres que moi.
He has more (less) books than I.
Il a plus de moutons que de vaches.
He has more sheep than cows.
Il est plus intelligent que moi.
He is cleverer than I.
Il court plus vite que moi.
He runs faster than I.
Il parle plus qu'il ne[1] travaille.
He talks more than he works.
Une chose plus commune qu'on ne[1] pense (Vigny).
A thing more common than one thinks.

(b) *With* **autant, tant, aussi, si**

Il travaille autant que moi.
He works as much as I.
Il n'a pas tant (autant) de livres que moi.
He has not as many books as I.
Il est aussi intelligent que moi.
He is as clever as I.
Il ne court pas si (aussi) vite que moi.
He does not run as (so) fast as I.
Il n'est pas si (aussi) riche que vous pensez.[2]
He is not as (so) rich as you think.

---

[1] **Ne** (without negative force) is usually present in the **que** clause in sentences of this kind. Where the subject of the **que** clause is a noun, inversion is frequent:

      Il est plus riche que ne pensent les autres.

[2] No **ne** is present in the **que** clause in sentences of this kind when the main clause is negative. Cf. note 1 to (*a*).

Note also such forms of expression as:

{ aussi vite que possible.
{ le plus vite possible.
as quickly as possible.

hauts comme des montagnes.
as high as mountains.

(c) *Comparison of Infinitives*

Where the comparison is between two courses of action, expressed by infinitives, the second infinitive is usually preceded by **de,** unless the infinitives are governed by another preposition:

Il vaudra mieux rester que de partir (Flaubert).
It will be better to stay than to go away.
Je tiens plus à écouter qu'à parler.
I am more anxious to listen than to talk.

(d) *Double Comparatives*

Plus je travaille, plus je deviens sage.
The more I work, the wiser I become.
Plus il a parlé, moins j'ai compris.
The more he talked, the less I understood.

(e) *With* **de plus en plus** *and* **de moins en moins**

Un problème qui se montrait de plus en plus compliqué.
A problem which appeared more and more complicated.
Des voitures de plus en plus élégantes.
Smarter and smarter cars.
Des provisions de moins en moins suffisantes.
Less and less adequate supplies.

XIV. NUMERALS

134. Forms of Cardinal Numbers

0 **zéro** [zero]	30 **trente** [trɑ̃:t]
1 **un, une** [œ̃, yn]	31 **trente et un** [trɑ̃:teœ̃]
2 **deux** [dø]	40 **quarante** [karɑ̃:t]
3 **trois** [trwɑ]	50 **cinquante** [sɛ̃kɑ̃:t]
4 **quatre** [katr]	60 **soixante** [swasɑ̃:t]
5 **cinq** [sɛ̃:k]	70 **soixante-dix** [swasɑ̃tdis]
6 **six** [sis]	71 **soixante et onze** [swasɑ̃teɔ̃:z]
7 **sept** [sɛt]	72 **soixante-douze** [swasɑ̃tdu:z]
8 **huit** [ɥit]	80 **quatre-vingts** [katrəvɛ̃]
9 **neuf** [nœf]	81 **quatre-vingt-un** [katrəvɛ̃œ̃]
10 **dix** [dis]	90 **quatre-vingt-dix** [katrəvɛ̃dis]
11 **onze** [ɔ̃:z]	91 **quatre-vingt-onze** [katrəvɛ̃ɔ̃:z]
12 **douze** [du:z]	100 **cent** [sɑ̃]
13 **treize** [trɛ:z]	101 **cent un** [sɑ̃œ̃]
14 **quatorze** [katɔrz]	150 **cent cinquante** [sɑ̃sɛ̃kɑ̃:t]
15 **quinze** [kɛ̃:z]	200 **deux cents** [døsɑ̃]
16 **seize** [sɛ:z]	201 **deux cent un** [døsɑ̃œ̃]
17 **dix-sept** [dissɛt]	1,000 **mille** [mil]
18 **dix-huit** [dizɥit]	1,001 **mille un** [milœ̃]
19 **dix-neuf** [diznœf]	2,000 **deux mille** [dømil]
20 **vingt** [vɛ̃]	1,000,000 **un million** [œ̃ miljɔ̃]
21 **vingt et un** [vɛ̃teœ̃]	2,500,000 **deux millions cinq cent mille**
22 **vingt-deux** [vɛ̃tdø]	600,000,000 **six cents millions**
23 **vingt-trois** [vɛ̃ttrwɑ]	1,000,000,000 **un milliard** [œ̃ miljɑ:r]

135. Notes on Spelling and Pronunciation

(a) (i) Cardinal Numbers below **un million** are adjectives, and precede the noun or noun-group they refer to:

Quatre grands arbres.　　Deux cents chevaux.
Four large trees.　　*Two hundred horses.*
Environ seize mille Juifs partirent (Maurois).
About sixteen thousand Jews went.

(ii) **Un** has feminine **une**, and agrees in gender with the noun it qualifies (but see also 136):

     une maison   vingt et une maisons

The remaining numeral adjectives are invariable for gender.

(iii) **Million** and **milliard** are masculine nouns. They are followed by **de** before the relevant noun:

     cinq millions de francs.   *five million francs.*

(*b*) Compound numbers which do not include **et** are, in correct usage, linked by a hyphen, but no hyphen is present before or after **cent** or **mille**:

     dix-sept;   quatre-vingt-cinq;   deux cent vingt-trois
                    trois mille cent quarante-huit.

(*c*) 21, 31, 41, 51, 61, and usually 71 are linked by **et,** with no hyphen. **Et** does not form part of any other number.

(*d*) (i) **Vingt** and **cent** take a plural s only when they are the last component of the number (but see also 136):

         quatre-vingts;   quatre-vingt-quatre
         trois cents;   trois cent cinquante

or when they stand before numeral nouns such as **million, milliard**:

         e.g. trois cents millions.

(ii) The *number* **mille** does not take a plural s (the *noun* **un mille** = *a mile* has a regular plural):

     quatre mille.   quatre milles.
     four thousand.   *four miles.*

(*e*) No **un** is present before **cent** or **mille** in the numbers 100 and 1,000.

         110 cent dix;   1,020 mille vingt.

(*f*) Numbers from 1,100 to 1,999 are often expressed as, for example, **treize cent quarante-six.**

(*g*) **Un** is written **l'un** in opposition to **l'autre** (see 222), and sometimes when followed by **de**;

         L'un des tableaux.   L'une des questions.

(*h*) In written figures above 1,000, French uses a full stop where English uses a comma: 2.000; 14.600.000.

A comma between figures in French represents a decimal point: 2,05 (*deux virgule zéro cinq*); 98,75 (*quatre-vingt-dix-huit virgule soixante-quinze*).

(*i*) The pronunciation given in the list in 134 is that of the individual words. Note that in a spoken sentence:

(i) The final consonant of **cinq, six, sept, huit, dix** is only sounded:

1. in liaison (the **x** of **six** and **dix** then being sounded [z]):

<blockquote>
cinq hommes [sɛ̃kɔm] but cinq livres [sɛ̃ livr]
six hommes [sizɔm]   six livres [si livr]
sept hommes [sɛtɔm]   sept livres [sɛ livr]
huit hommes [ɥitɔm]   huit livres [ɥi livr]
</blockquote>

2. when standing in the sense of an Ordinal (e.g. in dates, &c., see 136):

<blockquote>
le sept mai [sɛt]
Édouard Huit [ɥit]
</blockquote>

3. as final word in a phrase: j'en ai dix [dis].

(ii) The **f** of **neuf** is sounded [v] in liaison with **ans** and **heures**. Elsewhere in liaison, or as in (i) 2 and 3 above, it is sounded [f]:

<blockquote>
neuf heures [nœvœːr]
neuf enfants [nœfɑ̃fɑ̃]
le neuf juillet [nœf]
page neuf [nœf]
</blockquote>

Before consonants **neuf** may be pronounced [nœ] or [nœf].

(iii) The **t** of **vingt** is sounded before **et,** may be sounded in the numbers 22-29, and is not sounded in the numbers 81-99:

<blockquote>
vingt et un [vɛ̃teœ̃]
vingt-quatre [vɛ̃(t)katr]
quatre-vingt-un [katrvɛ̃œ̃]
</blockquote>

(iv) The **t** of **cent** is not sounded before **un**: deux cent un (døsɑ̃œ̃].

(v) Except in **dix-huit, vingt-huit,** there is no liaison or elision with the aspirates **huit, onze, huitième, onzième**:

<blockquote>
les onze livres [lɛ ɔ̃ːz]
le huitième mois [lə ɥitjɛm]
</blockquote>

136. Cardinals Used in the Sense of Ordinals

Cardinal Numbers are used to denote the day of the month,[1] the year, the title of a king, &c.,[1] the page.

They may also be used to denote acts, scenes, volumes, and chapters other than the first.

They then precede days of the month, but elsewhere follow the noun. In all these uses **un, vingt,** and **cent** are invariable:

le dix-huit mars.	Henri Quatre.	l'an dix-neuf cent.
the eighteenth of March.	*Henry the Fourth.*	*the year nineteen hundred.*
page un, page quatre-vingt.	scène vingt et un.	chapitre treize.
page one, page eighty.	*scene twenty-one.*	*chapter thirteen.*

137. Formation of Ordinal Numbers

(*a*) Ordinal Numbers are regularly formed by adding **-ième** to the last consonant of the corresponding Cardinal, e.g. **troisième, quatrième, trente-deuxième, mille trois cent cinquante-sixième,** &c., except that:

1. *First* = **premier** (fem. **première**). But **un** in compound numbers forms the ordinal **unième** (ynjɛm): **vingt et unième, quatre-vingt-unième; cent unième.**

2. **Second** (sɔgɔ̃) (fem. **seconde**) is an alternative to **deuxième,** and is preferred where there is no reference to third or subsequent items.

3. *Fifth* = **cinquième**; *ninth* = **neuvième.**

   la première fois   la vingt et unième année.
   la seconde partie   le deuxième et le troisième à gauche.

(*b*) The usage governing the presence of **et** or of hyphens in compound Ordinal Numbers is the same as for Cardinal Numbers (see 135 (*b*) and (*c*)).

---

[1] Except the first, see 138 (*b*).

138. Uses of Ordinal Numbers

(*a*) Ordinal Numbers precede the noun they qualify, and follow Cardinal Numbers.

They agree in gender and number with the noun they qualify or refer to:

La seconde fois.	Les deux premières semaines.
The second time.	*The first two weeks.*
Au troisième acte.	Elle est la première.
In the third act.	*She is the first.*

But if they in fact represent a singular noun, they remain singular:

Les quinzième et seizième siècles (= le quinzième et le seizième siècle).
The fifteenth and sixteenth centuries.

Note also the adverbial use:

Elle est arrivée la première.
She arrived first.

(*b*) The ordinal **premier** is used to denote the first day of the month, the first of a series of kings, &c., of that name, and the first act, scene, chapter, &c.:

Le premier mars.	François Premier.	Chapitre premier.
The first of March.	*Francis the First.*	*Chapter one.*
Acte premier.	Scène première.	
Act one.	*Scene one.*	

(*c*) Subsequent ordinals may also be used of chapters, acts, &c., instead of cardinals (cf. 136):

Chapitre troisième.	Acte cinquième.
Chapter three.	*Act five.*

In this use they follow the noun.

139. Fractions

(*a*) Fractions less than $\frac{1}{4}$ are expressed as follows, and are masculine in gender:

$$\frac{1}{5} \text{ un cinquième; } \quad \frac{7}{8} \text{ sept huitièmes}$$

(*b*) (i) The other fractions are:

$\frac{1}{2}$ {un demi une moitié	$\frac{1}{3}$ un tiers [tjɛ:r] $\frac{2}{3}$ deux tiers	$\frac{1}{4}$ un quart $\frac{3}{4}$ trois quarts

(ii) **Demi** is also an adjective. It precedes the noun it qualifies, to which it is linked by a hyphen, and is then invariable. Where it refers to a noun previously expressed, it stands separately, and then agrees in gender:

Une demi-bouteille.   Une bouteille et demie.
Half a bottle (a half-bottle).   *A bottle and a half.*

(iii) **Demi** is only found as a noun in arithmetic; elsewhere the noun is **moitié**:

La moitié de la population le suivit (Maurois).
Half the population followed him.

(*c*) Fractions (except **demi** as in (*b*) (ii) above) are followed by **de** before the relevant noun:

Trois quarts d'heure.   Quatre cinquièmes d'un pays.
Three-quarters of an hour.   *Four-fifths of a country.*

When the noun is preceded by the definite Article, or by a demonstrative or possessive, the fraction is itself also preceded by the definite article:

La moitié du temps.
Half the time.
Les trois quarts de ma fortune.
Three-quarters of my fortune.
Les neuf dixièmes de cette somme.
Nine-tenths of this sum.

(d) Fractions used adverbially are preceded by the preposition **à,** and (except **moitié** and **demi**) by the definite article:

> Peut-être était-il à moitié fou (Balzac).
> *Perhaps he was half mad.*
> Les peintures pendaient aux trois quarts hors de leur châssis (France).
> *The paintings were hanging three parts out of their frames.*

(e) Fractions may also be expressed, for example, **un sur dix.** Hence:

> Un habitant sur dix périt.
> *One in ten of the inhabitants perished.*
> Pendant dix-sept heures sur vingt-quatre (Verne).
> *For seventeen hours out of the twenty-four.*

But N.B. *per cent* = **pour cent.**

140. Collective Numerals

(a) These are, e.g.:

(i) une paire
a pair
un million
a million
un milliard
a thousand million
des milliers
thousands (indefinite number).

(ii) Nouns in **-aine,** expressing approximate quantities:

une huitaine	*about eight*	une trentaine	*about thirty*
une dizaine	*about ten*	une quarantaine	*about forty*
une douzaine	*a dozen*	une cinquantaine	*about fifty*
une quinzaine	*about fifteen* / *a fortnight*	une soixantaine	*about sixty*
une vingtaine	*about twenty* / *a score*	une centaine	*about a hundred*

(b) Collective Numerals are followed by **de** before the relevant noun:

Une paire de vases.   Des milliers d'insectes s'envolèrent.
A pair of vases.   *Thousands of insects flew up.*
Quelques douzaines de Juifs furent noyés (Maurois).
Several dozen Jews were drowned.

141. Numeral Adverbs

Numeral Adverbs are formed regularly from the ordinal: **premièrement, deuxièmement (secondement), troisième-ment,** &c., *first(ly), secondly, thirdly,* &c.

Note also the common alternatives: **d'abord** *at first,* **puis, ensuite** *then, next,* **en premier (second, troisième) lieu** *in the first (second, third) place.*

The common abbreviations **1°, 2°, 3°,** &c., stand for the Latin *primo, secundo, tertio,* &c.

142. Time by the Clock

(a) Full and Half Hours

Quelle heure est-il (à votre montre)?   *What is the time (by your watch)?*
Il est une heure, deux heures, midi, minuit   *It is one o'clock, two o'clock, twelve (midday), twelve (midnight)*
Il est trois heures et demie, midi (minuit) et demi   *It is half past three, half past twelve*
A midi précis. A quatre heures précises   *At noon sharp. Exactly at four o'clock*
Il est une heure sonnée, deux heures sonnées, midi sonné   *It has struck one, two, twelve*

N.B. 1. Impersonal **il** (see 174 (a)) is used in asking and telling time by the clock.

2. **Midi** or **minuit** (and not *douze heures*) is used for *twelve o'clock.*

3. **Demi, précis,** and **sonné** agree in gender and number when following **heure(s), midi, minuit.**

(b) Quarter Hours and Minutes

Il est quatre heures $\begin{cases} \text{et quart} \\ \text{un quart} \end{cases}$	*It is a quarter past four*
A cinq heures moins le (*or* un) quart	*At quarter to five*
Il est six heures vingt-cinq, midi dix.	*It is twenty-five past six, ten past twelve.*
A sept heures moins trois, à minuit moins dix-sept.	*At three minutes to seven, at seventeen minutes to twelve.*

N.B. 1. Time before the hour is expressed with **moins**.
　　 2. **Minute(s)** is usually omitted in French.

(c) Approximate Time

Vers midi	*About midday*
Vers (Sur) les quatre heures	*About four*
A dix heures environ	*At about ten*
Il est onze heures environ	*It is about eleven*
Il est près de six heures	*It is nearly six*

N.B. **Vers** and **sur** are not normally used after **être**.

(d) One o'clock in the morning, evening, a.m., p.m., &c.

A une heure du matin	*At one o'clock in the morning (1 a.m.)*
Il était quatre heures de l'après-midi	*It was four o'clock in the afternoon (4 p.m.)*
Dix heures du soir	*Ten o'clock in the evening (at night) (10 p.m.)*

(e) Length of Time

Cela a duré trois heures, une demi-heure, une heure et demie, un quart d'heure, trois quarts d'heure	*It lasted three hours, half an hour, an hour and a half, a quarter of an hour, three-quarters of an hour*

(f) Miscellaneous Idioms

A partir de neuf heures	*From nine o'clock (onwards)*

Au bout de vingt minutes	After twenty minutes
Toutes les cinq minutes	Every five minutes
De minute en minute	At intervals of a minute
Vous êtes en retard de quatre minutes	You are four minutes late
Ma montre avance (retarde) de cinq minutes	My watch is five minutes fast (slow)

(g) Abbreviations

(i) When time is written in figures, **heures** is abbreviated to **h.**, and the time is written, for example, **3 h., 3 h. 30, 3 h. 50,** &c. (but see also (ii) below).

(ii) In official style (time-tables, broadcast programmes, documents, &c.) time is measured by the 24-hour clock, the hours after noon being numbered 13–24:

Départ 2 h. 25.   Musique légère de 22 h. 30 à 23 h. 15.
Departure 2.25 a.m.   Light music from 10.30 to 11.15 p.m.

N.B. 24 h. or 0 h. (**zéro heure**) = *12 midnight.*
  0 h. 15 = *12.15 a.m.*

143. Time of Day

Ils sont arrivés le matin, l'après-midi, le soir, la nuit	They arrived in the morning, in the afternoon, in the evening, at night
La nuit il fait froid	At night(s) it is cold
De bon (grand) matin	Early in the morning
Avant le soir (la nuit)	Before evening (night)
Tous les matins	Every morning

144. Fois, Heure, Temps

(a) **Fois** represents a time which is, or could be one of a series of times or occasions:

Chaque fois qu'il pleuvait l'eau entrait par le toit.
Each time it rained the water came through the roof.

Cette fois je ne me trompais pas; le train arrivait.
This time I was right; the train was coming.

(b) **Heure** represents time considered with reference to the clock:

Quelle heure est-il?   A cette heure du matin.
What is the time?   *At that time in the morning.*
Le dîner est à quelle heure?
What time is dinner?

(c) **Temps** generally represents a length or period of time, or the right time (for something):

Je n'ai plus le temps d'y réfléchir (Chevallier).
I no longer have time to think about it.
En ce temps-là je devais garder le lit.
At that time I had to stay in bed.
Il est temps de partir.   Arriver à temps.
It is time to go.   *Arrive in time.*

(See also TIME in Appendix C.)

145. Dates and Days

(a) The *months* are: The *days of the week* are:

janvier	juillet	dimanche	jeudi
février	août [u]	(*Sunday*)	
mars	septembre	lundi	vendredi
avril	octobre	mardi	samedi
mai	novembre	mercredi	
juin	décembre		

N.B. 1. Months and days of the week are not spelt with a capital letter, unless they begin a sentence.

2. *It*, referring to a date or day of the week, is rendered by **ce** (see 174 (a)).

3. Months and days of the week are masculine.

(b) *Dates*

Quel jour (du mois) est-ce?⎫ Quel jour sommes-nous? ⎬	*What day (of the month) is it?*
C'est (Nous sommes) le pre- mier (1er), deux (2), trois (3) février	*It is the first, second, third of February*
Ce sera demain le 21 mai	*Tomorrow will be the 21st May*
C'était hier le 30	*Yesterday was the 30th*
Vers le 6 décembre	*About the 6th December*
Ils sont arrivés le 25 janvier au soir (au matin, &c.)	*They arrived on the 25th January in the evening (morning, &c.)*

N.B. 1. Cardinal Numbers are used to denote all days of the
month except the first.
   2. The date at the head of letters is written:
      le premier (1er) mars   le deux (2) avril.

(c) *Months*

En juin. Au mois d'août	*In June. In (the month of) August*
Un matin du mois de mai (Daudet)	*One May morning*
Environ trois mois après	*About three months afterwards*

(d) *Days of the Week*

(i)
Quel jour de la semaine est-ce?	*What day of the week is it?*
C'est mardi	*It is Tuesday*
Ils sont arrivés lundi, mercredi au soir	*They arrived on Monday, on Wednesday evening*
Du dimanche au lundi	*From Sunday to Monday*

(ii) On *Sundays*, &c. (i.e. *every Sunday*), is expressed with the
definite article, usually in the singular:

Il arrivait le dimanche (Flaubert)	*He used to come on Sundays*
Je vais chez mon professeur le jeudi matin (Pagnol)	*I go to my teacher on Thursday mornings*
Le lundi il n'y a pas de marché	*On Mondays there is no market*

(iii) Combined days and dates are expressed as follows:

Ils sont arrivés {le lundi, 14 novembre {lundi, le 14 novembre	*They arrived on Monday, 14th November*
Le dimanche, 20 février arriva (Bazin)	*Sunday, 20th February arrived*

(e) *Today, Yesterday, The Day Before, The Day After, &c.*

Ils sont arrivés aujourd'hui, hier, avant-hier	*They arrived today, yesterday, the day before yesterday*
Ils sont arrivés ce soir, hier soir, avant-hier soir	*They arrived this evening, yesterday evening (last night), the evening (night) before last*
Ils arriveront demain, demain soir, après-demain	*They will arrive tomorrow, tomorrow evening, the day after tomorrow*
Ils sont arrivés la veille, le lendemain	*They arrived the day before, on the following day*
Ils sont arrivés la veille au soir, le lendemain après-midi	*They arrived the previous evening, (on) the following afternoon*
D'aujourd'hui en huit (quinze)	*Today week (fortnight)*

(f) *Ago, Since*

Il y a trois jours, huit jours (une semaine), quinze jours	*Three days, a week, a fortnight ago*
Il y a aujourd'hui huit jours	*A week ago today*

Note also such forms of expression as:

Il y a de cela huit ans (France)	*That is eight years ago*
Il y avait quatre mois qu'il était parti (Daudet)	*It was four months ago that he had left*
Il y a si longtemps que vous nous avez quittés (Romains)	*It is such a long time since you left us*
Il n'y a pas un an que je t'ai fait capitaine (About)	*It is not a year since I made you captain*

(g) *Last* (= *Immediately Preceding*)

Il est mort jeudi dernier, la semaine dernière (passée), au mois de mai dernier, l'an dernier	*He died last Thursday, last week, last May, last year*
Hier soir au bal	*Last night at the dance*
J'ai mal dormi cette nuit	*I slept badly last night*

146. *An, année*, &c.

An, jour, matin, soir have feminine forms **année, journée, matinée, soirée.**

An usually follows Cardinal Numbers, and **année** Ordinals, and often Indefinites:

Trois ans après.	*Three years after.*
La troisième année de la guerre.	*The third year of the war.*
Pendant plusieurs années.	*For several years.*

Elsewhere the distinction is mainly one of style, the feminine form serving rather to focus attention on the actual passage of time within the period, or on the events it contains.

Compare:

Il resta trois ans à Marseille.
He stayed three years in Marseilles.
Nous avons eu trois années terribles.
We have had three terrible years.
Attendez un jour ou deux.
Wait a day or two.
Les affaires furent arrêtées pendant une journée (Maurois).
Matters were held up for a day.
Un soir j'ai vu les Monnet.
One evening I saw the Monnets.
J'ai passé une soirée chez les Monnet.
I spent an evening with the Monnets.

147. Seasons

The seasons are masculine nouns: **le printemps, l'été, l'automne**[1] [otɔn], **l'hiver** [ivɛːr], and are normally preceded by the definite article:

Pendant l'été.	*During the summer.*
Le début du printemps.	*The beginning of spring.*

N.B.	au printemps,	
	in spring,	
en été,	en automne,	en hiver.
in summer,	*in autumn,*	*in winter.*

148. Years

Dates of years are usually written in figures. When written in full, **mil** is used instead of *mille* for dates A.D. (but *The year 1000* is **L'an mille**).

1955 **mil neuf cent cinquante-cinq** or **dix-neuf cent cinquante-cinq** (the latter form more usual, especially in speech).

Note also: en 1306	en l'an 1290	jusqu'en 1815.
in 1306	*in the year 1290*	*until 1815.*

149. Age

Quel âge as-tu? J'ai treize ans.	*How old are you? I am thirteen.*
A quatre-vingts ans.	*At eighty (years of age).*
Âgé de trente ans.	*Thirty years old.*
Un garçon de treize ans.	*A boy of thirteen.*
Une femme d'une cinquantaine d'années.	*A woman of about fifty.*
Il a cinq mois de plus que moi.	*He is five months older than I.*

When giving age, **ans** should always be added.

---

[1] Occasionally feminine.

150. Dimensions

(a) The following forms of expression are available as required:

(i) Une planche longue de deux mètres ⎫
(ii) Une planche de 2m. de longueur ⎬ *A plank two metres long*
(iii) Une planche de 2m. de long ⎪
(iv) Une planche d'une longueur de deux mètres ⎭

(i) La planche est longue de deux mètres ⎫
(ii) La planche a 2m. de longueur ⎬ *The plank is two metres long*
(iii) La planche a 2m. de long ⎪
(iv) La planche a une longueur de deux mètres ⎭

(v) La longueur de la planche est de deux mètres   *The length of the plank is two metres*

(b) **Large** *broad, wide,* **largeur**; **épais** *thick,* **épaisseur**; **haut** *high,* **hauteur**; **profond** *deep,* **profondeur** are similarly used, except that **épais** and **profond** are not found in the construction of (iii).

(c) Other dimensions may usually be expressed as in (ii) or (iv):

Un cercle de 40 cm. de circonférence.
A circle of 40 cm. circumference.
La propriété a une superficie de 80 hectares.
The property has an area of 80 hectares.

(d) Note also the senses of prepositions as in:

La table a trois mètres de long *sur* un de large.
The table is three metres long by *one wide.*
Il a élargi la promenade *de* six pieds (Stendhal).
He widened the promenade by *six feet.*
Le parapet s'élève *de* quatre pieds au-dessus du sol (Stendhal).
The parapet rises four feet above the ground.

151. Distance

(a) Where a distance serves to locate a point, it is preceded by the preposition **à**:

A quelle distance sommes-nous de la gare?
How far are we from the station?
Nous sommes à un kilomètre environ de la gare.
We are about a kilometre from the station.
Il s'arrêta à quelques pas du bord.
He stopped a few feet from the edge.

(b) Note also:

Combien y a-t-il d'ici à Elbeuf?
How far is it (from here) to Elbeuf?
Il y a, d'ici au château, sept bons kilomètres (France).
It is a good seven kilometres to the castle.

(c) Distances may stand as an adverbial accusative after certain verbs of motion, such as **marcher,** or **courir** (or **faire** so used):

Courir cent mètres.   Il fit huit kilomètres à pied.
Run a hundred metres.   *He walked eight kilometres.*

(d) After other verbs of motion, the distance traversed is preceded by **de**:

Je reculai de quelques pas (Mérimée).
I stepped back a few paces.

152. Price

(a) Where a price expresses a rate, it is preceded by the preposition **à**:

Deux boîtes à cinquante francs.   Deux timbres à 20 frs.
Two boxes at fifty francs.   *Two 20 fr. stamps.*
Les meilleurs se vendent à quinze francs pièce.
The best ones are selling at fifteen francs each.

(b) After **coûter, payer, acheter,** and **vendre** (except as in (a) above), the price stands as an adverbial accusative, without a preposition:

> Cela m'a coûté mille francs.
> *That cost me a thousand francs.*
> Je l'ai vendu (acheté) mille francs.
> *I sold (bought) it for a thousand francs.*
> Je l'ai payé mille francs.
> *I paid a thousand francs for it.*

(c) A price which is the complement of the verb *être* is usually preceded by the preposition **de**:

> Le prix d'entrée est de 80 frs.
> *The entry price is 80 frs.*
> La hausse est de dix pour cent.
> *The increase is ten per cent.*

153. Rate

For expressions of rate, e.g. *price per article, per kilogram,* &c., *times per week, speed per hour,* &c., see 72.

XV. PERSONAL PRONOUNS

Conjunctive (or Unstressed) Pronouns

154. Forms of Conjunctive Pronouns

	Nom.	Acc.	Dat.	Gen.
1st sing.	je	me	me	
2nd sing.	tu	te	te	
3rd sing. masc.	il	le ⎱	lui, y	en
fem.	elle	la ⎰		
refl.		se	se	
1st plur.	nous	nous	nous	
2nd plur.	vous	vous	vous	
3rd plur. masc.	ils ⎱	les	leur, y	en
fem.	elles ⎰			
refl.		se	se	

Notes

1. **Tu** and **te** are normally used when speaking to a single person who is a close relative or an intimate friend. They are also used to any child, or an animal. Otherwise the 2nd Plural **vous** is normally used to address single persons. In this use it retains a plural verb, but its other agreements (with adjectives, participles, &c.) are singular, provided it refers to a single person:

> Madame, vous êtes imprudente, vous êtes sortie sans parapluie,

but:

> Mes enfants, vous êtes parfaitement libres.

2. The forms **me, te, nous, vous** are also reflexive (accusative or dative).

3. The vowel of **je, me, te, se, le, la** elides before a word beginning with a vowel or h-mute, and before **y**:

> j'ai; il m'ordonne; il s'est trompé; on l'y porta.

But **je** does not elide when inverted: **puis-je aller?** nor does **le** after an Imperative Affirmative: **faites-le entrer.**

4. For the use of **nous** or **vous** resuming subjects of different persons, see 62 (*c*).

155. *Il, elle*

(*a*) The Personal Pronouns **il, elle,** and their plurals **ils, elles,** refer to masculine or feminine nouns respectively, whether these are persons, animals, or things:

L'homme y était . . . il marchait derrière la voiture (Musset).
The man was there . . . he was walking behind the carriage.
Ma nièce avait levé la tête et elle me regardait (Vercors).
My niece had raised her head and was looking at me.
Je n'écoutais guère leurs histoires. Elles m'amusaient parfois (Vercors).
I hardly used to listen to their stories. Sometimes they amused me.

(*b*) But the Demonstrative Pronoun **ce** (invariable) is almost always found instead of **il, elle,** &c., when the words following are a tense of *être* plus the Indefinite Articles *un, une, des,* or *de*:

Il s'appelait Stenne. . . . C'était un enfant de Paris (Daudet).
His name was Stenne. . . . He was a child of Paris.
C'étaient des gamins de douze à quinze ans (Daudet).
They were urchins of twelve to fifteen.

156. Repetition of Subject Pronouns

(*a*) When the same pronoun is the subject of two or more verbs which follow one another closely, it may or may not be repeated. In most cases this is a matter of style:

Il traversa la pièce et ouvrit la porte (Vercors).
Je me croisai les bras, et j'attendis (Verne).

(*b*) It is almost invariably repeated when there is a change of tense:

Ils s'étaient levés, et ils descendaient la colline (Musset).

157. *Le, la, les*

Le, la, les refer to a masculine, feminine, or plural noun respectively:

> Il enleva le couvercle et le mit à côté.
> *He removed the lid and put it on one side.*
> Nous la reconduirons.
> *We will take her back.*

> Où sont tes souliers?   Je les ai cherchés partout.
> *Where are your shoes?*   *I have been looking for them everywhere.*
> La fenêtre est ouverte.   Ferme-la.
> *The window is open.*   *Close it.*

N.B. The Pronouns **le, les** do not (as do the Definite Articles *le, les*) combine with the Prepositions **de** and **à**:

> Je ne tiens pas à les conserver.
> Obligé de le faire parler.

158. Impersonal *le*

Le may be used, as object or complement, when the reference is to a fact, statement, idea, &c. It does not always have an equivalent in English:

> Eugène et son frère manquaient.   Il ne le remarqua pas.
> *Eugene and his brother were missing.*   *He did not notice it.*
> Ce que vous avez cru facile ne l'est pas (Balzac).
> *What you thought easy is not so.*
> Tu ne les avais pas, je le sais.
> *You had not got them, I know.*
> Une vraie héroïne, sans le paraître.
> *A real heroine, without appearing so.*
> A cette époque j'en étais le propriétaire. Je ne le suis plus.
> *At that time I was the owner. I am not any longer.*

159. Use of *Y*

(*a*) **Y** may retain its original meaning as an adverb, with the sense of *there* or *thither*, but its position is always that of an object pronoun (see 162):

Sachant que vous y seriez.
Knowing that you would be there.
Paul y fut envoyé.
Paul was sent there.

(*b*) As a Pronoun, **y** represents a Thing or Things in the Dative, or governed by the Prepositions **à, en,** or **dans**:

On entendait les ordres, mais on n'y obéissait plus.
They heard the orders, but they no longer obeyed them.
La maison n'était pas loin. Elle y courut.
The house was not far off. She ran to it.
Il y pensait sans cesse.
He was thinking of it all the time.
Je n'y ai aucune confiance (N.B. avoir confiance en).
I have no confidence in them.
Le château existe, mais il est impossible d'y pénétrer (N.B. pénétrer dans).
The castle exists, but it is impossible to get into it.

(*c*) Or it may be used impersonally, referring to a clause or idea:

S'il gardait le silence, c'est qu'il y était obligé (Musset).
If he kept silent, it was because he was compelled to do so.

160. Use of *En*

(*a*) **En** may retain its original meaning as an adverb, with the sense of *from there*, but its position is always that of an object pronoun (see 162). It does not always have an English equivalent:

Je n'en bougeais guère (Vercors).
I hardly budged from there.
Il y va à huit heures, et il en revient vers midi.
He goes there at eight o'clock and comes back about midday.

(*b*) As a pronoun, it may refer to a Thing or Things. It frequently refers to Persons in the plural, but very rarely, in modern French, to a Person in the singular. It represents these:

(i) in the Genitive (including the Partitive use):

Il en avait compris l'importance (Mérimée).[1]
He had realized the importance of it.
Pour en continuer la lecture (Bordeaux).
To continue the reading of it.
Le parfum du café me donnait grande envie d'en prendre (Duhamel).
The smell of the coffee gave me a great desire to have some.
Est-ce qu'il y en aura demain?
Will there be any tomorrow?
Je regrette, mais je n'en ai pas.
I am sorry, but I haven't got any.

N.B. **En** is always present in French to represent a noun which is understood in expressions of quantity, including numerals and indefinites:

Il en prit une poignée.	Il n'en a pas d'autres.
He took a handful.	*He has not any others.*
J'en ai trouvé huit.	Nous en avons perdu quelques-uns.
I found eight (of them).	*We have lost some.*

(ii) governed by the Preposition **de**:

Je n'en ai plus besoin.	Elle s'en souvient.
I no longer need it.	*She remembered it.*

Félicité lui en fut reconnaissante (Flaubert).
Felicity was grateful to her for it.

(*c*) It may also be used impersonally, referring to a clause or idea:

Ils disaient que s'il eût tué le colonel, il s'en serait vanté (Mérimée).
They said that if he had killed the colonel, he would have boasted about it.

---

[1] For the rules governing the use of **en** in a possessive sense see 182.

161. Repetition of Object Pronouns

(a) Where the same pronoun is the object of two or more verbs, it is usually present with all of them:

> Alors il la grondait et la battait.
> *Then he would scold and beat her.*
> Je me sentis mieux et me mis à délibérer (Erckmann-Chatrian).
> *I felt better and began to take thought.*

(b) But where the verbs are all in the same compound tense, the second pronoun object is often omitted (in this case the auxiliary is omitted also):

> Je m'étais repris et décidé (Vercors).
> *I had collected myself and made up my mind.*

162. Position of Object Pronouns

(a) With all forms of the verb except the Imperative Affirmative, object pronouns stand immediately *before* the verb (including its auxiliary *avoir* or *être*):

> Il lui donna le fusil.
> *He gave her the gun.*
> Vous ne me répondez pas.
> *You do not answer me.*
> La reconnaissez-vous?
> *Do you recognize her?*
> Ne vous êtes-vous jamais disputés? (Musset)
> *Have you never quarrelled?*
> Ne le tue pas.
> *Do not kill him.*

> Il s'était si bien caché.
> *He had hidden himself so well.*

> Pour ne pas la perdre.
> *So as not to lose it.*

(b) With the verb in the Imperative Affirmative, object pronouns stand *after* the verb, and are normally linked to it by hyphens. **Moi** and **toi** are then used instead of **me** and te (but see also 163 (b)):

> Prends-les;　pensez-y;　aidez-moi;　dépêchez-vous.
> *Take them;　think of it;　help me;　hurry up.*

CONJUNCTIVE PRONOUNS §§ 161-2

(c) Object Pronouns governed by **voici** or **voilà** precede them:

Les voilà! La voici qui rentre (Musset).
There they are! *There she is returning.*

(d) Pronouns which are objects of an Infinitive which is governed by another verb, normally stand immediately before the Infinitive:

Vous pouvez me sauver.
You can save me.
Je vais le leur rendre.
I am going to give it back to them.
Vous êtes bien bon d'être venu me voir (France).
You are very kind to have come to see me.

But pronouns which are objects of an Infinitive governed by **faire** or **laisser** precede the latter:[1]

Il vous le fera rendre.
He will make you give it back.
On vous y laissera aller.
You will be allowed to go there.

This position of the pronouns is sometimes found when the Infinitive is governed by a verb of motion or by **envoyer**:

Nous l'avons envoyé chercher.
We have sent (to look) for him.
J'avais pris l'habitude de l'aller voir (Vercors).
I had got into the habit of going to see him.

'Envoyé le chercher' and 'aller le voir' would also be permissible.

---

[1] The pronouns are, however, separated to avoid conflict with the rule in 163 (a) (iii):

Je vous ferai lui obéir.
I will make you obey him.

and to avoid a double accusative:

Je vous ferai m'écouter.
I will make you listen to me.

A reflexive pronoun object of an infinitive governed by **faire** is omitted:

Après avoir fait asseoir son singulier client (Balzac).
After making his peculiar client sit down.

163. Order of Object Pronouns

(a) *Before* the verb:

(i) If of different persons: **1st Person** ⎫ **—3rd Person—y—en**
                                    2nd Person ⎭

Je te le cède.   Qui vous l'a dit?
I give it up to you.   *Who told it you?*
Je m'y suis enfermée.   Je vous en ai parlé.
I shut myself up in it.   *I have spoken to you about it.*

(ii) If both are 3rd Person: **Accusative—Dative—y—en**

Elle le lui montra.   Je leur en donne.
She showed it to him.   *I give them some.*
Il s'y est installé.
He settled down in it.

(iii) But the Dative Pronouns **lui, leur,** and the Pronouns **me, te, se, nous, vous,** when they are *dative*, may not stand with any Accusative Pronoun except **le, la, les.**

     If an Accusative Pronoun other than **le, la, les** is present, these datives are rendered by the appropriate Disjunctive Pronoun (for list see 164), preceded by **à** and placed after the verb:

Parce que je m'intéresse à vous (Duhamel).
Because I am interested in you.
Vous vous abandonnez à moi (Balzac).
You are abandoning yourself to me.

(b) *After* the verb (i.e. in the Imperative Affirmative): **Accusative—Dative—y—en** (**m'** and **t'** are found, instead of **moi** and **toi,** before **y** and **en,** the apostrophe replacing the hyphens):

dites-le-nous;   donnez-m'en;   portez-les-y.
tell it to us;   *give me some;*   *take them there.*

But the rule as to datives, given in (a) (iii) above, also applies here:
Fiez-vous à moi.   *Trust me.*

Disjunctive (or Stressed) Pronouns

164. Forms of Disjunctive Pronouns

		Singular	Plural
1st Person		moi	nous
2nd Person		toi	vous
3rd Person	Masculine	lui	eux
	Feminine	elle	elles
Reflexive		soi (see 166).	

The considerations relating to the use of **toi** or **vous** are the same as for the Conjunctive **tu** and **vous** (see 154 n. 1).

165. Uses of Disjunctive Pronouns

(*a*) The Disjunctive forms of Personal Pronouns are those used when the Pronouns are governed by a preposition[1] or by **comme**:

Deux mains se tendirent vers lui (Maupassant).
Two hands were stretched towards him.

Tu es chez toi.
You are at home.

Ne vous moquez pas de moi (About).
Don't make fun of me.

Malgré moi.   Comme toi.
In spite of myself.   *Like you.*

---

[1] The use of the Disjunctive forms is normally limited to human beings. Therefore, where the pronoun governed by the preposition refers to a thing or things, some other form of expression is usually employed, e.g.:

(*a*) Sometimes **y** or **en** is applicable (see 159–60):

il y revint;	il y mit la main;	il en parle.
he came back to it;	*he put his hand in it;*	*he speaks of it.*

(*b*) Frequently an adverb is used (and the pronoun is not expressed) (see also 124):

On ne voyait au-dessus que son chapeau (Bazin).
One only saw his hat above it.

S'il y avait autre chose derrière (Augier et Sandeau).
Supposing there was something else behind it.

(*c*) Or some other means is used, as e.g. a demonstrative:

Voilà le poirier; derrière celui-là se trouvent les fraises.
There is the pear-tree; behind it are the strawberries.

(*b*) The Disjunctive forms are used where people are singled out or contrasted. (In English this is frequently expressed by an emphatic tone of voice.)

They may be so found instead of or in addition to Conjunctive forms:

> Lui ne jouait pas, bien entendu (Daudet).
> He *didn't play, of course.*
> Moi, je vais vivre à la campagne (Balzac).
> *Personally, I am going to live in the country.*
> Vous êtes à un bout de la maison, eux à l'autre (Mérimée).
> *You are at one end of the house, they at the other.*

The emphasis may be reinforced by: **seul, -même, aussi,** or a Cardinal Number:

> Lui seul pourrait le faire.
> *He alone could do it.*
> Les francs-tireurs . . . tombant eux-mêmes dans une embuscade (Daudet).
> *The partisans . . . themselves falling into an ambush.*
> Le colonel, furieux lui aussi, ne voulait voir personne (Daudet).
> *The colonel, furious too, would see no one.*
> La conversation reprit entre eux trois (Vercors).
> *The conversation was resumed between the three of them.*

The Disjunctive forms are also required when a pronoun:

(*c*) stands as the sole word in a sentence, or is in a phrase without a verb:

> Qui a parlé? Lui.
> *Who spoke? He (did).*
> Pas eux, alors? Non, lui, le borgne.
> *Not they, then? No, he, the fellow with one eye.*

(*d*) stands as the Antecedent of a Relative:

> Moi qui étais assis dans mon fauteuil (Vercors).
> *I, who was sitting in my arm-chair.*
> Eux qui viennent si rarement.
> *They who come so seldom.*

208

(e) forms part of a Double Subject or Object of a verb:

Ni toi ni moi, nous n'avons reçu d'éducation (Balzac).
Neither you nor I have received any education.
Il n'avait trouvé ni elle ni son père.
He had found neither her nor her father.
Ca convient à nous et à eux.
That suits us and them.

(f) is the Complement of *être* (see also 174 (a)):

Ce n'était pas elle.
It was not she.
Ce sont eux.
It is they.
Sans doute, mais je ne suis pas toi.
No doubt, but I am not you.

(g) stands after **que** in Comparative Sentences, or after **ne . . . que**:

Plus âgé que lui.
Older than he.
Je ne veux que toi.
I want only you.

166. Disjunctive Pronouns—Reflexive Forms

(a) The forms **moi, toi, lui, elle, nous, vous, eux, elles** are also the normal reflexive forms. They are sometimes reinforced by **-même**:

Il croit tout le monde plus fortuné que lui.
He thinks that everybody is better off than himself.
Vous manquez de confiance en vous-même.
You are lacking in confidence in yourself.

(b) The form **soi** is, in strict usage, found only to refer to an indefinite person or group of persons, to such an idea as is conveyed by **chacun, tout le monde, personne**, &c., and by other expressions which refer to types rather than individuals:

On devrait moins encore parler de soi (La Rochefoucauld).
Still less should one speak of oneself.
Chacun pour soi.
Each man for himself.
De tels gens ne pensent qu'à soi.
Such people only think of themselves.
Celui qui se défie de soi-même (La Rochefoucauld).
He who has no confidence in himself.

167. Note on the Dative and the Preposition *à*

(*a*) The *dative* Conjunctive Pronouns are the forms **me, te, se, nous, vous, lui, leur.** These are the forms which are used with a verb that takes the dative (e.g. *obéir*), or which can be constructed with the dative (e.g. *donner*):

je lui obéis;	j'y obéis;	je le lui donne;	promettez-moi.[1]
I obey her;	*I obey it;*	*I give it to her;*	*promise me.*

The dative of a Disjunctive Pronoun is only required when the dative Conjunctive may not be used (as in 163 (*a*) (iii)), and it is formed with the Preposition **à**:

Je vous présente à eux.
I introduce you to them.

(*b*) The Disjunctive forms are required when the Preposition **à** is *not dative*, e.g. after such verbs as *aller, penser,* &c.; the Conjunctive **y** being, however, used of Things:

Je vais à elle;	j'y vais;	je pense à elle;	j'y pense;
I go to her;	*I go to it;*	*I think of her;*	*I think of it;*
pensez à moi.			
think of me.			

[1] See 162 (*b*).

XVI. DEMONSTRATIVES

168. Forms and Use of Demonstrative Adjective

	Masc. Sing.	Fem. Sing	Plural
Before consonants, including h-aspirate	ce tapis ce hamac	cette fleur cette halle	ces chevaux ces harpes
Before vowel and h-mute	cet âge cet hiver	cette ombre cette herbe	ces amis ces histoires

Note liaisons in speech, **s** of **ces** then being sounded [z].

The Demonstrative adjective is only found preceding and qualifying a noun:

Allez ce soir à la gare.
Go to the station this evening.
Cet enfant va se blesser.
That child is going to hurt itself.
Cette explication lui suffisait (Bordeaux).
This (That) explanation satisfied him.
Donnez-lui ces lettres.
Give him these (those) letters.

169. Meaning of Demonstrative Adjective

It will be seen from the examples in 168 that **ce, cet, cette** are the equivalents of either *this* or *that*, and **ces** of *these* or *those*. It is only when the idea of *this* or *that* is emphatic that a distinction is made in French.

Then the idea of *this* (or of nearness in space or time) is conveyed by **-ci,** and the idea of *that* (or being less near) is conveyed by **-là,** both of these being attached to the noun by a hyphen. Similarly for the plural *these* and *those*:

C'est par cette porte-ci qu'on est entré.
It is by this door that they got in.

Il n'était pas content ce soir-là (Daudet).
That evening he was ill at ease.
Ces bêtes-là vivent cent ans (M. Renard).
Those (kind of) animals live a hundred years.

170. Repetition of Demonstrative Adjective

The Demonstrative is normally found preceding each noun to which it applies, including those in a series:

A qui sont ces chapeaux et ces pardessus?
Whose are these hats and coats?

171. Forms and Use of Demonstrative Pronouns

celui, fem. **celle,** masc. plur. **ceux,** fem. plur. **celles**
ceci, cela, ce, to which may be added: **il** (impersonal).

These, being pronouns, do not qualify a noun, as does **ce** in 168, but stand instead of a noun as, e.g. subject, object, &c., of a sentence:

> Je préfère celle-ci
> je sais cela
> c'est vrai; il pleut.

172. *Celui, celle, ceux, celles*

These forms are mainly used to refer to a masculine or feminine noun, previously expressed, and they agree with it in gender. They may be in their singular or plural forms, according to whether they mean one or more items.

(a) *without -ci or -là:*

celui, celle = *the one, that* (when it = *the one*)
ceux, celles = *the ones, those* (when it = *the ones*).

These ideas are also sometimes expressed in English by *'s,* as in: *My dog and my uncle's* (= *the one of my uncle*), and *My dogs and my uncle's* (= *the ones of my uncle*).

In these senses, **celui,** &c., are, in strict usage, always found in constructions where the following word is **de** or a Relative (**qui, que, dont,** &c.):

> Voici les billets! J'ai retrouvé celui qui manquait.
> *Here are the tickets! I have found the one which was missing.*
> Celui dont il parlait avait deux cheminées.
> *The one he was talking about had two funnels.*
> En attachant ses yeux noirs sur ceux de son mari (Mérimée).
> *Fixing her dark eyes on those of her husband.*
> Je préfère votre proposition à celle de Marie.
> *I prefer your idea to Mary's.*

It also conveys the idea of *the kind of person(s) who*, especially in the plural after **tous** (**toutes**):

> Celui qui a peur court le plus grand danger.
> *He who is afraid runs the greatest danger.*
> Tous ceux qui voudraient le suivre (Daudet).
> *All (those) who would be prepared to follow him.*[1]

(b) with *-ci* or *-là*:

celui-ci, celle-ci this (one).   **celui-là, celle-là** that (one).
ceux-ci, celles-ci these (ones).
ceux-là, celles-là those (ones).

> Quel est votre verre, celui-ci ou celui-là?
> *Which is your glass, this one or that?*
> Les pièces sont petites, mais celle-ci me plaît.
> *The rooms are small, but I like this one.*
> A faire des statuettes comme celle-ci (France).
> *Making statuettes like this (one).*

Celui-ci may also mean *the latter* (last mentioned), and **celui-là** *the former* (first mentioned):

> Johnson regarda le docteur. Celui-ci ne savait que faire (Verne).
> *Johnson looked at the doctor. The latter was at a loss what to do.*

---

[1] English may here omit the Demonstrative *those*, but in French **ceux,** &c., are never omitted.

173. *Ceci, cela*

(*a*) It was seen in 172 that **celui,** which has masculine and feminine forms, refers to a masculine or feminine noun previously expressed. **Ceci** and **cela,** which have only the one form, refer, as pronouns *this* and *that,* not to nouns or persons, but to such things as cannot have a gender, e.g.:

(i) facts, statements, or ideas:

Elle jase dans la loge du concierge, cela est sûr (France).
She is chattering in the porter's lodge, that is certain.
Elle sait que je suis faible, et cela m'ôte tout courage (France).
She knows that I am weak, and this[1] deprives me of all courage.
Ceci au moins est vrai . . . l'ennemi est vaincu.
This at least is true . . . the enemy is defeated.

(ii) when the reference is to some object which has not yet been given a name, and which consequently can have no gender:

Buvez ceci, mon voisin (Daudet).
Drink this, neighbour.
Ceci est mon palais (Saint-Exupéry).
This is my palace.

Cela ne m'appartient pas.   Cela est le plus grand danger.
That does not belong to me.   *That is the greatest danger.*

N.B. The Prepositions **voici** and **voilà** are often used in French in preference to **ceci est, cela est** for *this is, that is,* &c.:

Voici la sortie.   Voici ce qui était arrivé.
This is the way out.   *This is what had happened.*
Voilà tout !   Voilà les faits.
That is all!   *Those are the facts.*

(*b*) The shortened form **ça** may replace **cela** in conversational style:

Mais nous savons tout ça (Duhamel).   *But we know all that.*

---

[1] **Ceci** almost always refers to a statement, &c., that *follows*; **cela** to one that has *preceded.* **Ceci,** unlike the English *this,* is hardly ever used to refer to what has preceded.

(c) When the idea of *that* is very emphatic, **cela**, as subject of *être*, may divide up into **ce** and **là**:

> Ce n'est pas là un métier honnête (France).
> *That is not an honest trade.*

(d) **Cela** (and not *ce* or *il*) is also the French equivalent of *it* when the verb is other than *être*:

> Parlez votre langue maternelle; cela vous fatiguera moins (Verene).
> *Speak your native language; it will tire you less.*

> Cela me choque de vous trouver ainsi.
> *It shocks me to find you in this state.*

174. Ce[1] and *il* (Impersonal)

Ce or **il** is the French equivalent of *it*, when the subject of *être* (or of *devoir* or *pouvoir* governing *être*), the distinction being as follows:

(a) Where the complement of *être* is *not an adjective*, **ce** is used:

> Un beuglement formidable s'éleva. C'était un taureau (Flaubert).
> *A frightful bellowing arose. It was a bull.*

> Il prit un parti fort courageux; ce fut de s'avancer seul (Mérimée).
> *He took a very brave decision; it was, to go on alone.*

> C'est[2] ainsi que je l'ai trouvée (France).
> *It was thus that I found her.*

> Ce doit être une grande perte (Duhamel).
> *It must be a great loss.*

---

[1] For the personal use of **ce**, as in **c'est un Français** = *he is a Frenchman*, see 155.

[2] French frequently uses the Present **c'est**, where English uses a Past *it was*, when the reference is to a fact that is still valid at the time in question.

Ce pouvaient[1] être les pas de M. Alphonse (Mérimée).
It could be M. Alphonse's footsteps.

Qui est là? C'est moi, c'est nous, c'est un ami, c'est le chat, ce sont[1] eux, ce sont[1] des amis.
Who is there? It is I, it is we, it is a friend, it is the cat, it is they, it is some friends.

But **il** (and not *ce*) is used in telling time by the clock, and in similar statements relating to the time of day, and in a few such expressions as **il est temps**:

Quelle heure est-il?	Il était deux heures.
What is the time?	*It was two o'clock.*
Il était presque nuit (Mérimée).	Il est temps de partir.
It was almost night.	*It is time to go.*

(*b*) Where the complement of *être* is *an adjective*:

(i) **ce** is used where the adjective refers to something *previously* expressed:

Les hommes ne seront jamais égaux; ce n'est pas possible (France).
Men will never be equal; it is not possible.

Je l'essaierai, mais c'est difficile à[2] écrire.
I will try it, but it is difficult to write.

(ii) **il** is used, in careful writing and speech, where the adjective refers to something which *follows*:

Il est difficile d'écrire un tel livre.
It is difficult to write such a book.

Il m'était impossible de[2] ne pas le voir (France).
It was impossible for me not to see it.

Il était clair que le capitaine avait deviné (Verne).
It was clear that the captain had guessed.

---

[1] After **ce**, where the complement is 3rd Person Plural, it is usual, in careful writing and speech, for the verb to be 3rd Person Plural.

[2] Note the preposition before the infinitive in these constructions:

     c'est+adjective referring *back*: **à . . . c'est difficile à faire.**

     il est+adjective referring *forward*: **de . . . il est difficile de faire cela.**

175. Other Uses of *ce*

Ce is frequently found, as subject of *être*, preceded by a comma, and repeating the real subject of the sentence, as follows (in these uses it has no English equivalent):

(*a*) When the real subject is an infinitive. **Ce** is obligatory here if the complement is also a positive infinitive, but is optional otherwise:

> Vouloir, c'est pouvoir.
> *Where there's a will there's a way.*
> Écrire était un aveu (Balzac).
> *To write was an admission.*
> Prendre Berlin, ce n'était plus qu'une affaire de patience (Daudet).
> *Taking Berlin was now only a matter of patience.*

(*b*) When the real subject is a relative clause beginning **celui qui, ce qui**, &c.:

> Celui qui était le plus étonné, c'était le facteur.
> *The one who was the most astonished was the postman.*
> Ce qu'il y a de sûr, c'est qu'il était là (Daudet).
> *What is certain is that he was there.*

(*c*) Sometimes, when the real subject is a noun or pronoun.[1] This is an optional device of style, which serves to emphasize the subject by creating a pause after it by means of the comma and **ce**:

> La patience, c'était la première vertu à acquérir (Maurois).
> *Patience was the first virtue to acquire.*
> Cela, c'est pareil au vol.
> *That is equivalent to stealing.*

---

[1] Note also the following idiomatic sentence-forms, which are used to make an emphatic statement:

> C'est un fameux médecin que l'amour.
> *Love is a famous doctor.*
> C'est une folie (que) de la laisser seule.
> *To leave her on her own is an act of madness.*

176. Other Uses of *il*

Il is found, always with a 3rd Person Singular verb:

(a) As Subject of Impersonal Verbs:

Il y a des fleurs sur la table.
There are flowers on the table.
Il faut que tu reviennes.
You must come back.
Il ne s'agissait plus de son bonheur (Bordeaux).
It was no longer a question of his happiness.

(b) As subject of other verbs used impersonally. This is an optional device of style, which prepares the way for the real subject by making a preliminary reference to it with **il** (the opposite effect is achieved by **ce** as in 175 (c)):

Il se passait quelque chose d'extraordinaire (Daudet).
There was something extraordinary happening.
Il ne restait plus à la maison que son père et Marguerite (Bordeaux).
There now remained at home only his father and Marguerite.

(c) As subject of verbs describing general conditions of weather, &c., including *faire* in this use:

Il gèle dur.	Il avait tant neigé.
It is freezing hard.	*It had snowed so heavily.*
Il faisait très froid.	Il ne faisait pas de brise.
It was very cold.	*There was no breeze.*
Il fait nuit.	Il était sombre dans le couloir.
It is dark.	*It was dark in the passage.*

XVII. POSSESSIVES

177. Possessive Case of Nouns

The Possessive (Genitive) Case of Nouns is formed with the Preposition **de**. There is no equivalent of the English *'s* as in: *The man's hat* (see also 172) (*a*):

Les livres du garçon.   Le nom du vaisseau.   Les livres des garçons.
The boy's books.   *The ship's name.*   *The boys' books.*
La serviette d'un écolier. }
Une serviette d'écolier.   }
A schoolboy's satchel.
Une serviette de mon ami.
A satchel of my friend's.   }
One of my friend's satchels.}

178. Possessive Adjective

The Possessive Adjective always precedes and qualifies a noun (the Thing Possessed), indicating the person of its Possessor.

POSSESSOR	THING POSSESSED		
	Masc. Sing.	*Fem. Sing.*	*Plur.*
1st sing. *my*	**mon** frère	**ma** sœur	**mes** frères (sœurs)
2nd sing. *your*	**ton** „	**ta** „	**tes** „ „
3rd sing. *his, her, its*	**son** „	**sa** „	**ses** „ „
1st plur. *our*	**notre** „	**notre** „	**nos** „ „
2nd plur. *your*	**votre** „	**votre** „	**vos** „ „
3rd plur. *their*	**leur** „	**leur** „	**leurs** „ „

The masculine forms **mon, ton, son** are found qualifying a feminine singular noun, when they are followed by a word beginning with a vowel or h-mute:

mon idée;   mon héritière
mon autre sœur;   mon habile cousine.

179. Possessive Pronoun

The Possessive Pronoun stands instead of a noun (the Thing Possessed), representing it in a form which indicates the person of its Possessor.

POSSESSOR	THING POSSESSED			
	Masc. Sing.	Fem. Sing.	Masc. Plur.	Fem. Plur.
1st sing. *mine*	le mien	la mienne	les miens	les miennes
2nd sing. *yours*	le tien	la tienne	les tiens	les tiennes
3rd sing. *his, hers, its*	le sien	la sienne	les siens	les siennes
1st plur. *ours*	le nôtre	la nôtre	les nôtres	
2nd plur. *yours*	le vôtre	la vôtre	les vôtres	
3rd plur. *theirs*	le leur	la leur	les leurs	

NOTES

1. The Definite Article forms part of the Possessive Pronoun, and is always present.

2. The normal combination of the Definite Article with the Prepositions **à** and **de** takes place, giving, e.g. **au mien, des vôtres,** &c.

3. Note that **nôtre** [noːtr] and **vôtre** [voːtr] above are written with a circumflex accent, and are thus distinguished both in speech and writing from the Possessive Adjectives **notre** [nɔtr] and **votre** [vɔtr].

180. Use and Agreement of Possessive Adjective and Pronoun

(For the use and omission of the Possessive Adjective with Parts of the Body, see 73.)

(*a*) The Possessive Adjective is normally present before each noun to which it applies, including those in a series:

Il se remit à manger son pain et son fromage (Balzac).
He began eating his bread and cheese again.
Ils s'en allèrent avec leurs frères et leurs sœurs.
They went off with their brothers and sisters.

(*b*) The Possessive Adjective and Pronoun take the gender and number of the *Thing Possessed*. They agree with the *Possessor* in person only:

> Il m'avait présenté à sa femme et à son fils (Mérimée).
> *He had introduced me to his wife and his son.*
> Je connais sa maison comme la mienne (Mérimée).
> *I know his house as well as (I do) mine.*
> Si ma découverte s'accorde avec les siennes (Balzac).
> *If my discovery fits in with his (ones).*

(*c*) Neither the Possessive Adjective nor Pronoun shows the gender of the Possessor (e.g. **son** may mean *his, her,* or *its*). In most cases the gender, and consequently the identity, of the Possessor is clear from the context. Where there is ambiguity, the doubt may be resolved by adding the Preposition **à** and the appropriate Disjunctive Pronoun, or by the use of **propre**:

> C'est son livre à elle qui manque.
> *It is her book which is missing.*
> Son mari avait vendu le sien à lui.
> *Her husband had sold his one.*
> Ce n'est pas mon propre malheur qui m'afflige.
> *It is not my misfortune which is distressing me.*

(*d*) **Son, le, sien,** &c. are the Possessives which normally correspond to Indefinite Pronouns (**on, chacun, personne,** &c.):

> Autrement on ne retrouverait pas ses bagages.
> *Otherwise one wouldn't get one's luggage back.*
> Chacun avait apporté le sien.   *Each person had brought his.*

181. Possessive Pronoun as Complement of *être*

(*a*) When it is the complement of *être*, the Possessive Pronoun serves to *identify* the object referred to, by describing it as being the property of the Possessor:

> Non, c'est la petite maison en briques qui est la leur.
> *No, it is the little brick house that is theirs.*
> C'était bien le sien.   *It was indeed his one.*

(b) Where the main emphasis is on deciding *who is the possessor*, this is expressed, after *être*, by the Preposition **à** and a Disjunctive Pronoun:

> Cette fortune . . . elle est à toi; tu peux la dépenser (Balzac).
> *This fortune . . . it is yours; you can spend it.*
> Si tu étais à moi je te casserais le cou (Mérimée).
> *If you were mine I would break your neck.*

182. *En* Used in a Possessive Sense

(a) In careful writing and speech, **en** is frequently found in a possessive sense, where the possessor is a thing:

> Il en répandit le contenu (About).
> *He spread out its contents.*
> J'ai reçu vos lettres. L'écriture en était méconnaissable (Balzac).
> *I received your letters. Their handwriting was scarcely recognizable.*
> J'ai pu en saisir l'application.
> *I was able to grasp its application.*

(b) But the Possessive Adjective (and not *en*) is used where:

(i) The Thing Possessed is the subject of a verb which expresses an action (and not a state, as do, for example, *être, sembler, paraître, rester*).

> Nous sommes retournés au village, et sa beauté nous a frappés de nouveau.
> *We went back to the village, and its beauty struck us once more.*

(ii) The Possessor has been mentioned in the same clause:

> Je déteste ce pays et ses éternelles plaines.
> *I detest this country and its never-ending plains.*

(iii) The Thing Possessed is governed by a Preposition:

> Tu reconnaîtras leur auto à sa couleur.
> *You will recognize their car by its colour.*
> Il doutait de son existence.
> *He doubted its existence.*

183. Other Uses of Possessive Adjectives

(a) The Possessive Adjective is frequently used when addressing relatives respectfully, and, in the French Army, is used, with the appropriate rank, as the correct form of address to a superior officer (the English equivalent being simply: *sir*):

Bonjour, mon oncle, ma cousine.
C'est bien, mon capitaine, mon général.

(b) Note the following forms of expression:

Un de mes collègues.
A colleague of mine.
Un militaire de mes amis.
A soldier friend of mine.
Vous étiez de ses amis.
You were a friend of his.

(c) Note also the idiomatic use of the Possessive Adjective in such expressions as:

L'inspecteur vient; il faut aller à sa rencontre.
The inspector is coming; you must go and meet him.
Elle vola à son secours.
She rushed to help him.
Dites-lui cela de ma part.
Tell him that from me.

XVIII. RELATIVE PRONOUNS

184. Grammatical Note

(a) In the sentence:

He was in the train which had just arrived

which is the Relative Pronoun
which had just arrived is the Relative Clause
the train is what the Relative refers to—its Antecedent.

(b) The English Relatives *who, which, what,* and the French Relatives **qui, que, quoi, lequel** are the same in form as some Interrogative Pronouns (see Chapter XIX). As their Relative and Interrogative uses are not the same, it is important to be clearly aware which are involved.

185. Forms of Relative Pronouns

	Persons	*Persons and Things*
As subject		**qui**
As object or complement		**que**
In genitive, or combined with		**dont**
preposition **de**	**de qui**	**duquel**
After other prepositions, e.g.	**à qui**	**auquel**
	avec qui	**avec lequel**

Notes

1. The **e** of **que** is elided before a word beginning with a vowel or h-mute.

2. **Lequel** (fem. **laquelle,** masc. plur. **lesquels,** fem. plur. **lesquelles**) agrees in gender and number with the noun it refers to. **Lequel, lesquels,** and **lesquelles** combine with the Prepositions **à** and **de** to give the forms **auquel, duquel, auxquels, desquels, auxquelles, desquelles.**

186. Retention of Relative Pronoun

The Relative Pronoun, which is frequently omitted in English, is never omitted in French:

> Les lettres que je recevais.
> *The letters (which) I received.*
> Un homme que je connais.
> *A man I know.*

187. Position of Relative Pronoun

(*a*) In good usage the Relative should, wherever possible, immediately follow its Antecedent (French is more strict on this point than English):

> J'ai remarqué à l'exposition un tableau qui m'a intéressé.
> *I noticed a picture at the exhibition which interested me.*

(*b*) But a preposition governing the Relative separates it from its Antecedent:

> Le guide avec qui j'ai fait l'ascension.
> {*The guide with whom I made the ascent.*
> {*The guide whom I made the ascent with.*

N.B. It will be seen that in French a Preposition governing a Relative can only stand in one position, i.e. immediately before the Relative (but see also 192 (*d*)). It cannot be postponed as in English.

188. Agreement of Relative Pronouns

(*a*) The Relative Pronoun agrees with its Antecedent in *gender*, *number*, and *person*.

(*b*) In the case of **lequel**, the agreement in gender and number is shown by its form (see 185 n. 2):

> L'arbre derrière lequel il se cacha.
> Les idées vers lesquelles il était attiré.

(c) The remaining Pronouns (**qui, que,** &c.) are in the same form when Masc. or Fem. and Sing. or Plur., and they have the same form for each Person. However the agreement in gender, number and person exists in fact, and:

(i) The agreement in gender and number may be seen in any Adjectives or Participles in the Relative Clause:

> La chambre qui m'était destinée (Mérimée).

(ii) The agreement in number and person may be seen in the Verb in the Relative Clause:

> Vous qui avez de l'argent (Balzac).

(d) The *case* of the Relative Pronoun, as shown in the forms set out in 185, is that required by its function in the Relative Clause (i.e. whether it is subject, object, &c., or governed by a Preposition). Examples are given in the following sections.

189. *qui*—Subject

Refers to Persons or Things:

> Les gens qui ont perdu leur porte-monnaie (Romains).
> *People who have lost their purse.*
> Une petite chambre qui donnait sur la rue (Maupassant).
> *A little room which looked on to the street.*

190. *que*—Object

Refers to Persons or Things:

> C'est un homme que je ne connais guère.
> *He is a man whom I scarcely know.*
> Les lettres qu'il envoyait.
> *The letters which he sent.*

It may also stand as object to a double verb:

> Le train que j'ai vu arriver.
> *The train which I saw arrive.*

191. *que*—Complement

Refers to Persons or Things:

>Il n'est plus le grand général qu'il était.
>*He is no longer the great general he was.*

Que is also used as the Complement of Impersonal Verbs (or Verbs used impersonally):

>Prenez les boîtes qu'il y a sur le buffet.
>*Take the boxes which there are on the sideboard.*
>Les mesures qu'il faut.
>*The measures which are required.*

192. *dont*, *de qui*, *duquel*—Genitive, or Combined with *de*

(*a*) **Dont** is the commonest form, and may refer to Persons or Things:

>D'autres voyageurs, dont nous entendions les voix (Daudet).
>*Other travellers, whose voices we heard.*
>Un affreux caniche dont les pattes salissaient tous les meubles. (Flaubert).
>*A frightful poodle, whose paws dirtied all the furniture.*
>Une ville dont il avait oublié le nom.
>*A town, the name of which he had forgotten.*
>Vous avez fait quelque chose dont vous n'êtes pas très content (Duhamel).
>*You have done something which you are not very happy about.*

N.B. Where **dont** is present, the order of the sentence is such that **dont** stands between its Antecedent and the subject of the Relative Clause: **Un caniche dont les pattes . . .; une ville dont il. . . .**

(*b*) **De qui** is a less common equivalent of **dont,** when referring to persons. The order of the sentence is the same as when **dont** is used (but see also (*d*) below):

>Un homme de qui le passé m'était bien connu.
>*A man whose past was well known to me.*

227

(c) **Duquel,** &c., is a less common equivalent of **dont,** when referring to Things (and occasionally to Persons). When the subject of the Relative Clause is a pronoun, the order is the same as when **dont** is used (but see also (d) below):

> Une affaire de laquelle il refusait de parler.
> *A matter about which he refused to speak.*

When the subject of the Relative Clause is a noun, this stands between the Antecedent and **duquel**:

> Des événements l'importance desquels était considérable.
> *Events whose importance was considerable.*

Compare the word-order here with that where **dont** is used, as in the second example in (a) above.

(d) **De qui** or **duquel,** and not *dont,* are used when the Relative Clause begins with a Preposition:

> Cet homme, avec l'aide de qui je l'ai trouvé.
> *This man, with whose help I found it.*
> Un feu maigre, à la flamme duquel ils faisaient dégeler du biscuit (Daudet).
> *A meagre fire, by the flame of which they were thawing out some biscuit.*

N.B. The order in this type of sentence is

Antecedent—	Preposition and Noun it Governs	**de qui** or—**duquel**	Subject of Relative Clause
Cet homme	avec l'aide	de qui	je
Un feu maigre	à la flamme	duquel	ils

(e) It will be seen in the sections above that a noun to which **dont, de qui,** or **duquel** stand as Genitive is preceded by the Definite Article:

> Un caniche dont *les* pattes. . . .
> Une ville dont il avait oublié *le* nom.
> Un homme de qui *le* passé. . . .
> Un feu maigre, à *la* flamme duquel. . . .

193. *qui, lequel*—After Prepositions

(*a*) **Qui** is used of Persons (and see 187 (*b*), n.):

Ce Grec avec qui vous causiez (About).
That Greek whom you were chatting with.

(*b*) (i) **Lequel** is used of Things, and occasionally of Persons:

L'état dans lequel je me trouvais (Balzac).
The state in which I found myself.
Une princesse à laquelle il se dévouait (Maurois).
A princess to whom he devoted himself.

(ii) **Lequel** (and not *qui*) is used of Persons after the Prepositions **parmi** and **entre**:

Des ouvriers parmi lesquels il y avait quelques Espagnols.
Some workmen, among whom were a few Spaniards.

194. *où*

The Relative Adverb **où** is very frequently found (referring to Things only) expressing various ideas of place, time, and situation, e.g. *to which, towards which, at which, on which, in which*, &c. It is, in such cases, a shorter equivalent of **auquel, dans laquelle**, &c.:

Cet endroit où elle admettait peu de monde (Flaubert).
That place, to which she admitted few people.
Une chose en bronze où l'on pose les parapluies (Maupassant).
A bronze thing in which one puts umbrellas.
Au moment où nous revenions vers l'empereur (Balzac).
At the moment when (at which) we were returning towards the emperor.

195. *que*

The Relative Adverb **que** is sometimes used in the same way as **où** (see 194 above), mostly in expressions of time.

Un matin que le facteur n'était pas venu (Flaubert).
One morning when the postman had not come.
Du jour qu'ils sont arrivés (Daudet).
From the day when (that, on which) they arrived.

196. *Ce qui, ce que,*[1] *ce dont*

(*a*) **Qui, que, dont** are found preceded by **ce** when they would otherwise have no antecedent. This arises when the Relative has the sense of *the* (*a*) *thing which*:

> Ce qui la désolait principalement c'était d'abandonner sa chambre (Flaubert).
> *What principally distressed her was having to give up her bedroom.*
> C'est ce qu'il avait demandé.
> *It was what he had asked for.*
> Ce que j'avais aimé n'était qu'une ombre (France).
> *What I had loved was only a shadow.*
> Gamelin l'aida à descendre son paquet, ce dont le vieillard lui rendit grâces (France).
> *Gamelin helped him to get his package down, for which the old man expressed his thanks to him.*

(*b*) **Ce,** so used, may itself be governed by a Preposition:

> Après ce qui s'est passé (M. Renard). *After what has happened.*
> Il y a du vrai dans ce que dit le docteur (Verne).
> *There is some truth in what the doctor says.*

(*c*) **Ce** is also present with the Relative when the Antecedent is **tout** (= *everything*):

> Tout ce qui avait un air de mystère (Maurois).
> *Everything that had an air of mystery.*
> C'est tout ce que je peux dire.
> *That is all I can say.*

> N.B. 1. When the Antecedent is **tous** or **toutes**, the pronoun is **ceux, celles** (see 172 (*a*)).
> 2. Pronunciation: **tout ce qui** [tuski]: **tout ce que** [tuskə].

and usually after **voici** and **voilà** in the sense of *this is, that is*

> Voilà donc ce qui est arrivé.
> *That then is what happened.*

---

[1] For the use of **ce qui** and **ce que** in Indirect Questions see 204 and 206.

197. *quoi*[1]

Quoi is the form of the relative governed by a preposition:

(*a*) When it refers, not to an actual noun previously expressed (as do **qui** and **lequel** in 193), but to an event, fact, or idea:

A quoi il répondit que . . .
To which he replied that. . . .

Heureusement il avait ouvert la fenêtre, sans quoi il serait mort.
Fortunately he had opened the window, but for which he would have died.

(*b*) Where the antecedent is **ce**:

Ce à quoi je pense.
What I am thinking of.

N.B. Here the preposition *follows* **ce** and governs the relative **quoi** (**ce à quoi** = *the thing of which*). Compare 196 (*b*) above, where the preposition *precedes* and governs **ce** (**après ce qui** = *after the thing which*).

198. *lequel*—to avoid ambiguity

In written language only, **lequel** is sometimes used, in the Nominative, where the normal use of **qui** would leave some doubt as to which Antecedent was referred to:

La poignée du couteau, laquelle était en ivoire.
The handle of the knife, which was of ivory.

(Here **laquelle,** being feminine, must refer to **poignée.**)

If both Antecedents are of the same gender and number, **lequel** is considered to refer to the former one:

Une amie de sa sœur, laquelle venait parfois le dimanche.
A friend of his sister's, who sometimes came on Sundays.

[1] For the use of **quoi** in Indirect Questions see 209.

XIX. INTERROGATIVES

199. Grammatical Note

(*a*) The English Interrogatives *who? which? what?* and the French Interrogatives **qui? que? quoi? lequel?** are the same in form as some Relative Pronouns (see Chapter XVIII). As their Relative and Interrogative uses are not the same, it is important to be clearly aware which is involved.

(*b*) The English Interrogatives *what? which?* may be Adjectives (as in: *What reason? Which dog?*), or Pronouns (as in: *What did he say? Which do you want?*).

The French Adjective and Pronoun forms are not the same. The Interrogative Adjective is dealt with in 200, and the Interrogative Pronouns in 201 ff.

200. Interrogative Adjective—*quel?*

(*a*) **Quel?** (fem. **quelle**; masc. plur. **quels**; fem. plur. **quelles**) is only found qualifying a noun, and agrees with it in gender and number. It either precedes the noun immediately, or is separated from it by a tense of *être*.

(*b*) Referring to the noun it qualifies, it asks (in Direct or Indirect Questions) *what it is*, or *of what kind it is*:

Quelle maison?
Which house?
Quels clients réguliers?
What regular customers?
Quelle est cette jeune fille qui chante? (Musset)
Who is that girl singing?
Quelle est cette bête-là?
What is that animal?
Quel est le sens de cette expression? (Romains)
What is the meaning of that expression?
Vous savez dans quel état ça l'a mis (Maupassant).
You know what a state that put him into.

201. Interrogative Pronouns—*qui? que? quoi?*

	Persons	Things
As subject	qui? qui est-ce qui?	qu'est-ce qui?
As object or complement	qui? qui est-ce que?	que? qu'est-ce que?
After preposition, e.g.:	à qui? à qui est-ce que?	à quoi? à quoi est-ce que?

NOTES

1. The forms with **est-ce qui** and **est-ce que** are of fairly frequent use, especially in conversation.

2. The **e** of **que** in all the above forms is elided before a word beginning with a vowel or h-mute.

202. Agreement of *qui? que? quoi?*

(*a*) All the above pronouns are *3rd Person Singular Masculine*. Agreement in gender and number is shown in adjectives and participles:

> Qui est assez courageux?
> Qu'a-t il fait?
> Qu'est-ce qui s'est passé?

Agreement in number and person is shown in any verb of which they are the subject:

> Qui va là?
> Qu'est-ce qui est tombé?

(*b*) The *case-form* of Interrogative Pronouns depends on their function in the Interrogative Sentence (i.e. whether they are subject, object, &c., or governed by a preposition). It also depends on whether they refer to Persons or Things.

The forms required are set out in 201 above, and further examples are given in the following sections.

233

203. As Subject (Persons)—*qui? qui est-ce qui?*

Qui? in Direct or Indirect Questions; **qui est-ce qui?** in Direct Questions only:

> Qui donc m'aurait soupçonné? (M. Renard)
> *Who would have suspected me then?*
> Qui est-ce qui m'aidera à la combattre? (Romains)
> *Who will help me to fight it?*
> Il se demanda qui l'aurait pris.
> *He wondered who would have taken it.*

204. As Subject (Things)—*qu'est-ce qui? ce qui*

Qu'est-ce qui? in Direct Questions; **ce qui** in Indirect:

> Qu'est-ce qui vous y attire? (Romains)
> *What attracts you to it?*
> On ne sait jamais ce qui peut arriver (Maupassant).
> *One never knows what may happen.*

205. As Object (Persons)—*qui? qui est-ce que?*

Qui? in Direct or Indirect Questions; **qui est-ce que?** in Direct Questions only:

> Qui soupçonnez-vous?   Qui est-ce qu'il protège?
> *Whom do you suspect?*   *Whom is he protecting?*
> Je ne me rappelle plus qui j'ai rencontré.
> *I no longer remember whom I met.*

206. As Object (Things)—*que? qu'est-ce que? ce que*

Que? or **qu'est-ce que?** in Direct Questions: **ce que** in Indirect:

> Que vous a-t-elle dit?   Que faire?
> *What did she say to you?*   *What is to be done?*
> Qu'est-ce que vous croyez?
> *What do you think?*
> Sans dire ce qu'elle envoyait (Flaubert).
> *Without saying what she was sending.*

207. As Complement

(a) Of Persons (or where *Who?* is meant): **qui?** in Direct or Indirect Questions:

Qui êtes-vous?
Who are you?
Vous savez qui il est?
You know who he is?

(b) Of Things (or where *What?* is meant): **que?** or **qu'est-ce que?** in Direct Questions; **ce que** in Indirect:

Qu'êtes-vous?   Qu'est-ce? (*or*) Qu'est-ce que c'est?
What are you?   *What is it?*
Que deviendra ma fille? (About)
What will become of my daughter? (lit. *What will she become?*)
J'ai demandé ce que c'était.
I asked what it was.

N.B. 1. The above forms also stand as the Complement of Impersonal Verbs (or Verbs used impersonally):

Qu'est-ce qu'il y a dans le tiroir?
What is there in the drawer?
Que se passe-t-il?
What is happening?
Que m'importe?
What does it matter to me?
Il demanda ce qu'il y avait au feu.
He asked what was on the fire.

2. **Qu'est-ce que?** (**ce que c'est que** in Indirect Questions) is frequently used to ask for a definition (see also (d) below):

Qu'est-ce qu'un spectacle? (Balzac)
What is a show?
L'on vit ce que c'est qu'une guerre nationale (Daudet).
One saw what war on a national scale is.

235

(c) Similar senses to the above may be conveyed, before *être*, by **quel** (see 200 (*b*)).

(d) In conversation, the form **qu'est-ce que c'est que?** is sometimes used to make an emphatic inquiry:

> Qu'est-ce que c'est que ce jeune homme qui téléphone?
> *Who (ever) is that young man on the telephone?*
> Qu'est-ce que c'est que cette chose-là? (Saint-Exupéry)
> *What (ever) is that thing?*

208. Governed by Preposition (Persons)—*qui? qui est-ce que?*

Qui? in Direct or Indirect Questions; **qui est-ce que?** in Direct Questions only:

> A qui ai-je l'honneur de parler? (Balzac)
> *To whom have I the honour of speaking?*
> Avec qui est-ce qu'elle est venue?
> *Whom did she come with?*[1]
> Sachant à qui j'avais affaire (Balzac).
> *Knowing whom I had to deal with.*

209. Governed by Preposition (Things)—*quoi? quoi est-ce que?*

Quoi? in Direct and Indirect Questions; **quoi est-ce que?** in Direct Questions only:

> A quoi songe-t-il?
> *What is he dreaming of?*
> Avec quoi est-ce qu'on sert les petits pois?
> *What does one serve green peas with?*[1]
> Je ne vois pas en quoi je suis coupable (Pagnol).
> *I don't see in what way I am to blame.*
> Je lui ai demandé à quoi il pensait.
> *I asked him what he was thinking about.*

---

[1] Note that, in French, Prepositions governing Interrogatives must stand immediately before them. They cannot be postponed as in English.

236

XIX INTERROGATIVES §§ 207-11

210. To Express Possession

(*a*) The normal French rendering of *whose?* (*of whom?*), meaning possession, is **à qui?**

> A qui sont ces instruments?
> *Whose are these instruments?*
> A qui est le chien qui a mordu le facteur?
> *Whose dog bit the postman?*

(*b*) **De qui** is little used to ask a question as to possession. It is only found in simple sentences with *être*, when it is a question of identification rather than possession:

> De qui êtes-vous le représentant?
> *Whose representative are you?*
> De qui est-ce là l'empreinte?
> *Whose is that footprint?*

211. Other Uses of *quoi?*

(*a*) **Quoi?** is also found as sole word in a sentence, in the sense of the English *What?*

> Je sais quelque chose qui va les étonner. Quoi?
> *I know something that will surprise them. What?*

N.B. The use of **quoi?** in the sense of *What did you say?* is not polite. Expressions such as **Comment? Plaît-il? Vous dites?** are preferred.

(*b*) Note also the idiomatic use of **quoi?** followed by **de** and an adjective:

> Quoi de nouveau?
> *Anything new?* }
> *What's the news?* }
> Quoi de plus innocent?
> *What* }
> *What is (could be)* } *more innocent?*

212. Interrogative Pronoun *lequel?*

(*a*) **Lequel** has Fem. **laquelle**; Masc. Plur. **lesquels**; Fem. Plur. **lesquelles,** and agrees in gender with the noun it refers to.

(*b*) It is *3rd Person*, and is *singular or plural* according to whether it means one or more items. It has the same form for all cases.

(*c*) It combines with the Prepositions **à** and **de** in the same way as the Relative **lequel** (see 185 n. 2).

213. Uses of *lequel?*

(*a*) **Lequel?** is the form of the Interrogative Pronoun when the question implies the making of a choice, and may be used in Direct or Indirect Questions:

(i) The alternatives to choose from may already have been mentioned:

Voici Georges et Anne. Lequel est l'aîné?
Here are George and Anne. Which is the elder?

(ii) Or they may be mentioned in what follows:

Je me demande auquel de ces employés on montre son passeport.
I wonder which of these officials one shows one's passport to.
Laquelle me va mieux, la bleue ou la rose?
Which suits me best, the blue one or the pink?

(iii) Or the fact that there is an alternative may be implied:

Lequel est le train de Vincennes?
Which is the Vincennes train?

(iv) The alternatives may be actions. In this case **lequel** is masculine:

Lequel vaudrait mieux, parler ou se taire?
Which would be better, to speak or to say nothing?

(b) **Qui?** followed by **de** or **d'entre** is often found instead of **lequel** before a Personal Pronoun:

Qui de nous   } a pu le faire?   *Who of us*   } *can have done*
Qui d'entre eux }   *Who of (among) them* }   *it?*

(c) Note the following idiomatic use of **lequel?** in conversation:

J'accepte, mais à une condition. Laquelle? (About)
I accept, but on one condition. What is it?
Il est l'auteur de plusieurs livres. Lesquels?
He is the author of several books. What are they?

214. *que! quoi! quel!* in Exclamations

(a) **Que**! in the sense of *how much! to what extent!*

(i) as an adverb:
Que je suis heureux!   *How happy I am!*

(ii) as a pronoun, followed by **de** and a noun:
Que d'argent gaspillé!
What a lot of money thrown away!
Dans cette salle, que de mères, que d'enfants avaient vécu! (Bazin)
In this room, how many mothers, how many children had lived!

(b) **Quoi**! as sole word in a sentence, expressing surprise or indignation:

Quoi! C'est vous?
What! It's you?
Quoi! L'on ne peut jamais vous parler tête-à-tête? (Molière)
What! Can one never have a word with you alone?

(c) **Quel**! is the adjective form:

Quelle journée!   Quels affreux vêtements!
What a day!   *What frightful clothes!*

XX. INDEFINITE ADJECTIVES, PRONOUNS, &c.

(For **aucun, nul, pas un, personne, rien** see 249 ff.)

215. *autre* (plural *autres*)

1. **other** (adj. or Pron.) usually preceded by appropriate Article or Demonstrative or Possessive	Prenez une autre (mon autre, cette autre) canne.[1] *Take another (my other, this other) stick.* D'autres docteurs l'auraient sauvée (Flaubert). *Other doctors would have saved her.* Il fit comme les autres. *He did like the others.* Il n'en a pas d'autres. *He hasn't any others (other ones).* Entre autres choses. *Among other things.*
2. **different**	Mon avis est autre. *My view differs.* C'est un autre homme. *He is a different man.*
3. Special sense with *nous* or *vous*, placing in class apart (no English equivalent)	Voici ce qui nous tue, nous autres petits détaillants (Balzac). *This is what is killing us small retailers.*
4. Other idioms	L'autre jour; autre part; de temps à autre. *The other day; elsewhere; from time to time.*

216. *autre chose* (Masculine)

something else	C'est autre chose qui m'a retenu (Pailleron). *It is something else which kept me.*

[1] **Une autre canne** means *another* (i.e. *a different*) *stick*. Cf. **Encore une canne,** which means *another* (i.e. *an additional*) *stick*.

240

217. *chaque* (**Invariable**)

1. **each** (adj.)	·Vous vous arrêterez chaque fois que je vous le dirai (Romains). *You will stop each time I tell you to.*
2. **every** (= **each and every**). In correct French only with sing. noun	Chaque jour apportait quelque chose de nouveau. *Every day brought something new.*

218. *chacun* (**Feminine *chacune***)

1. **each** (pron. = **each one**). Agrees in gender with noun referred to	Il a parlé à chacun des invités. *He spoke to each of the guests.* Les oranges coûtent 15 francs chacune. *The oranges cost 15 francs each.*
2. **each** (= **everyone**) Masc. invariable	Il faut que chacun fasse sa tâche en ce monde (France). *Each must perform his task in this world.* Chacun pour soi. *Every man for himself.*

219. *certain* (**Regular Feminine and Plural Forms**)

1. **certain** (indefinite sense). Precedes noun: may or may not be preceded by *un(e)* in sing.	Il y a un certain charme à se trouver auprès d'un être dangereux (Mérimée). *There is a certain attraction in finding oneself next to a dangerous character.* Certain geste pourrait le toucher (Pagnol). *A certain gesture might move him.* Il y a certaines raisons pourquoi . . . *There are certain reasons why . . .*
2. **certain** (= **definite, sure**). Follows noun	. . . les entraîner à une mort certaine (Verne). *. . . drag them to certain death.*
3. As masc. plur. pron. **certain individuals**	Certains des amis de son père (Maurois). *Certain of his father's friends.* Certains ont fait la remarque que . . . *Certain people made the observation that . . .*

220. *de quoi*

Sufficient quantity of, sufficient reason for. Usually followed by infin.	Elle possédait de quoi se vêtir (Flaubert). *She had enough to wear.*
	Il y avait là de quoi faire guillotiner ma grand-mère (France). *There was enough there to have my grandmother guillotined.*

221. *différent, divers* (Regular Feminine and Plural Forms)

1. Preceding noun; in plur. only: **of more than one kind.** Do not require a preceding *de*	Par différents détours il avait gagné le château. *By various detours he had reached the castle.*
	Diverses personnes ont raconté la chose (La Bruyère). *Various people have told of the matter.*
2. Following noun: **not of the same kind**	J'y vais aussi, mais pour une raison bien différente. *I am going there too, but for a very different reason.*

222. *l'un(e) . . . l'autre* (Plural *les un(e)s . . . les autres*)

(These are the forms of the Pronouns **un** and **autre** when used in contrast to each other.)

(*a*) *With separate vbs.*	L'un travaillait pendant que l'autre dormait. *One worked while the other slept.*
	Les uns avaient vendu, les autres avaient acheté (About). *Some had sold, others had bought.*
(*b*) *With same vb.* (frequently emphasizing a reflexive or other pronoun). Note various senses, and that prepositions and *que, et, ou* stand between *l'un* and *l'autre*	Les deux frères s'aideront l'un l'autre. *The two brothers will help one another.*
	Les convives se disaient les uns aux autres . . . (Maurois). *The guests were saying to each other . . .*
	Ils se serrèrent les uns contre les autres (Daudet). *They huddled one against the other.*
	Ils sont aussi ignorants l'un que l'autre (Musset). *They are each as ignorant as the other.*
	Marchant l'un et l'autre sans faire le moindre bruit (Mérimée). *Both walking without making the slightest noise.*
	L'un ou l'autre suffira. *Either will be sufficient.*
	Elles ne s'attendaient ni l'une ni l'autre à cette conclusion (About). *Neither of them was expecting this conclusion.*

223. *même* (Plural *mêmes*)

1. Adj. Preceding noun or as complement: **same**

Ils réfléchissaient aux mêmes choses (Bazin).
They were thinking of the same things.
Ces deux cartes ne sont pas les mêmes.
These two maps are not the same.

2. Adj. Following noun **very, self** (also when attached to Disjunctive Pron. by hyphen) (see 165 (*b*), 166)

Les canons mêmes étaient déjà rouillés.
The very guns were already rusted.
Elle est la bonté même.
She is kindness itself.
Ils l'ont vu eux-mêmes.[1]
They saw it themselves.

3. Adv. (invariable): **even**. Usually follows verb, and precedes *pas* if present

Il est probable et même certain que ... (France).
It is probable and even certain that ...
Je ne savais même pas qu'elle existât (France).
I did not even know that she existed.
Même les oiseaux se turent.
Even the birds fell silent.

4. Other idioms

Cela revient au même.
That comes to the same thing.
Il fit de même.
He did likewise.
Il en est de même des lapins.
It is the same with rabbits.
Nous irons quand même (tout de même).
We shall go all the same.

224. *On* (Invariable)

Agreements with **on** are normally masculine singular. The corresponding Reflexive is *se*, Disjunctive *soi*, and Possessive *son*, &c.

1. **one** (= people in general, or any such people as are here involved)

On n'est jamais si heureux ni si malheureux qu'on s'imagine (La Rochefoucauld).
One is never as fortunate or as unfortunate as one thinks one is.

---

[1] The *self* which is expressed by **même** serves to emphasize the identity. Distinguish from the reflexive *self*, which is rendered by a reflexive pronoun. Cf. **Ils se sont vus dans le miroir** = *They saw themselves in the mirror.*

On se lasse de tout.
One gets tired of everything.
On doit céder.
One must give way.
On entre par la grande porte.
One goes in by the main door.

2. Undefined person(s) responsible for the action. Frequently = English Passive (see 61)

On vient.
Someone is coming.
On frappe à la porte.
There is a knock at the door.
On me l'a dit aussi.
I have been told so too.
On m'a volé.
I have been robbed.
On la pria d'être ma marraine (France).
She was asked to be my godmother.

N.B. **On** is only found in the Nominative (i.e. as subject). Its other cases are supplied usually by *vous*:

L'employé vous donne un bulletin d'enregistrement.
The official gives one a registration receipt.
On a un ami qui s'intéresse à vous (Mérimée).
One has a friend who is interested in one.

225. *pareil* (Regular Feminine and Plural Forms)

1. Adj. Preceding noun: **such** (often uncomplimentary sense). May or may not be preceded by *un(e)* or *de*

Surpris de le voir à pareille heure (Mérimée).
Surprised to see him at such an hour.
Assez fatigué pour pouvoir dormir dans un pareil gîte (Mérimée).
Sufficiently tired to be able to sleep in such a lodging.

2. Adj. Following noun or as complement: **of the same kind**

Il cherchait une fleur pareille.
He was looking for a similar flower.
Les deux cas ne sont pas pareils.
The two cases are not alike.

3. Pronoun: **the like, the equal**

Lui et ses pareils.
He and the like of him.
Elle n'a pas sa pareille pour la couture.
She has not her equal for sewing.

226. *plusieurs* (Plural Invariable)

1. Adj. Precedes noun: **several** (adj.), **a number of**

Après avoir essayé plusieurs sujets de conversation (Mérimée).
After trying several subjects of conversation.
Il a plusieurs propriétés aux environs de Tours.
He has a number of properties around Tours.

2. Pron. **several** (pron.), **a number.** As object can only be used with *de* or *en*

Plusieurs de ces pommes sont déjà mûres.
Several of these apples are already ripe.
Plusieurs ont refusé de venir.
Several have refused to come.
Il vit plusieurs de ses collègues.
He saw several of his colleagues.
Des dictionnaires? J'en ai plusieurs.
Dictionaries? I have several.

227. *quelque*[1] (Plural *quelques*)

1. Adj. sing. **some kind of, some quantity of**

Seriez-vous venu demander quelque service? (Balzac).
Have you by chance come to ask some service?
Il a sans doute quelque raison.
He has doubtless some reason.
A quelque distance de sa couche (Mérimée).
Some distance from his bed.

2. Adj. plur. **a small number of**

Des parties de chasse avec quelques amis (Maupassant).
Some hunting expeditions with a few friends.
Il n'en restait que quelques miettes.
Only a few crumbs were left.

3. Adv. (invariable) **approximately**

Il marcha quelque deux cents pas (Mérimée).
He walked some (about a) hundred yards.

228. *quelque chose* (Masculine)

Something. Adj. qualifying it preceded by *de*

Quelque chose m'est arrivé.
Something has happened to me.
Quelque chose de fâcheux.
Something annoying.

[1] For uses with subjunctive see HOWEVER, WHATEVER in Appendix C.

229. *quelqu'un* (Feminine *quelqu'une*, Plural *quelques-un(e)s*)

1. Invariable masc. pron. **somebody.** Adj. qualifying it preceded by *de*

   Je ne sais ... mais quelqu'un m'a dit (Mérimée).
   I don't know ... but somebody said to me.
   Quelqu'un d'inattendu.
   Someone unexpected.

2. Variable pron. agreeing in gender with noun referred to. Sing.= **(some)one** Plur.= **some, a few** followed by *of*. Used only with *de* or *en*

   Quelqu'un de ces individus a dû le savoir.
   (Some)one of these individuals must have known it.
   Quelques-unes de ces lettres sont incompréhensibles.
   A few of these letters are unintelligible.
   Elle examina les bas et en reprisa quelques-uns.
   She examined the stockings and darned some of them.

230. *tel* (Regular Feminine and Plural Forms)

Agrees in gender and number with the noun it qualifies or refers to:

1. Preceding noun: **such.** Usually preceded by *un(e)* in sing. and *de* in plur.

   Avec une telle voiture[1] et de tels chevaux.
   With such a carriage and such horses.
   Votre ami m'a rendu de tels services (Labiche et Martin).
   Your friend has rendered me such services.

2. As complement, or with *que* in comparative phrase: **such as, like**

   Elle était telle qu'il me l'avait dépeinte (Mérimée).
   It was like he had described it to me.
   Telle est la vérité.
   Such is the truth.
   Plusieurs êtres minuscules, tels que les fourmis.
   Several tiny creatures, such as ants.

N.B. **Tel** cannot qualify another adjective. The idea of *such* is then expressed by **si** or **tellement**:

De si bonnes raisons.
Such good reasons.
Un si large fleuve.
Such a wide river (so wide a river).
Des idées tellement dangereuses.
Such dangerous ideas.

[1] This is the only permissible order: the order *telle une* is not correct in the sense of *such a.*

246

231. Adjective *tout* (Fem. *toute*, Masc. Plur. *tous* [tu], Fem. Plur. *toutes*)

(a) Followed by Article (or Demonstrative or Possessive):

1. **all**

Tous les crimes que le bandit va commettre (Mérimée).
All the crimes which the bandit is going to commit.

Je m'intéresse à {
toutes ces choses-là.
tout ceci.
tous ceux qui sont authentiques.
}

I am interested in {
all these things.
all this.
all which are authentic.
}

Tous les Anglais avaient quelque chose de travers dans la tête (About).
All English people were a bit funny in the head.

2. **all of**

Il a mangé tout le gâteau.
He has eaten all of the cake.

3. **the whole, a whole**

Toute la famille allait à pied (Maurois).
The whole family went on foot.

. . . qui vous révèlent toute une existence (Daudet).
... which reveal a whole existence to you.

4. **the whole of**

Pendant tout son voyage.
For the whole of his journey.
Le plus précieux de toute ma bibliothèque.
The most precious in the whole of my library.

5. **every** (plural)

Tous les jours;   tous les deux mois;
Every day;   every other month;
tous les cinq ans.
every five years.

(b) Without Article, &c.:

1. In sing. **any** (= **any and every**)

Une protection assurée contre toute mauvaise rencontre (Mérimée).
A sure protection against any evil encounter.
A toute heure.
At any hour (At all times).

2. In plur. in certain idioms only: **all**	De toutes sortes.	*Of all kinds.*
	De tous côtés.	⎰ *In all directions.* ⎱ *From all directions.* *On all sides.*
	De toutes parts.	*On (from) all sides.*
	De toutes couleurs.	*Of all colours.*
	Au-dessus de toutes choses.	*Above all things.*

N.B. The adjective **tout** is normally present before each noun to which it applies, including those in a series:

Je sentis toute ma fatigue et toute ma tristesse se fondre (France).
I felt all my weariness and sadness melt away.

232. Pronoun *tout* (Masculine Singular Invariable)

1. **everything.** Frequently precedes Past Participles and Dependent Infinitives	Jusqu'alors tout avait été simple (Balzac). *Up to then everything had been simple.* Vous n'avez pas tout vu. *You have not seen all.* Il voulait tout admirer. *He wanted to admire everything.*
2. Sums up a series of things	Les ruches, la vigne, la maison, tout t'appartient (Daudet). *The hives, the vine, the house, all are yours.*

233. Plural Pronoun *tous* [tus] (Feminine *toutes*)

1. **everyone** (usually only masc. **tous**)	Il s'est fait détester de tous. *He has made himself detested by everyone.*
2. **all, all of** (pron.), referring to or emphasizing noun or another pronoun	Il essaya plusieurs portes; toutes étaient fermées à clef. *He tried several doors; all were locked.* Ils étaient tous montés avec nous (Pailleron). *They had all got in with us.* Le lendemain nous apparut à tous d'une longueur considérable (Verne). *The next day appeared of considerable length to all of us.*
3. Sums up a series of persons	Jardinier, bonne, chauffeur, tous furent renvoyés. *Gardener, maid, chauffeur, all were dismissed.*

234. Adverb *tout*

1. **quite, completely.** Avec des yeux tout ronds d'étonnement.
   Normally invariable, *With eyes quite round with astonishment.*
   but agrees with fem. Elle est tout exceptionnelle.
   sing. or plur. adj. be- *It is quite exceptional.*
   ginning with con- Toute seule elle regardait.
   sonant or h-aspirate *All alone she was watching.*
   Elles s'arrêtèrent toutes haletantes.
   They stopped quite out of breath.

2. Concessive use,[1] regu- Tout épuisé qu'il était, il ne voulait pas se rendre.
   larly with indicative, *Exhausted though he was, he would not give in.*
   but subjunctive be- Je fais un métier d'homme, toute femme que
   coming common. je suis.
   Agreement as in (1) *I do a man's job, in spite of being a woman.*
   above. Tout invraisemblable que cela paraisse.
   However unlikely it may seem.

235. *tous (les) deux* (Feminine *toutes (les) deux*)

1. **both** (pron.). Refers Une vieille femme et une petite fille, toutes les
   to or emphasizes noun deux de couleur de suie (Mérimée).
   or another pronoun *An old woman and a little girl, both the colour of soot.*
   Ils le regardaient tous deux avec inquiétude.
   They were both looking at him apprehensively.
   Je leur ai donné un bon soufflet à tous deux.
   I gave them both a good slap.

2. Similar construction Ils étaient tous trois perdus dans une forêt
   with other numerals (Maurois).
   They were all three lost in a forest.

N.B. The adjective *both* is expressed by **les deux**:

Prenez les deux autos si vous en avez besoin.
Take both (the) cars if you need them.

236. *tout le monde* (Masculine Invariable)

Everybody, Agree- Tout le monde était endormi.
ments are sing. *Everybody was asleep.*

N.B. *The whole world* is expressed by **le monde entier**.

---

[1] For concessive use of **tout** with **en** and Gerund, see 35 (*b*).

XXI. PREPOSITIONS AND CONJUNCTIONS

PREPOSITIONS

The finding of appropriate French equivalents for English prepositions presents considerable difficulties, as the prepositions of both languages have a great variety of senses, which rarely coincide and, where they overlap, only do so incompletely. For instance, in a number of cases the French equivalent of the English *for* may be **pour,** but in a number of other cases it is not so. Conversely *for* is by no means always the appropriate translation of the French **pour.**

The only reliable guide to the correct use of French prepositions is to acquire by careful reading a true feeling of what these prepositions convey to a Frenchman. Meanwhile a preliminary guide to this is given in APPENDIX B, and some initial help in finding French equivalents of English prepositions in certain common contexts may be obtained from the INDEX and from APPENDIX C.

237. Construction of Prepositions

(*a*) A preposition may govern a noun or pronoun, e.g. **pour la patrie, avec eux.**

The Prepositions **à** and **de** combine with certain forms of the Definite Article to give, for example, **au, des** (see 70, 179 n. 2).

Special forms of Personal, Relative, and Interrogative Pronouns may be required when governed by a Preposition. (See the appropriate chapters.)

(*b*) A preposition may also govern a verb.

(i) In the case of **en,** the form is the Gerund (the same in form as the Present Participle—see Chapter IV):

Il l'amusait en lui racontant des histoires (Flaubert).
He entertained her by telling her stories.

(ii) When governed by any other preposition the form of the verb is the infinitive (**après** almost always governs the Perfect Infinitive):

> Avant de me déshabiller.
> *Before getting undressed.*
> Le sommeil fut long à venir.
> *Sleep was long in coming.*
> Le roi décida de saisir leurs biens (Maurois).
> *The king decided to seize their property.*
> Après avoir fermé la porte.
> *After closing the door.*

(c) The Prepositions **à, de,** and **en** are normally present before each word or word-group that they govern, including those in a series:

> Consacrer sa vie à lire et à prendre des notes (Maurois).
> *To devote his life to reading and note-taking.*
> Ceux de Clémentine et de sa fille (France).
> *Those of Clementine and her daughter.*
> L'école était très forte en latin et en grec (Maurois).
> *The school was very strong in Latin and Greek.*

Conjunctions

238. Co-ordinating Conjunctions

The principal Co-ordinating Conjunctions are:

> **et** (notes 1 and 2) *and*;
> **ou** (note 2) *or*;
> **(ni) . . . ni** (*neither*) . . . *nor* (see 250 (g));
> **mais** *but*;
> **car** *for*;
> **aussi, ainsi** (note 3) *so, therefore*;
> **donc** *therefore*;
> **ainsi que** *as well as*.

They do not affect the construction of the sentence:

> Mais je songeais aux différences (Romains).
> *But I was thinking of the differences.*
> Car on m'écoute avec attention (Romains).
> *For they are listening to me attentively.*
> Je louai une chambre, ainsi qu'un piano (Romains).
> *I rented a room, as well as a piano.*

NOTES

1. Where **et** links the last of a series of words or phrases it is not preceded by a comma:

> Une main durcie, endolorie et froide (France).
> *A hand roughened, sore, and cold.*
> On nous apporte des confitures, des pipes et du café (Daudet).
> *They bring us some preserves, pipes, and coffee.*

Et is present before a relative clause where the latter adds to the sense of a preceding adjectival phrase:

> Un homme posté dans la rue et qui l'accosta quand il sortit (Balzac).
> *A man stationed in the street, who accosted him when he came out.*
> Cette puissance particulière à l'homme et que l'on nomme la volonté (Balzac).
> *That power peculiar to mankind which is called will.*

2. The use of **et . . . et** (= *both . . . and*) and **ou . . . ou** (= *either . . . or*) is mainly in literary language. Elsewhere the first **et** or **ou** is omitted.

Soit . . . soit is also an equivalent of *either . . . or* in literary language.

3. Inverted word-order may follow the conjunction **aussi** (but not **ainsi**) = *so, therefore*:

> Aussi gagne-t-il beaucoup d'argent (Balzac).
> *So he earns a lot of money.*

239. Subordinating Conjunctions

These introduce a subordinate clause, and require the verb to be in the indicative or subjunctive, as indicated below. The principal Subordinating Conjunctions are:

Verb in Indicative		*Verb in Subjunctive*	
ainsi que	*just as (similarity)*	à condition que	*on condition that*
alors que	*(at a time) when, whereas*	afin que	*in order that*
		à moins que (note 1)	*unless*
à mesure que	*(in proportion) as*	au (en) cas que	*in case*
		avant que	*before*
à peine . . . que	*scarcely . . . when*	bien que / quoique	*although*
après que	*after*	de crainte que / de peur que (note 1)	*for fear that*
au (dans le) cas ou	*in the event of*	de façon que / de manière que / de sorte que	*so that (purpose— see 241 (d) (ii))*
aussitôt que / dès que	*as soon as*	en admettant que	*admitting that*
comme	*as (time or cause)*	jusqu'à ce que	*until (note 3)*
		loin que	*far from*
de façon que / de manière que / de sorte que	*so that (conse-quence—see 241 (d) (ii))*	non que	*not that*
		pour que (note 4)	*in order that*
		pourvu que	*provided that, if only*
depuis que	*since (time)*		
lorsque / quand (note 2)	*when*	sans que	*without*
		soit que . . .	*whether . . .*
maintenant que	*now that*	soit que . . .	*or . . .*
parce que	*because*		
pendant que	*while*		
puisque	*since (reason)*	N.B. The tense of the subjunc-
selon que	*according as*	tive verb will depend partly
si	*if*	on the sequence of the sen-
tandis que	*while, whereas*	tence. The principles are the
tant que	*as long as*	same as those in 48.
vu que	*seeing that*	

253

Dès qu'il l'apercevait il commençait à rire (Flaubert).
As soon as he saw him he would begin laughing.
On est entré dans sa maison pendant qu'il était sorti (Mérimée).
His house was entered while he was out.
Je réciterai jusqu'à ce que vous m'arrêtiez (Stendhal).
I will recite until you stop me.
Quoique mes souvenirs soient bien confus (Balzac).
Although my recollections are very confused.

NOTES

1. Where **à moins que,** or **de peur (crainte) que** introduce a possibility in the affirmative, **ne** (without negative force) is present before the verb:

Nous sortirons à moins qu'il ne pleuve.
We will go out unless it rains.
Il se cacha de peur que son père ne le battît.
He hid for fear that his father might beat him.

2. **Où** (or **que**), and not *quand* or *lorsque*, are used to introduce a clause which qualifies a noun expressing time (e.g. *the moment when, the day when,* &c.). See 194, 195.
Quand, or **quand même,** followed by the Conditional or Conditional Perfect may have the sense of *even if.*

Et quand je comprendrais, croyez-vous que je reviendrais? (Balzac)
And even if I did understand, do you think I would return?
Quand même ils seraient restés, nous les aurions chassés dehors.
Even if they had stayed, we should have chased them out.

3. *Wait until* (conjunction) is **attendre que** with subjunctive. But see also UNTIL in Appendix C.

4. **Pour que** introduces a clause qualifying **assez** or **trop** (cf. **pour** 14 in Appendix B):

L'effort était assez grand pour qu'il en tirât quelque vanité (Mérimée).
The effort was sufficiently great for him to derive some pride from it.

240. Repetition of Subordinating Conjunctions

(*a*) Where the sense of a subordinating conjunction applies to a further clause, the conjunction itself is not usually repeated, but **que** is used instead. The verb after **que** is then in the same mood as the verb in the original clause:

> Quand des nuages s'amoncelaient et que le tonnerre grondait (Flaubert).
> *When clouds were piling up and the thunder was growling.*
> Pour que vous en profitiez et que l'affaire aille plus vite.
> *So that you may profit from it and so that the matter may proceed more quickly.*

(*b*) Where the conjunction whose sense is repeated is **si** (conditional), the mood after **que** is subjunctive:

> Si le temps s'éclaircit et qu'ils soient toujours là.
> *If the weather clears up and they are still there.*

Que is not thus used to repeat **si** as found in indirect questions (see 244).

(*c*) Occasionally **que** may replace another conjunction entirely:

> Le métayer n'avait pas fait dix pas que (= quand) l'infirme glissa (Bazin).
> *The farmer had not taken ten steps when the sick man fell.*
> Approche-toi que (= pour que) je te voie mieux (Saint-Exupéry).
> *Come nearer, so that I can see you better.*

241. Grammatical Note on Prepositions and Conjunctions

English Prepositions frequently have the same form as Conjunctions, e.g. *after* is a Preposition in *after dinner*, and a Conjunction in *after he left*.

In French the Conjunction form always differs from the Preposition, and they may not be interchanged. It should therefore be noted that:

(a) (i) The *Preposition* form is the one which governs a *word*, i.e. a noun, pronoun, or, in French, an infinitive (for the construction with **en** see 237 (b) (i)):

Après son arrivée.   Avant moi.   Sans bouger.
After his arrival.   *Before me.*   *Without moving.*

(ii) The *Conjunction* form is the one which introduces a *clause* with finite verb (i.e. a verb in a tense):

Après qu'on eut libéré les prisonniers.
After they had set the prisoners free.
Avant qu'il eût détaché son amarre (Daudet).
Before he had cast off his mooring.

(b) (i) While many French Prepositions may govern an Infinitive, they can only do so if there is *no change of subject* (i.e. if the subject of the infinitive is the same as that of the main clause):

Pour le savoir elle interrogea M. Bourais (Flaubert).
In order to find out she questioned M. Bourais.
Justin me regardait sans répondre (Duhamel).
Justin looked at me without answering.

(ii) Where there is a *change of subject* the sense can only be conveyed by a Conjunction and Clause:

Elle parlait bas pour que son père ne l'entendît pas (Mérimée).
She spoke in a low tone so that her father should not hear her.
Colette était animée de pensées sérieuses sans que sa gaieté la quittât jamais (Barrès).
Colette was moved by serious thoughts without her light-heartedness ever leaving her.

(iii) A Conjunction and Clause must also be used where the corresponding preposition cannot take an infinitive (e.g. **depuis**), or where there is no corresponding preposition (e.g. to **bien que**):

Depuis qu'il est ici, il a engraissé.
Since being here he has put on weight.
Bien qu'il s'affaiblît déjà, il força un sourire.
Although already getting weaker, he forced a smile.

(*c*) Some common French Preposition and Conjunction forms, which have a single English equivalent, are contrasted in the following list. Selection depends on the context (see (*a*) and (*b*) above).

after	après la guerre	*after the war*
	après avoir mangé	*after eating*
	après qu'il fut arrivé	*after he had arrived*
before	avant moi	*before me*
	avant de partir	*before leaving*
	avant qu'ils partent	*before they leave*
since (time)	depuis l'été	*since the summer*
	depuis qu'il est sorti	*since he went out*
while	en parlant	*while speaking*
	pendant qu'il travaillait	*while he was working*
because	à cause de vous	*because of you*
	parce qu'il est malade	*because he is ill*
without	sans aide	*without help*
	sans bouger	*without moving*
	sans qu'il l'aperçût	*without his noticing it*
until	jusqu'à la fin	*until the end*
	jusqu'à ce qu'il fût sorti	*until he had gone out*
unless	à moins de tomber, j'y arriverai	*unless I fall, I shall get there*
	à moins qu'il ne tombe, tout ira bien	*unless he falls, all will be well*
for fear of	il hésitait, de peur (crainte) de tomber	*he hesitated, for fear of falling*
	je me tus, de peur (crainte) qu'il ne tombât	*I kept silent, for fear of his falling*

(*d*) Note, similarly, ways of expressing purpose:

(i) No change of subject (English *in order to, so as to*)—**pour** or **afin de** with Infinitive, or **de façon (manière) à** in the sense of *in such a way as to*:

Il le dit pour (afin de) prévenir les autres.
He said it to (in order to, so as to) warn the others.
Il tendait son mouchoir de manière à cacher la lettre.
He held out his handkerchief, so as to conceal the letter.

(ii) Change of subject (English *in order that, so that*)—**pour que** or **afin que** with Subjunctive:

257

Il le dit pour que (afin que) les autres entendissent la vérité.
He said it in order that (so that) the others should hear the truth.

The sense of the English *so that*, meaning *in such a way that*, when it expresses a *purpose*,[1] is conveyed by **de sorte (façon, manière) que** with Subjunctive:

Il le dit de sorte que les autres le comprissent.
He said it so that (in such a way that) the others should understand it.

[1] When *so that* expresses a *consequence*, it is conveyed by **de sorte que**, &c., followed by the Indicative:

Il ne dit rien, de sorte que les autres s'inquiétèrent.
He said nothing, so that the others became anxious.

XXII. QUESTIONS AND ANSWERS

242. Direct Question with No Interrogative Word

(e.g. Has he gone? Is the man there?)

(a) If the subject is a Personal Pronoun (or **on** or **ce**), subject and verb are inverted, and linked by a hyphen (*Simple Inversion*):[1]

Me reconnaissez-vous?	L'as-tu vue?
Do you recognize me?	*Did you see her?*
Ne doit-on pas descendre?	Est-ce singulier?
Shouldn't one go down?	*Is it strange?*

(b) If the subject is any other pronoun, or a noun, the subject is not inverted, but is repeated by the appropriate subject-pronoun attached to the verb as follows (*Complex Inversion*):

La chambre était-elle ouverte?
Was the room open?
Les autres sont-ils partis aussi?　　　*Have the others gone too?*

(c) Either of the above types of question may be introduced by **Est-ce que?** The order of the rest of the sentence is then that of a statement. This construction is particularly common in speech:

Est-ce que vous allez continuer comme ça? (Labiche et Martin)
Are you going to go on like that?
Est-ce que ces dames sont prêtes? (Labiche et Martin)
Are these ladies ready?

---

[1] For reasons of sound, the inversion of **je** in the Present Indicative, as in **aimé-je? prends-je?** &c., is fairly rare, the *est-ce que* construction (see 242 (c)) being preferred in speech and writing. But **ai-je? dis-je? dois-je? fais-je? suis-je? vais-je? vois-je? veux-je?** are in common use; also **puis-je**, which is preferred to **peux-je?**

-t- is inserted between verb and pronoun subject where the verb ends in a vowel: **parle-t-il? va-t-elle? ira-t-on?**

(*d*) Very frequently in speech, and also in writing, such questions are asked simply by giving the statement form an interrogative intonation (shown in writing by the question-mark):

Tu ne déjeunes pas avec nous? (Daudet)
Aren't you having dinner with us?

243. Direct Question Introduced by Interrogative Word

(e.g. *Who is there? What has happened? Why (when, &c.) did he go?*)

(*a*) If the question is introduced by **qui? quel? lequel?** as subject or complement, they precede the verb:

Qui étaient mes prétendants? (Pagnol)
Who were my suitors?
Quelles sont vos relations habituelles? (Pagnol)
What are your usual contacts?
Lequel partira le premier?
Which will leave first?

(*b*) If the question is introduced by **que?** noun and pronoun subjects follow the verb (Simple Inversion):

Que vous a-t-il dit? (Pagnol)
What did he say to you?
Que doit penser ce jeune homme? (Mérimée)
What must this young man be thinking?

(*c*) Otherwise:

(i) If the subject is a Personal Pronoun (or **on** or **ce**), there simple inversion of subject and verb:

Qui ont-ils retenu?   A quoi pensez-vous?
Whom did they keep behind?   *What are you thinking of?*
Quel âge as-tu?
How old are you?
Pourquoi n'attaque-t-on pas? (Daudet)
Why don't they attack?

(ii) If the subject is any other pronoun, or a noun:

1. Complex inversion (see 242 (b)) is required:
after **pourquoi?**

> Pourquoi le docteur Knock refuserait-il? (Romains)
> *Why should Doctor Knock refuse?*

if the verb has an object (other than a reflexive pronoun):

> Qui ton frère a-t-il amené?   *Whom did your brother bring?*
> Comment ce dernier paiera-t-il sa part? (Maurois)
> *How will the latter pay for his share?*
> Quand les ouvriers l'ont-ils commencé?
> *When did the workmen begin it?*

or if the sense of the verb is completed otherwise:

> Les cloches d'Alsace seraient-elles en retard? (Bazin)
> *Would the chimes of Alsace be behind?*

and, preferably, with a compound tense:

> Par qui cette nouvelle a-t-elle été annoncée?
> *By whom was this piece of news announced?*

2. Elsewhere, simple and complex inversion are alternative:

> De quoi s'effrayent les femmes? (Balzac)
> *What are women frightened of?*
> Combien de temps durera cette plaisanterie? (Musset)
> *How long will this joke go on?*
> Quand tout cela finirait-il? (Daudet)
> *When would all this finish?*

(d) Where questions are introduced by the longer Interrogative Pronouns (**qui est-ce qui? qu'est-ce que?** &c.), or by **quand? pourquoi?** &c., followed by **est-ce que,** the order of the rest of the sentence is then that of a statement.

This construction is especially frequent in speech, particularly to avoid the awkward inversions as in 243 (c) (ii):

> Qu'est-ce que vous dites?   *What are you saying?*
> Qui est-ce que le gouverneur a félicité?
> *Whom did the governor congratulate?*
> Pourquoi est-ce que l'auto n'est pas restée ici?
> *Why didn't the car stay here?*

244. Indirect Question Introduced by *si*

An indirect question which queries the action of the verb itself is introduced by **si**, without inversion.

Je me demande si vous me reconnaissez.
I wonder if you recognize me.
Il ne savait pas si la chambre était ouverte.
He did not know if (whether) the room was open.

245. Indirect Question Introduced by Interrogative Word

(*a*) There is no inversion:

(i) If the subject is a Personal Pronoun (or **on** or **ce**):

Il n'a pas dit qui il avait interrogé.
He did not say whom he had questioned.
Je ne sais ce que vous en pensez (Musset).
I don't know what you think of it.
J'ignore pourquoi je vous aime (Pagnol).
I don't know why I love you.
Tu sais dans quelle position je me trouvais (Augier et Sandeau).
You know the position I was in.

(ii) If **qui, ce qui, quel, lequel** are the subject or complement:

Je ne sais
⎧ qui l'a fait.
⎨ qui vous êtes.
⎩ ce qui s'est passé.
  quel est cet individu.
  lequel est le mien.

I don't know
⎧ who did it.
⎨ who you are.
⎩ what happened.
  who that individual is.
  which is mine.

(iii) In the indirect form of such questions as in 243 (*c*) (ii) (the *est-ce que* construction cannot be used in indirect questions):

J'ignore
⎧ qui ton frère a amené.
⎨ pourquoi le docteur Knock refuserait.
⎩ comment ce dernier paiera sa part.
  quand les ouvriers l'ont commencé.

(*b*) Otherwise a noun subject is usually inverted where the normal order would result in a lame ending to the sound of the sentence:

Il m'a dit où se trouvait l'hôtel de ville.
He told me where the town hall was.
Figurez-vous ce que souffrent ces infortunés!
Think what these unfortunate people are suffering!

246. Other Question Idioms

(*a*) The kind of question which seeks confirmation of a statement just made it rendered in French only by **n'est-ce pas?**

C'est la femme du capitaine, n'est-ce pas? (Bazin)
It is the captain's wife, isn't it?
Il t'a fait de beaux discours, n'est-ce pas? (Musset)
He made you pretty speeches, didn't he?
Ils ont été parfaits, n'est-ce pas? (Bazin)
They were perfect, weren't they?
Tu ne tarderas pas, n'est-ce pas?
You won't be long, will you?

(*b*) The kind of English question which expresses polite interest in what has been said is conveyed variously in French, e.g.:

Il a de beaux meubles. Vraiment?
He has some beautiful furniture. Has he?
J'ai dû l'attendre deux mois. Pas possible!
I had to wait two months for it. Did you really?

(*c*) Note also the French idioms for short questions of the following kind:

J'étais en retard. Et vous?
I was late. Were you (What about you)?
Les grands bagages restent là. Et les autres?
The heavy luggage stops there. What about the rest?
Sortez-vous ou non?
Are you going out or aren't you?

247. Answers

(a) **Oui** = *Yes*; **non** = *no*. **Si** = *yes*, when this has a contra-dictory effect:

Êtes-vous là? Oui.   L'a-t-il permis? Non.
Are you there? Yes.   *Did he allow it? No.*
Retirez-vous, oui ou non?   (Labiche et Martin)
Do you withdraw, yes or no?
Il n'y a pas de couvercle? Si, dans le tiroir.
Is there no lid? Yes, in the drawer.

(b) **Oui, non,** and **si** may be variously reinforced, with some such senses as those given:

Mais oui!	*Oh yes!*	Mais non!	*Oh no!*
Oui vraiment!	*Yes indeed!*	Non pas!	*Not at all!*
Mais si!	*Oh yes (it is)!*	Mon dieu non!	*No, indeed!*
Si vraiment!	*Yes indeed (it is)!*	Que (non) pas!	*Definitely not!*

(c) The single answers **oui, non,** or **si** tend to be regarded as abrupt, and are frequently modified by, for example, a word of address, or by repeating the verb of the question. These are also the French equivalents of such English answers as: *Yes, he was. No. I didn't*:

Cette place est libre? Oui, monsieur. (*or*) Oui, elle est libre.
Is this place free? Yes (it is).
Est-ce que ton frère l'a fait? Non, maman. (*or*) Non, il ne l'a pas fait.
Did your brother do it? No (he didn't).
Tu ne pars pas? Si, je pars.
You aren't going away? Yes, I am.

(d) Note also the use of **oui** and **non** in e.g.:

Je crois que oui,[1] que non.   Il répondit que oui, que non.
I think so, I think not.   *He answered yes, no.*
Vous verrez que non (Musset).   *You will see I won't.*

---

[1] There is no elision before **oui**.

XXIII. NEGATION

248. *non* and *pas*

(*a*) **Non** is the French word for direct negative answers (see 247).

(*b*) **Non** is, in careful language, the word which negatives components of the sentence other than the verb, i.e. *nouns, noun clauses, pronouns, adjectives, &c.* It may be reinforced by **pas**:

Le clerc, non moins étonné, salua le colonel (Balzac).
The clerk, no less astonished, bowed to the colonel.
Ils virent non pas des hommes, mais des bêtes (Dumas).
They saw not men, but animals.
J'ai remarqué qu'il était absent, mais non qu'il avait emporté le sac.
I noticed that he was absent, but not that he had taken the bag away.

In familiar language, **pas** alone is frequently found:

Pas par là !
Not that way!
Ah non, pas moi !
Oh no, not me!
Un très gros paquet, mais pas très lourd (France).
A very big parcel, but not very heavy.

249. Forms of Negative Expressions *ne . . . pas*, &c.

The principal negative expressions which *accompany a verb* are formed by **ne** combined with one or other of the following words:

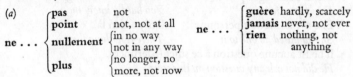

(*a*)

ne . . .	pas	not	ne . . .	guère	hardly, scarcely
	point	not, not at all		jamais	never, not ever
	nullement	in no way / not in any way		rien	nothing, not anything
	plus	no longer, no more, not now			

265

(b)

ne . . .	personne	{ nobody / not anybody
	que	only
	aucun	{ no (adj.)
	nul	{ none (of)
	pas un	{ not any (of)

| ne . . . | nulle part | { nowhere / not anywhere |
| | ni (. . . ni) | { neither . . . nor / not either . . . or |

NOTES

1. **Point** is now mainly used in literary language. Elsewhere *not* is rendered by **pas** and *not at all* by, for example, **pas du tout, certainement pas.**

2. **Pas un** has a stronger force than **aucun** or **nul,** and conveys the idea of *not (a single) one.*

3. **Personne** and **rien** are masculine singular pronouns. (But the noun **une personne,** meaning *a person* (of either sex), is feminine.)

4. **Aucun, nul,** and **pas un** have regular feminine forms. They may be pronouns or adjectives, and are normally used in the singular only.

5. **Non plus** may be found reinforcing some of the above expressions in the sense of *(not, nor) . . . either.* (See examples in 250 (b) (i), (c), 252 (a).)

6. A preceding **de** is required with adjectives and participles qualifying **rien** or **personne**:

Je ne sais rien de meilleur (Maupassant). *I know nothing better.*
Il n'y a personne d'intéressé. *There is nobody interested.*

250. Position of *ne . . . pas,* &c.

(a) With a *simple tense,* or with the *imperative,* **ne** and **pas,** &c., are separated by the verb and any conjunctive pronoun objects:

Ne m'interrogez pas.   Tu ne me connais guère.
Don't question me.   *You hardly know me.*
Elle n'y admettait personne.   Il n'y a rien là.
She admitted no one to it.   *There is nothing there.*
Il ne fit aucune question à ce sujet (Mérimée).
He did not ask any question on this score.

(b) With a *compound tense*, or *perfect infinitive*:

(i) **Ne** and **pas,** and other expressions in 249 (a), are separated by the auxiliary and any conjunctive pronoun objects:

Il ne l'a pas trouvé non plus.
He did not find it either (Nor did he find it).
Je n'y avais jamais réfléchi (Vigny).
I had never thought about it.
Je suis content de n'avoir pas vu ça (Bazin).
I am glad not to have seen that.

(ii) **Personne,** and other expressions in 249 (b), follow the Past Participle (but see also (e) below):

Il n'en a découvert nulle trace.
He discovered no trace of it.
Il est stupide de n'avoir renseigné personne.
It is stupid not to have informed anybody.

(c) With an *interrogative tense* the position is as in (a) or (b) above, as required, except for the presence of the pronoun subject, which is attached to the verb:

Ne suis-je pas ton frère? (Musset)
Am I not your brother?
N'as-tu pas souri tout à l'heure? (Musset)
Didn't you smile a moment ago?
Votre collègue n'a-t-il obtenu aucune réponse non plus?
Didn't your colleague get any answer either?

(d) With a *present infinitive*:

(i) **Ne** and **pas,** and other expressions in 249 (a) (including usually **rien**), stand together before the infinitive:

Elle aima mieux ne pas la revoir (France).
She preferred not to see her again.
Le meilleur moyen de ne rien comprendre (Barrès).
The best way not to understand anything.

(ii) **Ne** and **personne,** and other expressions in 249 (*b*), are separated by the infinitive:

Bien surpris de ne voir personne (Saint-Exupéry).
Much surprised not to see anyone.

(*e*) The exact position of **personne**, and other expressions in 249 (*b*), is determined by the balance and sense of the sentence. While they most frequently follow the verb immediately as in the examples above, they may also occupy a later position, e.g.:

Il n'a montré cette carte à personne.
He has shown this map to no one.
Je n'ai trouvé ton cousin nulle part à la gare.
I did not find your cousin anywhere in the station.

(*f*) Similarly, the position of **que**, in the expression **ne . . . que**, is immediately before the words to which the idea of *only* applies:

Je ne vous demande que votre amitié (Pagnol).
I ask only for your friendship.
Elles ne sont comme cela que le dimanche (Bazin).
They are like that only on Sundays.
Vous ne m'avez fait la cour que pour vous divertir (Musset).
You have only been paying attentions to me to amuse yourself.

N.B. **Ne . . . que** cannot be used to apply the idea of *only* to the subject (including an infinitive subject), and some other rendering is required, e.g.:

Un seul homme peut l'approcher (Bazin).
Only one man can get near him.
Il n'y a que les imbéciles qui font cela.
Only fools do that.
Rien que le voir me ferait du bien.
Only to see him would do me good.

Nor can it apply to the action of the verb itself. This sense is usually conveyed by the expression **ne faire que**:

L'autre ne fit que rire (Daudet).
The other only laughed.

(g) The constructions of **ne ... ni ... ni** should be noted (see also 251):

> Tu ne voulais revoir ni ce bois ni cette fontaine (Musset).
> *You did not want to see either this wood or this fountain again.*
> Ni Toussaint ni son fils n'entendirent (Bazin).
> *Neither Toussaint nor his son heard.*
> Il ne boit, ni ne fume, ni ne danse.[1]
> *He neither drinks, nor smokes, nor dances.*

(h) **Jamais, rien, personne, aucun, nul, pas un,** and **ni** (see (g) above) may begin a sentence, **ne** remaining in its usual place:

> Personne ne le saura.   Pas un mot ne fut dit.
> *Nobody will know it.*   *Not a word was said.*
> Aucun de mes élèves n'y a jamais réussi (Pagnol).
> *None of my pupils has ever succeeded in it.*

N.B. There is no inversion after **jamais**:

> Jamais je n'oublierai son regard farouche (Mérimée).
> *Never shall I forget his wild look.*

251. Double Negatives

Where the meaning permits, the sense of **ne** may be completed by a combination of, e.g. **jamais rien, plus personne,** &c. The order of the combinations is that of the lists in 249, e.g. **jamais** precedes **rien, rien** precedes **personne, personne** precedes **nulle part.**

> N.B. The sense does not permit any combination with **pas** or **point,** except that these may be followed by **ni,** and **ne ... pas que** may be used to render *not only* (see example in 78 (d)).
> On ne voyait plus personne.
> *They could no longer see anyone.*

---

[1] Note that, when a series of finite verbs is negatived by **ne ... ni ... ni,** correct usage requires the presence of **ne** with each.

Les grandes personnes ne comprennent jamais rien (Saint-
Exupéry).
Grown-ups never understand anything.

Mon dessein n'est pas de réformer notre langue, ni d'abolir
des mots (Vaugelas).
My intention is not to reform our language, nor to abolish words.

252. Omission of *ne*

(*a*) In a phrase, where there is no verb, the negative expressions
in 249 may be present without *ne*, but they *retain their negative force*:

Vous vous réconcilierez avec elle? Jamais! (Labiche et Martin)
You will make it up with her? Never!

Personne. Nul signe de vie (Mérimée).
No one. Not a sign of life.

Je n'en sais rien encore. Ni moi non plus (Labiche et Martin).
I know nothing about it yet. Nor do I. (No more do I).

(*b*) (i) When used with a verb, some of the expressions in 249
may be present without *ne*, but they are then *not negative in force*:

Si le modèle a jamais existé (Mérimée).
If the model ever existed.

(ii) In particular, **rien, personne,** and **aucun** are found, without
ne, in the senses of *anything, anybody, any,* &c., where there is a
negative idea in the context, especially after **sans.** *Or,* after **sans,** is
rendered by **ni**:

Aussi se garda-t-il de parler à personne (Maurois).
Therefore he refrained from speaking to anybody.

Il défendit expressément qu'on touchât à rien (France).
He expressly forbade anyone to touch anything.

Dites-moi si vous savez rien de plus navrant (Daudet).
Tell me if you know anything more heartbreaking.

Sans avoir rien trouvé.
Without having found anything.

Il est sorti sans pardessus ni chapeau.
He has gone out without coat or hat.

253. Omission of *pas*

(*a*) **Pas** is omitted in certain set expressions, e.g.:

Il n'importe.   A Dieu ne plaise!   Qu'à cela ne tienne!
It doesn't matter.   *God forbid!*   *That is no obstacle!*
N'ayez crainte!
Never fear!

(*b*) In literary style, **pas** is frequently omitted:

(i) With **pouvoir, cesser, oser**, and **je ne saurais** (= *I cannot*) governing a positive infinitive (expressed or understood):

Je ne puis l'accepter.   Je ne puis.
I cannot accept it.   *I can't.*
Des idées qu'il n'osait exprimer (Maurois).
Ideas which he did not dare to express.

(ii) With **savoir** introducing a clause:

Je ne sais comment cela se fait (Maurois).
I don't know how it comes about.
Je ne sais trop ce qu'elle est (France).
I don't know exactly what it is.

(iii) In conditional clauses introduced by **si**:

Si ce ne fut mon discours, c'était ma pensée (France).
If it wasn't what I said, it was what I thought.

Quand voulez-vous qu'il travaille, si ce n'est la nuit? (M. Renard)
When do you expect him to work, if not at night?

(*c*) When used with **depuis que, il y a ... que, voilà ... que, pas** (or **point** or **plus**) is present with a simple tense, but omitted with a compound tense. Thus e.g.:

Il y a deux ans que je ne le vois plus.
Voilà deux ans que je ne l'ai vu.
Deux ans se sont écoulés depuis que je ne l'ai vu.
I have not seen him for two years.
It is two years since I saw him.

ALPHABETICAL LIST OF VERB CONSTRUCTIONS

Constructions with Object and with Infinitive

(For verbs taking subjunctive see 45 ff.)

qn. = quelqu'un   qc. = quelque chose
so. = someone   sg. = something
after à: (D) = Dative (see 51 ff.); (ND) = Not Dative (see 55)

s'abstenir de qc., de faire qc.	abstain from sg., from doing sg.
accuser qn. de qc., de faire qc.	accuse so. of sg., of doing sg.
acheter qc. à (D) qn.	buy sg. from so.
achever qc., de faire qc.	finish sg., doing sg.
il s'agit de qc., de faire qc.	it is a question of sg., of doing sg.
aider qn. à faire qc.	help so. to do sg.
aimer, see 30.	
(aller, see 55), aller faire qc.	go and do sg.
s'amuser de qc., à faire qc.	be amused at sg., amuse oneself doing sg.
apercevoir qc.	notice sg.
s'apercevoir de qc.	perceive sg.
apprendre qc., à faire qc.	learn sg., to do sg.
apprendre qc. à (D) qn., à qn. à faire qc.	teach so. sg., so. to do sg.
approcher qc., de qc.	bring sg. near, approach sg.
s'approcher de qc.	approach sg.
(arriver, see 55), arriver à faire qc.	succeed in doing sg.
assister qn., assister à qc.	assist so., be present at sg.
attendre qc., s'attendre à (ND) qc.	wait for sg., expect sg.
s'attendre à faire qc.	expect to do sg.
avertir qn. de qc., de faire qc.	warn so. of sg., to do sg.
avoir beau faire qc.	do sg. in vain.
se battre avec/contre qn.	fight (with) so.
blâmer qn. de qc./qc. à (D) qn., qn. de faire qc.	blame so. for sg., for doing sg.
cacher qc. à (D) qn.	hide sg. from so.
cesser de faire qc.	cease doing sg.

charger qc. de qc., qn. de faire qc.	load sg. with sg., entrust so. w doing sg.
se charger de faire qc.	undertake to do sg.
commander qc., à (D) qn. de faire qc.	order sg., so. to do sg.
commencer qc., à/de faire qc.	begin sg., to do sg.
comparer qc. à (ND)/avec qc.	compare sg. to/with sg.
compter sur qn., faire qc.	count on so., on doing sg.
condamner qn. à faire qc.	condemn so. to do sg.
conseiller qc. à (D) qn., à qn. de faire qc.	advise so. sg., so. to do sg.
consentir à (D) qc., à faire qc.	consent to sg., to do sg.
consister en qc., à faire qc.	consist in sg., in doing sg.
consoler qn. de qc.	console so. for sg.
continuer qc., à/de faire qc.	continue sg., doing sg.
convenir à qn.	be suitable for so.
convenir de qc., de faire qc.	agree about sg., to do sg.
craindre qc., de faire qc.	fear sg., doing sg.
(croire, see 58), croire faire qc.	think one is doing sg.
décider qc./de qc., de faire qc., qn. à faire qc.	decide sg., to do sg., induce so. to c sg.
se décider à faire qc.	make up one's mind to do sg.
défendre qc. à (D) qn., à qn. de faire qc.	forbid so. sg., so. to do sg.
se défier de qn.	mistrust so.
déjeuner de qc.	lunch on sg.
demander qc. à (D) qn., with infin. see 30.	ask so. for sg.
se dépêcher de faire qc.	make haste to do sg.
dépendre de qc.	depend on sg.
déplaire à (D) qn.	displease so.
désirer qc., faire qc.	desire sg., to do sg.
devoir, see 64.	
dîner de qc.	dine on sg.
dire qc. à (D) qn., with infin. see 58.	tell so. sg.
se diriger vers qc.	make one's way to sg.
disposer de qc.	dispose of sg.
dissuader qn. de faire qc.	dissuade so. from doing sg.
douter de qc.	doubt sg.
se douter de qc.	suspect sg.
échanger qc. pour/contre qc.	exchange sg. for sg.
écouter qc., qn. faire qc.	listen to sg., to so. doing sg.
s'efforcer de/à faire qc.	make an effort to do sg.
empêcher qc., qn. de faire qc.	prevent sg., so. from doing sg.
employer qc. à faire qc.	employ sg. for doing sg.
emprunter qc. à (D) qn.	borrow sg. from so.
encourager qc., qn. à faire qc.	encourage sg., so. to do sg.

enlever qc. à (D) qn. — take sg. away from so.

enseigner qc. à (D) qn., à qn. à faire qc. — teach so. sg., so. to do sg.

entendre qc., with infin. see 27 (f), (g) (ii). — hear sg.

entreprendre qc., de faire qc. — undertake sg., to do sg.

entrer dans qc. — enter sg.

envoyer qc., qn. faire qc. — send sg., so. to do sg.

espérer qc., faire qc. — hope for sg., to do sg.

essayer qc., de faire qc. — try sg., to do sg.

s'étonner de qc., de faire qc. — be astonished at sg., at doing sg.

éviter qc., de faire qc. — avoid sg., doing sg.

exceller en/dans/à qc., à faire qc. — excel at sg., at doing sg.

excuser qc., qn. de qc., de faire qc. — excuse sg., so. sg., doing sg.

s'excuser de qc., de faire qc. — apologize for sg., for doing sg.

se fâcher de qc., de faire qc. — be annoyed at sg., at doing sg.

se fâcher contre qn. — be annoyed with so.

se fâcher avec qn. — fall out with so.

faillir faire qc. — nearly do sg.

faire qc., and with infin. see 27 (g) and 54. — do sg.

se fatiguer à faire qc. — wear oneself out doing sg.

être fatigué de qc., de faire qc. — be tired of sg., of doing sg.

falloir (il faut), see 65.

feindre qc., de faire qc. — feign sg., pretend to do sg.

féliciter qn. de qc. — congratulate so. on sg.

se fier à (D) qn. — trust so.

finir qc., de faire qc. — finish sg., doing sg.

forcer qn. à/de faire qc. — compel so. to do sg.

fournir qc. à (D) qn./qn. de qc. — supply so. with sg.

s'habituer à (ND) qc., à faire qc. — become used to sg., to doing sg.

se hâter de faire qc. — make haste to do sg.

hésiter à faire qc. — hesitate to do sg.

s'intéresser à (ND) qc. — be interested in sg.

inviter qn. à qc., à faire qc. — invite so. to sg., to do sg.

jouer, see 58.

jouir de qc. — enjoy (=have use of) sg.

jurer de faire qc. — swear to do sg.

laisser qc., and with infin. see 27 (g) and 54. — leave sg.

louer qc., qn. de qc. — praise sg., so. for sg.

(manquer, see 58), manquer de faire qc. — fail to do/nearly do sg.

se marier à/avec qn. — marry so.

méditer qc., de faire qc. — meditate sg., doing sg.

se méfier de qn. — mistrust so.

mêler qc. à (D) qc.

mix sg. with sg.

menacer qn., de faire qc.

threaten so., to do sg.

mériter qc., de faire qc.

deserve sg., to do sg.

se mettre à faire qc.

start to do sg.

se moquer de qn.

make fun of so.

mourir de qc., de faire qc.

die of sg., of doing sg.

négliger qc., de faire qc.

neglect sg., to do sg.

nuire à (D) qn.

harm so.

obéir à (D) qn.

obey so.

obliger qn. à ⎱ faire qc.
être obligé de⎰

compel so. ⎱ to do sg.
be compelled⎰

offrir qc. à qn., de faire qc.

offer so. sg., to do sg.

omettre qc., de faire qc.

omit sg., to do sg.

ordonner qc., à (D) qn. de faire qc.

order sg., so. to do sg.

oser qc., faire qc.

dare sg., to do sg.

ôter qc., qc. à (D) qn.

remove sg., take sg. away from so.

oublier qc., de faire qc.

forget sg., to do sg.

paraître faire qc.

seem to be doing sg.

pardonner qc. à (D) qn., à qn. de faire qc.

forgive so. sg., so. for doing sg.

parvenir à (ND) qc., à faire qc.

reach sg., succeed in doing sg.

se passer de qc.

do without sg.

payer, see 58.

pendre à (ND) qc.

hang from so.

penser, see 58, and with infin., see 30.

permettre qc. à (D) qn., à qn. de faire qc.

allow so. sg., so. to do sg.

persister dans qc., à faire qc.

persist in sg., in doing sg.

persuader qn., qn. de qc./qc. à (D) qn., qn. de faire qc.

persuade so., so. of sg., so. to do sg.

se plaindre de qc., de faire qc.

complain of sg., of doing sg.

plaire à (D) qn.

please so.

pouvoir, see 66.

préférer qc. à (D) qc., faire qc.

prefer sg. to sg., to do sg.

prendre qc. à (D) qn., and see 57 (b).

take sg. from so.

prendre garde à (ND) qc., and with infin. see 30.

beware of sg.

se préparer à faire qc.

make ready to do sg.

prévenir qn. de qc.

warn so. of sg.

prier qn. de faire qc.

beg so. to do sg.

profiter de qc.

profit by sg.

promettre qc. à (D) qn., à qn. de faire qc.

promise so. sg., so. to do sg.

punir qn. de qc., de faire qc.

punish so. for sg., for doing sg.

se rappeler qc.

recall sg.

275

récompenser qn. de qc.	reward so. for sg.
réfléchir à (ND) qc.	reflect about sg.
refuser qc., de faire qc.	refuse sg., to do sg.
regarder qc., qn. faire qc.	look at sg., watch so. doing sg.
regretter qc., de faire qc.	regret sg., doing sg.
se réjouir de qc.	rejoice at sg.
remercier qn. de qc., de faire qc.	thank so. for sg., for doing sg.
renoncer à (ND) qc.	renounce sg.
se repentir de qc.	repent of sg.
répondre à (D) qc./qn.	answer sg./so.
reprocher qc. à (D) qn., qn. de faire qc.	reproach so. with sg., so. for doing sg.
résister à (D) qc.	resist sg.
ressembler à (D) qn.	resemble so.
réussir à qc., à faire qc.	succeed in sg., in doing sg.
rire de qc.	laugh at sg.
risquer qc., de faire qc.	risk sg., doing sg.
savoir, see 67.	
sembler faire qc.	seem to do sg.
sentir qc., faire qc.	feel sg., feel sg. done.
(servir, see 58), servir à faire qc.	be useful for doing sg.
songer à (ND) qc., à faire qc.	think of sg., of doing sg.
souhaiter qc., faire qc.	wish sg., wish to do sg.
soupçonner qn. de qc., de faire qc.	suspect so. of sg., of doing sg.
souper de qc.	sup on sg.
se souvenir de qc.	remember sg.
succéder à (D) qn.	succeed so.
suffire à (D) qc., à faire qc.	be sufficient for sg., for doing sg.
il suffit de faire qc.	it is sufficient to do sg.
survivre à (D) qn.	survive so.
tâcher de faire qc.	try to do sg.
taire qc.	be silent about sg.
tarder, see 30.	
tendre à faire qc.	tend to do sg.
tenir qc., tenir à faire qc.	hold sg., be anxious to do sg.
tenter qc., de faire qc.	attempt sg., to do sg.
trembler de qc., de faire qc.	tremble at sg., at doing sg.
user, see 58.	
valoir, see 68.	
se vanter de qc., de faire qc.	boast of sg., of doing sg.
venir, see 58, and with infin. 30.	
vivre de qc.	live on sg.
voir qc. and with infin. see 27 (f) and 54.	see sg.
voler qc. à (D) qn.	steal sg. from so.
vouloir qc. and with infin., see 69.	want sg.

SOME FRENCH PREPOSITIONAL USES

A (for idioms of price, rate, distance, see 72, 151, 152)

1. Place to or at which (with Geographical Names see 75)	Aller **au** marché Le vase tomba **à** terre Il descendit **à** la gare Rester **à** genoux	Go **to** (the) market The vase fell **to** the ground He got out **at** the station Remain **on** one's knees
2. Location (cf. **dans** 1) including parts of body	Demeurer **à** la campagne **Au** premier étage Son fusil **à** l'épaule Une canne **à** la main Avoir mal **au** pied	Live **in** the country **On** the first floor His gun **on** his shoulder A stick **in** one's hand Have a pain **in** one's foot
3. *In contact with*	Suspendu **au** mur	Hanging **on** the wall
4. Time to or at which (with days, dates, time of day see 142, 145)	**Au** commencement de la guerre **Au** temps de Pasteur Du matin **au** soir	**At** the beginning of the war **At** (**in**) the time of Pasteur From morning **to** night
5. Manner (cf. **de** 4, **avec** 2)	**A** voix basse **A** l'espagnole	**In** a low voice **In** the Spanish manner
6. Means (cf. **de** 5, **avec** 3, **par** 6) including means of transport, or method of operation (see also 113 (*a*) (ii))	Aller **à** bicyclette, **à** cheval, **à** pied Traverser **à** la nage Casser **à** coups de marteau Murailles peintes **à** la chaux Un bateau **à** vapeur	Go **by** bicycle, **on** horseback, **on** foot Swim across Break **with** blows of a hammer Whitewashed walls A steamer
7. Purpose (see also 113 (*a*) (ii))	Une tasse **à** thé Quelque chose **à** manger	A tea-cup Something **to** eat
8. Permanent descriptive feature (with parts of body see 73 (*d*) (ii))	Une pièce **à** trois fenêtres La maison **aux** tuiles rouges	A room **with** three windows The house **with** red tiles
9. Possession	Ces souliers sont **à** Jean Un appartement **à** moi	These shoes are John's A flat of my own

10.	Forming infin. phrase defining an adj.	Le premier **à** vous féliciter	The first **to** congratulate you
		Long **à** venir	Long **in** coming
		Facile **à** manier	Easy **to** handle
		Amusant **à** écouter	Amusing **to** listen to
11.	Conditional	**A** vrai dire	**To** tell the truth
		A tout prendre	Considering all things
12.	Invocation	**A** moi! **A** l'assassin!	Help! Murder!
13.	Dative	Montrer, parler **à** quelqu'un	Show **to,** speak **to** somebody
		Demander **à** quelqu'un	Ask **of** somebody
		Impossible **à** un enfant	Impossible **for** a child
14.	Governing infin. dependent on numerous vbs. (see 28)	Réussir **à,** se décider **à** faire	Succeed **in** doing, make up one's mind **to** do

Après

1.	*After* of time	**Après** sa mort	**After** his death
2.	*After* of place where idea of sequence of events	**Après** moi sur la liste	**After** me on the list
		Fermer la porte **après** soi	Shut the door **behind** one
3.	Object pursued	Courir **après** les honneurs	Seek **after** honours

Auprès de

1.	Close proximity, *beside* (cf. **près de** 1)	Il reste **auprès de** sa mère	He stays **beside** his mother
		Il tenait son aide **auprès de** lui	He kept his assistant **with** him
2.	Comparison	Ses maux ne sont rien **auprès des** nôtres	His troubles are nothing **compared to** ours
3.	*In the sight of*	Fort estimé **auprès de** ses chefs	Of high standing **with** his superiors

Avant (de)

1.	*Before* of time, plus **de** before infin.	**Avant** le soir	**Before** evening
		Avant de s'asseoir	**Before** sitting down
2.	*Before* of place where an idea of sequence of events	Il y a deux arrêts **avant** Dijon	There are two stops **before** Dijon
3.	Preference (cf. **sur** 4)	La patrie **avant** tout	One's country **above** all

278

Avec

1. Accompanying	Venez **avec** moi	Come **with** me
2. Accompanying circumstance or feature (cf. **à** 8, **de** 4)	Parler **avec** amertume	Speak bitterly
	Il le dit **avec** un sourire	He said it **with** a smile
	Cette maison **avec** son joli jardin	This house **with** its pretty garden
3. Means or instrument, usually where in some way emphatic (cf. **de** 5, **par** 1)	Je l'ai coupé **avec** le canif que je portais	I cut it **with** the penknife I was carrying
	Avec un peu plus de patience on l'aura	**With** a little more patience one will get it

Chez

1. At or to the abode of	Rester **chez** nous	Stay at our **house,** at (our) **home**
	Trouver **chez** le quincaillier	Find at the ironmonger's
	Aller **chez** l'épicier	Go to the grocer's
	Revenir de **chez** eux	Return from their **house**
2. *Among, with,* referring to characteristics or customs	**Chez** les honnêtes gens cela ne se fait pas	**Among** respectable people that is not done
	Chez lui c'est une habitude	**With** him it is a habit
3. *In the works of*	Il n'y en a pas **chez** La Fontaine	There are not any **in** La Fontaine(**'s writings**)

Dans

(**Dans** is not normally found governing nouns which have no defining word such as an Article, Possessive, &c.)

1. Place in or into which, especially where idea of enclosure emphatic (cf. **à** 2)	**Dans** l'armoire	**In** the cupboard
	Porter **dans** les bras	Carry **in** one's arms
	Dans un fauteuil	**In** an arm-chair
	Sortir **dans** la rue	Go out **into** the street
	Habiter **dans** Paris même	Live right **in** Paris
2. Place or circumstances in which, where noun has defining word (cf. **en** 1, 2, 8)	**Dans** un train rapide	**In** an express train
	Dans son enfance	**In** his childhood
	Dans l'histoire	**In** history
	Il vivait **dans** une joie fiévreuse	He lived **in** feverish happiness
3. Time at the end of which (cf. **en** 3)	Les soldes commencent **dans** deux jours	The sales begin **in** two days' **time**
	Dans quelques jours ils auront disparu	**In** a few days they will have disappeared

4. *Out of*, with vbs. of taking, &c. (see 57 (*b*))	Prendre **dans** sa poche	Take **from** one's pocket
	Lire **dans** des livres	Read **from** books

De

(for uses with Time of Day, Dimensions, &c., see 142 (*d*), 150, 152 (*c*))

1. Point of departure in space, time, or number	S'éloigner **de** la ville	Go away **from** the town
	Loin **de** la maison	Far **from** the house
	Du matin au soir	**From** morning to night
	De jour en jour	**From** day to day
	De 20 à 30 personnes	**From** 20 to 30 people
2. *From* or *to* with expressions of direction	Aller } {**de** tous côtés Venir } {**de** toutes parts	Come **from**} all directions Go **in** }
3. Origin	Cela vient **de** ton père	That comes **from** your father
	Une blessure **de** la guerre de 1914	A wound **from** the 1914 war
4. Manner (cf. **avec** 2, **à** 5) especially with **manière** and **façon**	Répondre **d'**une voix basse	Answer **in** a low voice
	D'une manière (façon) agréable	**In** a pleasant manner
	De toutes ses forces	**With** all one's might
	D'un seul coup	**At** one go
	De la sorte	**In** such a way
5. Agent, instrument, means, cause, especially figurative or not emphatic (cf. **avec** 3, **par** 1)	Accompagné **d'**un enfant	Accompanied **by** a child
	Ce tableau est **de** Poussin	This picture is **by** Poussin
	Surmonté **d'**un drapeau	Surmounted **by** a flag
	Frappé **d'**une idée	Struck **by** an idea
	Sauter **de** joie	Jump **for** joy
6. *Of* the name of	La ville **de** Paris	The city **of** Paris
	Le mois **d'**avril	The month **of** April
7. Quality possessed	Un homme **de** génie	A man **of** genius
	Un objet **de** valeur	An object **of** value
8. Material (cf. **en** 5)	Une courroie **de** cuir	A leather strap
9. Contents or composition	Une tasse **de** thé	A cup **of** tea
	Une botte **de** paille	A bundle **of** straw
10. Genitive (including adjectival use—see 84 (*a*), 113 (*a*) (i))	Les amis **de** mon frère	My brother's friends
	La vente **de** la ferme	The sale **of** the farm
	Les vacances **d'**été	The summer holidays
	Un médecin **de** campagne	A country doctor

11.	Forming adjectival expressions which qualify expressions of quantity (cf. 131 (*b*))	Un mot **de** trop	A word too many
		Cinq mille hommes **de** tués	Five thousand men killed
		Trois ans **de** plus	Three years more
12.	Number greater or less than (cf. 132)	Cela a duré plus (moins) **de** deux ans	That lasted more (less) **than** two years
13.	Measure of difference	Plus long **de** trois mètres	Longer **by** three metres
		C'est trop **de** douze	It is twelve too many
14.	Defining superlatives	Les plus belles montagnes **du** monde	The most beautiful mountains **in** the world
		La première fois **de** sa vie	The first time **in** his life
15.	After certain adjs., especially of emotion	Content **de** les voir	Pleased **to** see them
		Fâché **de** l'entendre	Annoyed **at** hearing it
16.	After numerous vbs. (see 29, 56)	Remercier **d'**un service	Thank **for** a service
		Ordonner **de** partir	Order **to** leave

Depuis

1.	*Since* of time	**Depuis** sa mort	**Since** his death
2.	Time elapsed (cf. **pendant** 1, **pour** 2)	Abandonné **depuis** trente-deux ans	Abandoned **for** thirty-two years
		Je suis ici **depuis** trois heures	I have been here **for** three hours
3.	*From* of place or time, especially opposed to **jusqu'à**	**Depuis** les semailles jusqu'à la moisson	**(Right) from** the sowing to the harvest
		L'horizon, **depuis** le château jusqu'aux phares	The horizon, **from** the castle to the lighthouses

Dès

	Point of time at which action begins	**Dès** huit heures	**From** eight o'clock **onwards**
		Dès son enfance	**From** his childhood **up**
		Je le ferai **dès** mon retour	I will do it **as soon as** I return

PREPOSITIONAL USES

En

(for uses with Months, Years, and Seasons see 145 (*c*), 147, 148)

En is usually only found in the following uses when the noun is not particularized by the Article:

1. Place in or into which (cf. **dans** 2) (with Geographical Names see 75 (*b*))	Aller **en** prison Être **en** ville **En** pleine campagne	Go **to** prison Be **in** town **In** the depths of the country
2. Means of transport where idea of *in* is present (cf. **à** 6, **par** 5)	Aller **en** auto, **en** avion	Go **by** car, **by** air
3. Time taken or required (cf. **dans** 3)	On y arrive **en** quelques jours Il fut achevé **en** quatre mois	One gets there **in** a few days It was finished **in** four months
4. Progression	De temps **en** temps De lieu **en** lieu	From time **to** time From place **to** place
5. Material (cf. **de** 8)	Un cendrier **en** cuivre Bâti **en** briques	A copper ash-tray Built **of** bricks
6. Dress	**En** toilette de dimanche	**In** Sunday clothes
7. *In the role or guise of*	Se conduire **en** homme du monde Traiter **en** enfant Vêtu **en** pirate	Behave **like** a man of the world Treat **like** a child Dressed **like** a pirate
8. Figurative *in* (cf. **dans** 2)	**En** sûreté. **En** colère Causer **en** allemand **En** mon pouvoir **En** quelques phrases	**In** safety. **In** anger Chat **in** German **In** my power **In** a few sentences
9. After certain vbs. (see 57)	Consister **en** quelques bottes de paille	Consist **of** a few bundles of straw
10. With gerund (see 35, 237 (*b*) (i)	**En** entrant	**On, while, by** going in

En is found with nouns particularized by the Article normally only in certain set expressions, e.g.:

en l'air	in the air	en l'honneur de	in honour of
en l'an 1900	in the year 1900	en $\left\{\begin{array}{l}\text{la présence}\\\text{l'absence}\end{array}\right\}$ de	in the $\left\{\begin{array}{l}\text{presence}\\\text{absence}\end{array}\right\}$ of
en l'église de Ste Marie		In St. Mary's Church	

282

PREPOSITIONAL USES

(a) *Entre*

1. Places between which	**Entre** Paris et Chartres	**Between** Paris and Chartres
	Entre les barreaux	**Between** the bars
2. *Among* (=**parmi** (des))	Il sera **entre** amis	He will be **among** friends
3. Times between which	**Entre** 9 et 10 heures	**Between** $\begin{cases} \text{9 and 10 o'clock} \\ \text{9 and 10 hours} \end{cases}$
4. Choice	Hésiter **entre** les deux	Hesitate **between** the two
5. Reciprocal	Ils s'aidaient **entre** eux	They helped each other

(b) *D'entre*

1. Partitive *of* before Disjunctive Prons.	Quelques-uns **d'entre** eux	Some **of** (**amongst**) them
2. *From among* (*between*)	Arraché **d'entre** ses griffes	Snatched **from** its claws

(a) *Hors*

1. *Out of, outside,* in certain set expressions	**Hors** ligne	**Out of** the ordinary
	Hors la loi	Outlawed
2. *Except*	Personne **hors** nous	No one **besides** ourselves
	Hors lui on est prêt	**Apart from** him we are ready

(b) *Hors de, au dehors de*

Outside, out of	**Hors de** la ville	**Out of, outside** the town
	Au dehors de la maison	**Outside** the house
	Au dehors de l'Angleterre	**Outside, out of** England
	Hors d'haleine	**Out of** breath

(a) *Jusque*

Extent, mainly with other preps. and certain advbs.	**Jusqu'**ici	**As far as** this. **Up to** now
	Jusque-là	**As far as** that. **Up till** then
	Jusque dans sa chambre	**Right** into his bedroom

283

(b) *Jusqu'à*

1. Extent of place or time, also opposed to **depuis**	**Jusqu'à** la haie	**As far as** the hedge
	Jusqu'à sept heures	**Until** seven o'clock
	Depuis le commencement **jusqu'à** la fin	From the beginning **to** the end
2. Figurative extent	Il ira **jusqu'à** 300 francs	He will go **up to** 300 francs
	Je n'irai pas **jusqu'à** le faire arrêter	I will not go **as far as** having him arrested
	J'ai tout perdu **jusqu'aux** vêtements	I have lost everything, **even** my clothes

Par

1. Agent, instrument, especially if emphatic and/or literal (cf. **de** 5, **avec** 3)	Choisi **par** ses camarades	Chosen **by** his friends
	Tué **par** une chute de terre	Killed **by** a fall of earth
	Faire construire **par** un architecte	Have built **by** an architect
2. Reason	Se marier **par** amour	Marry **for** love
3. Particular circumstances of weather, &c.	Ne sortez pas **par** cette pluie	Don't go out **in** this rain
	Ils partirent **par** une belle matinée de juin	They set off **on** a fine June morning
4. *lying at length on, along, through*	Étendu **par** terre	Stretched out **on** the ground
	L'arbre tomba **par** terre	The tree fell **to** the ground
	Avancer **par** le sentier	Proceed **along** the path
	Errer **par** les rues	Wander **about** the streets
	Par toute la maison	**Through**out the house
	Regarder **par** la fenêtre	Look **through** (**out of**) the window
	Je l'ai su **par** lui	I learnt it **through** him
5. Way, manner (cf. **à** 5, 6)	Venez **par** ici	Come this **way**
	Voyager **par** chemin de fer, **par** Calais	Travel **by** rail, **via** Calais
	Avancer **par** sauts et **par** bonds	Proceed jerkily
6. Distribution	Sortir **par** groupes, **par** deux et trois, deux **par** deux	Come out **in** groups, **in** twos and threes, two **by** two
	Trois fois **par** jour	Three times a day
7. With infin. after **finir** and **commencer**	Finir **par** le perdre tout à fait	Finish **by** losing it completely

Pendant

1. Time during which (cf. **depuis** 2, **pour** 2)	Il sortit **pendant** l'après-midi	He went out **during** the afternoon
	Il y resta **pendant** six ans	He remained there **for** six years
2. Extent of place where an idea of duration of events	Le train ralentit **pendant** deux kilomètres	The train slowed down **for** two kilometres

Pour

1. *Intended for*	Une lettre **pour** vous	A letter **for** you
2. Time intended (cf. **depuis** 2, **pendant** 1)	Il est à Paris **pour** un mois	He is in Paris **for** one month
	Hospitalité **pour** deux nuits	Hospitality **for** two nights
3. Place intended	Partir **pour** l'Amérique	Leave **for** America
	En route **pour** l'Orient	Bound **for** the East
4. *For the sake of*	Mourir **pour** la patrie	Die **for** one's country
5. *On behalf of*	Agir **pour** un autre	Act **for** someone else
6. *In favour of*	Parler **pour** la paix	Speak **in favour of** peace
	Ils sont **pour** nous	They are **on** our **side**
7. *By reason of*	Estimé **pour** sa dureté	Valued **for** its hardness
8. *In exchange for*	Quelque chose **pour** son travail	Something **for** his work
	Rendre coup, **pour** coup	Return blow **for** blow
9. Personal concern	**Pour** moi, j'abstiendrai	Personally, I shall abstain
	Il est clair **pour** moi que ...	It is clear, **as far as** I am **concerned,** that ...
10. *Towards*, after some adjs. of feeling (cf. **vers** 3)	Il a été bon **pour** moi	He has been kind **to** me
	Sois généreux **pour** ces gens	Be generous **to** these people
11. *By way of*	Il l'aura **pour** guide	He will have him **as** a guide
	Pour couverture il avait un sac	**For** a blanket he had a sack
12. *As being*	Il me prend **pour** un sot	He takes me **for** a fool
13. *Considering*	**Pour** son âge, **pour** un enfant, il lit bien	**For** his age, **for** a child, he reads well
14. Purpose, with infin. (see 241 (*d*) (i)) including after **assez** and **trop** (cf. 239 n. 4)	**Pour** l'achever	**In order to** finish it
	Pour n'être pas vu	**So as** not **to** be seen
	Il est assez habile, trop paresseux, **pour** le faire	He is clever enough, too idle, **to** do it

Près de

1.	*Near* of place	**Près de** la ville	**Near** the town
2.	*Nearly* of time or number (see also 142 (*c*))	Il est **près de** midi	It is **nearly** twelve o'clock
		Près de cent hommes	**Nearly** a hundred men
3.	*On the verge of*	**Près de** s'affaisser	**On the verge of** collapse

Sans

(The Article is not present after **sans**, except for the Definite Article in the sense where the English has *the*, see 71 (*a*))

1.	*Without*	**Sans** cadre	**Without** a frame
		Sans nouvelles	**Without** any news
		Sans l'aide de ses parents	**Without** the help of his parents
		Il me regardait **sans** répondre	He looked at me **without** answering
2.	*But for*	**Sans** ce secours inespéré je périssais	**But for** this unexpected assistance I should have perished

Sauf

1.	*Except for*	Aucun bruit, **sauf** le tic-tac de la pendule	No noise, **except** the ticking of the clock
2.	*Except in case of*	**Sauf** accidents	**Barring** accidents
		Sauf correction	**Subject to** correction

(a) Sous

1.	*Under*, literally	**Sous** un immense tilleul	**Under** an immense lime-tree
2.	*Under*, figuratively	**Sous** Napoléon	**Under** Napoleon
		Sous le règne de Louis XIV	**In** the reign of Louis XIV
		Sous le pouvoir de	**In** the power of
		Sous peine de mort	**Under** pain of death
		Sous le nom de	**Under** the name of
		Sous clef	**Under** lock and key
		Sous prétexte de	**Under** pretext of
		Sous mes yeux	**Before** my eyes
3.	*Within* of time	**Sous** trois jours	**Within** three days
		Sous peu	**Before** long

(b) *Au-dessous de*

1. *Completely under*	**Au-dessous de** la table	**Under** the table
2. Inferiority	**Au-dessous de** la moyenne	**Below** average

Sur. (for uses with numbers, hours, &c., see 139 (*e*), 142 (*c*), 150 (*d*))

1. Place on or on to which, especially completely on, or supported by (cf. **à** 2, 3)	Le verre est **sur** la table	The glass is **on** the table
	Un bateau **sur** l'eau	A boat **on** the water
	Assis **sur** son épaule	Seated **on** his shoulder
	Le chat saute **sur** le toit	The cat jumps **on to** the roof
2. Figurative *on*	La fenêtre donne **sur** la rue	The window looks **on to** the street
	Je n'ai pas d'argent **sur** moi	I have no money **on** me
	Des observations **sur** le mariage	Some observations **on** marriage
	Agir **sur** des renseignements incertains	Act **on** doubtful information
	Sur un air de Grieg	**On** an air of Grieg
	Sur un ton maussade	**In** a sulky tone
3. Immediately following	**Sur** cela. **Sur** quoi	Where**upon**
	Il est **sur** mes pas	He is **on** my tracks
4. Preference (cf. **avant** 3), or superiority	**Surtout**	**Above all, especially**
	Sur toutes choses	**Above** all things
	L'emporter **sur**	Prevail **over**
	Autorité **sur**	Authority **over**
5. Objective	Avancer **sur** Paris	Advance **on** Paris
	Tirer **sur** l'ennemi	Fire **on** the enemy
6. *From off*, with vbs. of taking (see 57 (*b*))	Prendre **sur** le rayon	Take **off** the shelf

Vers, envers

1. *Towards*, of place	**Vers** le sud	**Towards** the south
2. *Towards*, of time	**Vers** la fin du concert	**Towards** the end of the concert
3. *Towards*, of feelings or behaviour (usually **envers**) (cf. **pour** 10)	Bien disposé **envers** (**vers**) moi	Well disposed **towards** me
	Il a agi charitablement **envers** eux	He has acted charitably **towards** them.

SOME TRANSLATION PROBLEMS

The words dealt with in this list present some common problems of translation which cannot conveniently be dealt with in the Index.

The list only deals with the principal aspects of the words concerned, and does not attempt to replace a dictionary. The references to sections of the Grammar indicate where further examples or information may be found. In the case of prepositions, reference may also be made to Appendix B.

ABOUT

1. = *approximately*
   environ trois kilomètres   **à peu près** la moitié
   about three kilometres   *about* half
   vers midi   **près de** huit heures (142 (*c*))
   about noon   *about* (=*nearly*) eight o'clock
   vers le 4 juin (145 (*b*)) *about* 4th June

2. = *concerning*
   parler **d'**un événement
   speak *about* an event
   un discours **au sujet des** métaux
   a talk *about* metals

3. = *around*
   la campagne **autour** de Paris
   the country *about* Paris

4. = *up and down*
   errer **par** les rues
   wander *about* the streets

5. = *of*
   il pensait **aux** vacances (58)
   he was thinking *about* the holidays

6. = *just going to*
   il était **sur le point de partir**
   he was *about* to leave

ABOVE

1. adverb
   mettez le nom **au-dessus** (117)   put the name *above*
   la chambre **d'en haut**   l'étage **supérieur**
   the room *above*   the floor *above*

   preposition

2. —place or superiority
   au-dessus de la porte   **au-dessus de** la moyenne
   above the door   *above* average

3. —preference
   surtout   **sur** toutes choses   la patrie **avant** tout
   above all   *above* all things   one's country *above* all

AFTER

1. adverb (also = afterwards)

il vint **après**   quelques moments **après**
he came *after*   a few moments *after*
le moment **d'après**   the moment *after*

2. conjunction

après qu'il fut arrivé (239, 241 (c))
after he had arrived

3. preposition

après la réunion (241)
after the meeting
au bout de quelques minutes il sortit (142 (f))
after a few minutes he went out
il courut **après** moi   il est **après** moi sur la liste
he ran *after* me   he is *after* me on the list

ALONG

1. = *the length of*

il y avait des gardes **le long de** la route
There were guards *along* the road

2. = *by way of*

On y va **par** un petit sentier
One goes to it *along* a little path

AS

1. adverb—in comparison

aussi bien **que** moi   *as* well *as* I
il n'est pas **si/aussi** fort **que** moi (133 (b))
he is not *as* strong *as* I
il a **autant de** livres **que** moi (119, 133 (b))
he has *as many* books *as* I

2. —*as though*

il était **comme** mort (121 (b))
he was *as though* dead

conjunction

3. —time

comme il descendait l'escalier
as he was going down the stairs

4. —proportion

à mesure que l'eau s'abaissait
as the water went down

5. —cause

parce qu' (comme) il est malade
as he is ill

6. —*as if, as though*

comme si elle eût peur (121 (b) 3)
as though she was afraid

7. —*as long as*

tant qu'ils étaient là (239)
as long as they were there

8. —*as soon as*

aussitôt (dès) que je reviendrai (20 (a), 239)
as soon as I come back

AS (*contd.*)

9. —*as well as*	le chat, **ainsi que** le chien, en mourut (238)	
	the cat, *as well as* the dog, died from it	
10. preposition	faites **comme** les autres (121)	
	do *as* the others	
	se déguiser **en** pirate	
	disguise oneself *as* a pirate	
	il l'aura **pour** guide	
	he will have him *as* guide	
11. —*as far as*	**jusqu'à** la haie *as far as* the hedge	
12. —*as if to*	**comme pour** l'effrayer (121 (*b*))	
	as if to frighten him	

AT

1. generally **à**	à la gare	à Dijon	à trois heures
	at the station	*at* Dijon	*at* three o'clock
	à ce moment-là	*at* that time	
2. *at house or shop of* —**chez**	**chez** vous	**chez** l'épicier	
	at your *house*	*at* the grocer's	
3. emotion	s'étonner **de**	content **de**	
	be astonished *at*	pleased *at*	
4. State of affairs	**en** guerre *at* war	**en** paix *at* peace	

BE

1. description, location	les pommes **sont** pourries
	the apples *are* rotten
	le fer **est** chaud (cf. 2 and 4 below)
	the iron *is* hot
	il **est** là la salle à manger **se trouve** en bas
	he *is* there the dining-room *is* downstairs
2. personal feelings	il **a** chaud, froid (cf. 1 and 4)
	he *is* hot, cold
	ils **ont** faim, soif, sommeil
	they *are* hungry, thirsty, sleepy
3. age	il **a** quinze ans he *is* fifteen
4. weather	il **fait** chaud, froid (cf. 1 and 2 above), beau temps
	it *is* hot, cold, fine
	il **fait** du vent, du brouillard
	it *is* windy, foggy
5. duty, or destiny	je **dois** prononcer un discours
	I *am* to make a speech
	il **devait** mourir jeune he *was* to die young

BEFORE, IN FRONT OF

1. adverb	deux mois **auparavant** (**avant**) (117)	
	two months *before*	
	il a **déjà** parlé	
	he has spoken *before*	
2. conjunction	**avant qu'**ils sortissent (239, 241 (*c*))	
	before they went out	
preposition		
3. —place	**devant** la Mairie	
	in front of the Town Hall	
4. —time or	**avant** la guerre	**avant** moi sur la liste
sequence	*before* the war	*in front of* me on the list
5. —preference	l'honneur **avant** tout	
	honour *before* all	
6. —governing	**avant de** parler (241 (*c*))	
infinitive	*before* speaking	

BEHIND

1. adverb	rester **derrière** être **en arrière** (117 (*c*))	
	remain *behind* be *behind*	
preposition		
2. —place	**derrière** la porte	
	behind the door	
3. —sequence	**après moi** dans la queue	
	behind me in the queue	

BY

1. literal or emphatic	frappé **par** une balle	construit **par** un architecte
	struck *by* a bullet	built *by* an architect (see also 54 (*d*))
2. figurative and when usual construction after verb —**de**	frappé **d'**une idée	un tableau **de** Corot
	struck *by* an idea	a picture *by* Corot
	surmonté **d'**un drapeau	aimé **de** tous
	surmounted *by* a flag	loved *by* all
	atteint **d'**une maladie	
	attacked *by* a disease	
3. governing verb	**en** tournant le bouton (237 (*b*) (i))	
	by turning the handle	

BY (*contd.*)

4. means of transport   **à** bicyclette   **à** pied   **en** voiture
                            by bicycle   *by* foot   *by* car
                            par le chemin de fer
                            by rail

5. measure of   plus âgé **de** trois ans (128 (*e*))
    difference   older *by* three years

6. dimensions   six mètres de long **sur** un de large (150 (*d*))
                      six metres long *by* one wide

7. distribution   aller **par** deux èt trois, deux **par** deux
                      go *by* twos and threes, two *by* two

FOR

1. conjunction   **car** il ne sera pas content
                      for he will not be pleased

   preposition

2. —generally **pour**   **pour** moi   **pour** la patrie   coup **pour** coup
                      for me   *for* one's country   blow *for* blow

3. —time
   (*a*) —action   en 1941 il a demeuré $\begin{cases} \text{dix mois à Paris} \\ \text{à Paris } \textbf{pendant} \text{ dix mois} \end{cases}$
      completed   in 1941 he lived in Paris *for* ten months
   (*b*) action   je suis ici **depuis** deux heures (24)
      continuing   I have been here *for* two hours
                      quand je l'ai vu il travaillait **depuis** quatre mois
                      when I saw him he had been working *for* four months
   (*c*) —proposed   je suis à Paris **pour** trois jours
      duration   I am in Paris *for* three days

4. —cause   sauter **de** joie   se marier **par** amour
                      jump *for* joy   marry *for* love

5. —after certain   remercier **de**   blâmer **de**   punir **de**
    verbs = *on the*   thank *for*   blame *for*   punish *for*
    grounds of   pardonner **de**
                      pardon *for*

6. —dative   impossible **à** un enfant
                      impossible *for* a child

7. —*buy, sell, pay for*   je l'ai acheté (vendu) mille francs (152)
                      I bought (sold) it *for* a thousand francs
                      je l'ai payé mille francs (152)
                      I paid a thousand francs *for* it
                      j'ai payé le dîner (58)
                      I paid *for* the dinner

FROM

1. generally **de**	loin **de** la maison	**de** trois à quatre heures
	far *from* the house	*from* three to four o'clock
	une lettre **de** ma sœur	dites-lui cela **de ma part**
	a letter *from* my sister	tell him that *from* me
	on sert le dîner **à partir de** six heures (142 (*f*))	
	dinner is served *from* six o'clock	

2. with **jusqu'à**	**depuis** le commencement jusqu'à la fin
	(right) *from* the beginning to the end

3. point of time when action began	**dès** huit heures il travaillait à son tableau
	from eight o'clock he was working at his picture
	depuis son arrivée il n'a pas cessé de parler
	from the time he arrived he did not stop talking

4. after verbs of taking, &c.	prendre **dans** un tiroir, **sur** un rayon (57 (*b*))
	take *from* a drawer, *from* a shelf
	boire **dans** un verre drink *from* a glass

5. with countries	(see 75)

GO IN, GO OUT, GO UP, GO DOWN, &C.

1. *in*	il **entra**	il **entra dans** la maison	
	he *went in*	he *went into* the house	
	il **entra en courant**	he *ran in*	

2. *out*	il **sortit**	il **sortit de** la maison
	he *went out*	he *went out of* the house
	il **sortit en courant**	he *ran out*

3. *up*	il **monta**	il **monta** l'escalier	il **se leva**
	he *went up*	he *went up* the stairs	he *got up*
	il **s'approcha** d'elle		
	he *went up* to her		

4. *down*	il **descendit** il **descendit** l'escalier
	he *went down* he *went down* the stairs

5. *across, over*	il **traversa** la rue il **traversa** le pont
	he *went across* the street he *went over* the bridge
	il **traversa** le fleuve **à la nage**
	he *swam across* the river

6. *away, off*	il **partit** le train **partit**
	he *went away* the train *went off*
	un coup de fusil **partit** a shot *went off*

7. *on*	il **alla sur** le pont il **continua** sans s'arrêter
	he *went on* deck he *went on* without stopping

293

HOWEVER

1. connective adverb **ce-pendant, pour-tant, toutefois**

pourtant je m'y opposerai
however, I shall resist it
il y a **toutefois** des conditions
there are, *however*, conditions

2. in concessive clause **tout . . . que** (234.2) or **quelque** (invariable) or **si**, both with **que** and subjunc. sometimes rendered *though* in Eng.

tout inexpérimenté **que** je suis
however inexperienced I am/may be
quelque optimiste **qu'**on soit
however optimistic one may be
quelque vite **qu'**on y aille
however fast one goes
si importante **que** soit cette subvention[1]
however considerable this subsidy may be
considerable *though* this subsidy may be

3. = *in whatever way*

faites-le **comme** vous voudrez
do it *however* you like
de quelque manière qu'on s'y prenne
however one sets about it

IN, INTO

1. adverb (go *in*) preposition

(see GO above)

2. —generally **dans**
   (a) especially if = *enclosed by*

dans un compartiment   **dans** un fauteuil
in a compartment   *in* an arm-chair
dans une boîte
in a box

   (b) or if followed by definite article

dans le bateau   **dans** l'histoire   sortir **dans** la rue
in the boat   *in* history   go out *into* the street

   (c) or when noun is qualified

dans une grande prison   **dans** une joie fiévreuse
in a large prison   *in* feverish happiness

3. —in many figurative and other expressions where no definite article or qualifying word—**en**[2]

en paix   **en** colère   **en** prison   **en** voiture
in peace   *in* anger   *in* prison   *in* a car
en ville   **en** fleur
in town   *in* flower

[1] Note also this possible order:
cette subvention, **si** importante soit-elle.
this subsidy, however *considerable it may be.*
[2] See under **en** in Appendix B.

4. —direction	**du** côté de Paris *in* the direction of Paris	**de** l'autre côté *in* the other direction
5. —in fractions	un **sur** dix périt (139 (*e*)) one *in* ten perished	
6. —countries	(see 75)	
7. —manner	**à** voix basse *in* a low voice **de** cette façon *in* that way	**d'**une voix très basse *in* a very low voice
8. —months and years	**en** juin **au mois de** juin (145 (*c*)) *in* June *in* (*the month of*) June **en** (**l'an**) 1945 (148) *in* (*the year*) 1945	
9. —parts of body	porter **à** la main carry *in* one's hand	avoir mal **à** la jambe have a pain *in* one's leg
10. —seasons	(see 147 n.)	
11. —with superlatives	la plus grande ville **du** monde the biggest city *in* the world	
12. —time at the end of which	le train part **dans** une heure the train leaves *in* an hour	
13. —time within which or required	il l'a achevé **en** deux heures he finished it *in* two hours	
14. —time of day	ils sont arrivés le matin (143) they arrived *in* the morning à deux heures **du** matin (142 (*d*)) at two o'clock *in* the morning ils sont arrivés le 6 juin **au** matin (145 (*b*)) they arrived on 6th June *in* the morning	
15. —towns	il demeure **à** Paris, **à** Londres, **au** Havre he lives *in* Paris, *in* London, *in* Le Havre	
16. —weather	ne sortez pas **par** cette pluie don't go out *in* this rain	
17. *in order to, in order that*	(see 241 (*d*))	

JUST (adv.)

1. = *exactly* or *quite*	**juste** ici *just* here **juste** au moment où *just* when	**juste** alors *just* then	**tout** près *just* near voilà **justement** ce qui est arrivé that is *just* what happened

JUST (adv.) (contd.)

2. = *equally*

je cours **tout** aussi vite que vous
I run *just* as quickly as you do

3. = *only*

un **seul**   une fois **seulement**   il **ne fit que** rire
just one   *just* once   he *just* laughed

4. = *recently*

tout à l'heure   **nouvellement** arrivé
just now   *just* arrived

5. *have just*
   had just

ce livre **vient de** paraître
this book *has just* been published
il **venait de** s'asseoir
he *had just* sat down

LIKE

1. = *be fond of*

j'**aime** les beaux paysages   l'idée **me plaît**
I *like* beautiful scenery   I *like* the idea

2. = *wish*

je **voudrais** les emporter tout de suite
I *would like* to take them straight away
il **aurait voulu** danser
he *would like to have* danced
he *would have liked to* dance

3. = *of the same kind
   as*

il **ressemble à** son père   c'est tout **comme** chez
he *is like* his father   nous
    it is just *like* at home

Un homme **tel que** mon   A man *like* my uncle
oncle

4. = *in the same way
   as*

je pense **comme** vous   il parle **comme** un Fran-
I think *like* you   çais
    he speaks *like* a French-
    man

OF

1. generally **de**

la porte **de** la maison   il parlait **de** lui
the door *of* the house   he was speaking *of* him
l'amour **de** la patrie   un homme **de** génie
love *of* one's country   a man *of* genius

2. between numeral
   or indefinite, and
   disjunctive pron.

l'un **d'entre** eux   quelques-uns **d'entre** nous
one *of* them   some *of* us

3. material or com-
   position

un manche **en** ivoire
a handle *of* ivory
il consistait **en** deux boîtes carrées
it consisted *of* two square boxes

296

ON, ON TO

1. generally **sur** especially if = *supported by*	assis **sur** une chaise sitting *on* a chair **sur** cela je n'ai pas d'argent **sur** moi there*upon* I have no money *on* me	sauter **sur** la table jump *on to* the table
2. = *attached to*	suspendu **au** mur hanging *on* the wall	
3. location, including with parts of body	**au** premier étage *on* the first floor	un fusil **à** l'épaule a gun *on* one's shoulder
4. dates and days	il viendra mardi he will come *on* Tuesday il partit le lendemain (145) he left *on* the next day	il est venu le 5 he came *on* the 5th
5. governing verb	**en** entrant (237 (*b*) (i)) *on* entering	

OUT, OUT OF, OUTSIDE (see also GO above)

1. adverb	jeter **dehors** throw *out*	être **au dehors** be *outside*	maman est **sortie** mother is *out*
2. preposition	**hors de** danger *out of* danger	**en** (or **au**) **dehors de** la ville *outside* the town
3. —with verbs of taking, &c.	prendre **dans** sa poche take *out* of one's pocket	lire **dans** un livre (57 (*b*)) read *out of* a book
4. —in fractions	quatre **sur** cinq (139 (*e*)) four *out of* five	
5. —= *by reason of*	il le fit **par** amitié he did it *out of* kindness	

OVER (see also GO above)

1. = *above*	**au-dessus de** la porte *over* the door	**au-dessus de** cent *over* a hundred
2. = *over and across*	sauter **par-dessus** la haie jump *over* the hedge	
3. superiority	régner **sur** reign *over*	autorité **sur** authority *over*

SELF

1. Reflexive acc. or dat.	je **me** suis blessé I have hurt *myself* elle **s'**est vue dans le miroir she saw *herself* in the glass	je **me** dis I say to *myself*

297

SELF (*contd.*)

2. Reflexive after
   prepositions
   il la garde pour **lui(-même)**
   he is keeping it for *himself*
   tu le fais malgré **toi**
   you do it in spite of *yourself*

3. Reflexive **soi**
   only with in-
   definites, e.g.
   on, chacun
   on ne devrait pas toujours parler de **soi(-même)**
   one should not always be talking about *oneself*
   chacun pour **soi**
   each man for *himself*

4. Emphasizing sub-
   ject or object
   ils l'ont compris **eux-mêmes**
   they realized it *themselves*
   cela attaque le président **lui-même**
   that is an attack on the president *himself*

5. = *nothing else
   than*
   elle est la bonté **même**
   she is kindness *itself*

SINCE

1. adverb
   je ne l'ai pas vu **depuis**
   I have not seen him *since*

   conjunction

2. —cause
   puisqu'il est très intelligent (239)
   since he is very intelligent

3. —time
   depuis qu'il l'a rencontré (24, 239, 241 (*c*))
   since he met him
   il y a si longtemps **que** je l'ai vu (145 (*f*))
   it is such a long time *since* I saw him

4. preposition
   depuis la guerre (24, 241 (*c*))
   since the war

SO

1. = *to such an extent*
   il est **si** grand
   he is *so* big
   il va **si** vite
   it goes *so* fast
   c'est **tellement** difficile
   it is *so* difficult
   une peinture **si** célèbre
   so famous a picture

2. = *in this way*
   et **ainsi** de suite
   and *so* on
   ne me tourmente pas **ainsi**
   don't pester me *so*

3. = *therefore*
   alors tu ne viens pas?
   so you are not coming?
   donc il n'y a rien à faire
   so there is nothing to be
   done
   aussi nous devons ⎫
   aussi devons-nous ⎭ économiser
   so we shall have to do some saving

TRANSLATION PROBLEMS

SOON

1. = *before long*   on aura **bientôt** une nouvelle autoroute
   soon we shall have a new motorway
   bientôt la pluie cessa
   soon the rain stopped
2. = *early*   vous êtes arrivé si **tôt**/trop **tôt**
   you have arrived so *soon*/too *soon*

AS SOON AS (see AS 8)

SOONER

3. = *earlier*   j'y arriverai plus **tôt** que vous
   I shall get there *sooner* than you
   tôt ou tard
   sooner or later
4. = *rather*   j'aimerais **mieux** rester à la maison
   I would *sooner* stop at home
   plutôt la mort que le déshonneur
   Sooner death than disgrace
5. *no sooner ... than*   **sitôt** dit, **sitôt** fait
   no sooner said *than* done
   à peine eut-il quitté la maison **que** ...
   no sooner had he left the house *than* ...

SUCH

1. qualifying a noun   **un tel** homme   **de telles** gens
   such a man   *such* people
   une raison **pareille**
   such a reason
2. qualifying an adjective   de **si** grands bâtiments
   such big buildings
   une année **aussi** catastrophique
   such a disastrous year
   des idées **tellement** dangereuses
   such dangerous ideas

THERE IS, THERE ARE

1. existence, location, occurrence   **il y** en **a** qui sont malhonnêtes
   there are some who are untrustworthy
   il y a une poignée derrière
   there is a handle at the back
   il y eut une explosion
   there was an explosion

THERE IS, THERE ARE (*contd.*)

2. becomes visible or clear	**le voilà**	**voilà** la maison
	there he is	*there is* the house
	voilà l'explication	
	there is the explanation	

THROUGH

1. penetration	la balle lui passa **à travers** l'oreille
	the bullet went *through* his ear
	ils continuèrent **au travers d'**un bois épais
	they went on *through* a thick wood
2. = *by way of*	je l'ai vu **par** la fenêtre
	I saw him *through* the window
	on y arrive **par** une petite cour
	one gets there *through* a little yard
3. = *by reason of*	perdre **par** négligence
	lose *through* carelessness
	pour avoir manqué le train
	through having missed the train
4. = *by agency or means of*	c'est **par** lui que je l'ai trouvé
	it is *through* him that I found it
	cela s'est fait **par** un truc
	it was done *through* a trick

TILL, UNTIL

1. conjunction	restez là **jusqu'à ce qu'**il vienne (239, 241 (*c*))	
	stay there *till* he comes	
—wait *until*	attendez **qu'**il vienne (45 (*f*))	
	wait *until* he comes	
2. preposition	**jusqu'au** soir	**jusqu'à** l'arrivée du train (241 (*c*))
	until evening	*until* the arrival of the train
3. —in negative sentences	**pas avant** minuit	
	not until midnight	
	il **ne** viendra **qu'à** dix heures	
	he will *not* come *till* 10 o'clock	

TIME

1. occasion (which is or could be repeated)	cette **fois** je n'en dirai plus
	this *time* I will say no more about it
	gardez-le pour une autre **fois**
	keep it for another *time*
	quatre **fois**; plusieurs **fois**; **quelquefois**; **parfois**
	four *times*; several *times*; *sometimes*; *at times*
	de **temps** en **temps**
	from *time* to *time*

2. point of time

à ce **moment**-là ⎱
à cet **instant** ⎰ il se cachait derrière le mur
at that *time* he was hiding behind the wall

3. length of time

je marche depuis **longtemps**
I have been walking *a long time*
il n'avait pas le **temps** de le faire
he had not *time* to do it
tout le **temps** ⎱
pendant tout ce **temps** ⎰ la pluie tombait
all this *time* the rain was coming down
consacrer son **temps** à des recherches
devote one's *time* to research

4. right time for
something

ce n'est pas le **temps** de ⎱
le **moment** pour ⎰ faire cela
it is not the *time* to do that
arriver à **temps**, à **temps** pour la répétition
arrive in *time*, in *time* for the rehearsal

5. time with refer-
ence to the clock

je ne savais pas l'**heure**
I did not know the *time*
A cette **heure**-là les magasins seront fermés
At that *time* the shops will be closed
l'**heure** du dîner   à chaque **heure** du jour
dinner-*time*   at any *time* of the day
arriver avant l'**heure**, à l'**heure** exacte
arrive before *time*, exactly on *time*

6. period, season,
epoch, circum-
stances

en ce **temps**-là ⎱
à cette **époque** ⎰ je gagnais plus qu'aujourd'hui
at that *time* I earnt more than I do now
il y a chômage, à l'**heure** actuelle
there is unemployment at the present *time*
à cette **saison** il n'y a guère de légumes
at this *time* there are hardly any vegetables
en **temps** de guerre   au **temps** de Richelieu
in *time* of war   in the *time* of Richelieu
le bon vieux **temps**   les **temps** sont durs
the good old *times*   *times* are hard

TO

1. generally **à**

aller **à** la gare, **à** Paris
go *to* the station, *to* Paris
de cinq **à** six heures
from five *to* six o'clock

TO (*contd.*)

2. dative (see 167)	parler **à** un ami	je **lui** parle
	speak *to* a friend	I speak *to him*
	montrer un livre **à** des amis	
	show a book *to* some friends	
	il le **leur** montre	
	he shows it *to them*	
	inconnu **à** mon frère	
	unknown *to* my brother	
3. progression	de temps **en** temps	
	from time *to* time	
	de lieu **en** lieu	
	from place *to* place	
4. *to house* or *shop of*	aller **chez** Pierre, **chez** l'épicier	
	go *to* Peter's *house*, *to* the grocer's	
5. purpose, including after **assez** and **trop**	il l'a fait **pour** la fâcher	
	he did it *to* annoy her	
	je suis trop fatigué **pour** travailler	
	I am too tired *to* work	
6. with countries	(see 75)	
7. attitude towards	cruel **envers** les bêtes	
	cruel *to* animals	
	il a été bon **pour** moi	
	he has been kind *to* me	
8. forming infinitive	(see Chapter III)	

UNDER

1. Literally **sous**, **au-dessous de** (latter usually = *completely under*)	**sous** un immense tilleul	
	under an immense lime-tree	
	au-dessous de la table	
	under the table	
2. figuratively	**sous** Napoléon	
	under Napoleon	
	sous peine de mort	
	under pain of death	
	sous le nom de	
	under the name of	
	sous cet aspect	
	under this aspect	
3. = *less than*	**au-dessous de** dix ans	
	under ten years old	

WHATEVER

1. = *the*	ce **qui** te plaira	
	do *whatever* you like	

2. *no matter what*
   quoi qui (subject)
   quoi que (object or complement) with subjunc.

   quoi qui survienne, reste calme
   whatever happens, remain calm
   quoi qu'en puissent dire ses confrères
   whatever his colleagues may say about it
   quoi que ce soit qui vous tracasse[1]
   whatever it is that is worrying you

3. = *no matter of what kind or amount*
   quelque(s) or, with *être*, **quel(les) que**, with **que** and subjunc.

   quelques espérances **qu'**il ait pu conserver
   whatever hopes he may have been able to retain
   quels que soient les services **qu'**il t'ait rendus
   whatever may be the services he has done you

4. = *at all* (in negative context)

   il **n'**a **aucun** désir de se corriger
   he has no desire *whatever* to reform
   ne dis **rien du tout**
   say nothing *whatever*

WHOEVER

   celui qui/que with indic.
   qui que[2] (complement of *être* only)
   otherwise **qui que ce soit qui/que**[3] with subjunc. or, in formal language **quiconque**[4] (subject only) with indic.

   celle que j'ai vue, ce n'était pas votre fille
   whoever (*whomever*) I saw, it was not your daughter
   qui que vous soyez, sortez-en immediatement !
   whoever you are, come out at once !
   qui que ce soit qui m'ait pris mon portefeuille n'y trouvera rien
   whoever took my wallet won't find anything in it
   quiconque se présentera comme candidat devra . . .
   whoever offers himself as a candidate will be required to . . .

[1] **quoi que ce soit** (not followed by *qui* or *que*) = *anything whatever*. It is only used at the end of a phrase:
   Elle ne veut se priver de **quoi que ce soit.**
   She will not deny herself *anything* (*whatever*).
[2] Note also **quel que**, with subjunctive, in the sense of *whatever quality of person*:
   Quels qu'ils soient, je ne les admets pas.
   Whoever they may be, I am not letting them in.
[3] **Qui que ce soit**, not followed by *qui* or *que*, = *anyone whatever*. It is only used at the end of a phrase:
   Je ne veux pas le confier à **qui que ce soit.**
   I do not want to entrust it to *anyone*.
   Elle m'interdit de parler à **qui que ce fût** (Simenon).
   She told me not to speak to *anyone at all.*
[4] **Quiconque** at the end of a phrase = *anyone* (*else*):
   Il semblait comprendre cela mieux que **quiconque** (Simenon).
   He seemed to realize that better than *anyone else.*

TRANSLATION PROBLEMS

WITH

1. = *accompanied by* (literal or figurative)—**avec**	il sortit **avec** son camarade he went out *with* his friend	
	répondre **avec**[1] un sourire answer *with* a smile	
	agir **avec** prudence act *with* prudence	le jardin **avec** sa belle pelouse the garden *with* its fine lawn
2. instrument— emphasized	il l'attacha **avec** un bout de ficelle he tied it *with* a piece of string	
3. figurative and after many verbs —**de**	couvert **de** gloire covered *with* glory	content **de** ses efforts pleased *with* one's efforts
	rempli **d'**eau filled *with* water	chargé **de** pierres loaded *with* stones
4. physical characteristic	l'homme **à** la barbe noire (73 (*d*)) the man *with* the black beard	
	la maison **aux** volets verts the house *with* the green shutters	
	une boîte **à** roulettes a box *with* wheels	
5. physical attitude	il les reçut les bras ouverts (73 (*d*)) he received them *with* open arms	

WITHOUT

1. preposition (note omission of Indefinite and Partitive Articles)	**sans** cadre *without* a frame	**sans** nouvelles *without* (any) news
	sans l'aide de ses parents *without* the help of his parents	
2. conjunction	il disparaît **sans qu'**on le remarque he disappears *without* anyone noticing	

[1] Cf.: répondre **avec** un sourire
answer *with* a smile (i.e. answer, smiling at the same time);
répondre **d'**un sourire/par un sourire
answer *with* a smile (i.e. answer by smiling).

EXERCISES

The Exercises follow the pattern of the Grammar itself, and are not graded in order of difficulty. It is, however, fairly easy to select sentences relating to the ground actually covered.

The vocabulary, even in the more advanced sentences, has been kept as simple as possible.

The numbers in brackets refer to Grammar Sections.

USE OF TENSES (13, 14)

1. 1. I am looking for a job.
   2. Do you find that the meals are expensive?
   3. The photographers were waiting, but the singer did not appear.
   4. In half an hour we shall be at the frontier.
   5. This camera does not work very well.
   6. He did say it. I am not lying.
   7. The soldier realized that he had been talking too much.

USE OF TENSES (15, 16)

2. Indicate whether the Imperfect or Past Historic would be used when translating the verbs printed in italics.

When we *started* (1) next morning we *could* (2) see on our left the Knoll. The sides of it *sloped* (3) down towards us. Mount Terror *was* (4) connected with the Knoll by a great drift of snow. For three weeks we *slogged* (5) up towards the moraine where we *were going* (6) to build our hut. We *chose* (7) a moderately level piece of moraine where we might escape a good deal of the winds which we *knew* (8) were common. Altogether things *looked* (9) very hopeful when we *turned* (10) in to the tent.

USE OF TENSES (16–18)

3. These sentences are taken from an English translation of a French novel. Re-translate them, with special attention to the use of past tenses. Inverted commas indicate conversation (see 17 (b)).

    1. 'He brought me presents for my daughters.'
    2. He talked very little, and what he said was always interesting.
    3. He drank his coffee and went into the dining-room.
    4. There was a knock at the door and Lucas appeared.
    5. The gun was no longer in the flat.
    6. Maigret tried to imagine the scene.
    7. 'I asked her to make me some coffee, and she went out to buy some croissants.'
    8. As he was going out again an idea struck him.
    9. He did not want to miss the slightest chance.
    10. How did he spend his evenings?

USE OF TENSES (19, 20)

4.   1. After the police had left the two men came out of the cellar.
    2. They closed the gates as soon as the last person had crossed the line.
    3. Meanwhile the mechanic had quickly removed the old tyre.
    4. I will write to you again when I have time.
    5. After we have painted the inside we will do the outside.
    6. He said he would start as soon as the coach was full.
    7. They would know better when they had received all the results.

WILL, SHALL, WOULD, SHOULD (21)

5.   1. If we don't hurry we shall be late.
    2. Will you carry the bottles and glasses, please?
    3. Frequently he would forget what they were talking about.
    4. The doctor says I should stay in bed until Monday.
    5. She knew she was wrong, but she wouldn't admit it.

6. I should be very surprised if they have reached Switzerland.
7. I will not give my money to people like that.
8. Would someone help me to find the owner of this car?

TENSES AFTER SI = IF (22)

6.
1. If I receive no answer I shall write again next week.
2. If we had two thousand pounds, there would be no problem.
3. What can we do if you have lost the key?
4. If the rain should continue, the whole town would be threatened.
5. If you came back on Thursday I could give you some more.
6. If he had driven straight on he would have fallen into the canal.
7. Tell me straight away, if I am not doing enough.
8. If you see the same car again you should inform the police.
9. What if the old man were to catch us?
10. If we could help you, we would certainly do so.

TENSES WITH VENIR DE, DEPUIS, &c. (23, 24)

7.
1. A goods train had just passed, and the gates were still closed.
2. I have just learnt the news through my cousin.
3. This factory has been making furniture for 120 years.
4. He had been stealing his employer's money for several years.
5. Since our son went to the United States we have been alone.
6. Since we have been living in London we have seen better films.
7. I have had eight different jobs since the war.

INFINITIVE (25, 31, 32)

8.
1. Eating too much can be very dangerous.
2. They were talking of sending me to a new school.
3. What was he to do? How could he reach the other side?
4. Invite that woman? You must be mad!
5. He is not a man to decide quickly.
6. A thing to be done without delay.

7. House for sale, kitchen, dining-room, three bedrooms, &c.
8. We are very happy to be able to help you.
9. I have no desire to be present.
10. The quickest way would be to ring up the station.

INFINITIVE (27–29)

9. Write *faire quelque chose*, or *à faire quelque chose*, or *de faire quelque chose* after each of the following to indicate the appropriate infinitive construction.

accuser	craindre	éviter	mériter	préferer
aider	défendre	faire	se mettre	refuser
apprendre	devoir	il importe	ordonner	réussir
cesser	empêcher	s'intéresser	permettre	sembler
conseiller	entendre	laisser	persister	vouloir

INFINITIVE (30)

10.
1. Come and see my new car. I have just bought it.
2. You must make up your mind to do it before Friday.
3. Take care not to break the glass.
4. I am only asking to see it.
5. Have you ever thought of spending your holidays in a boat?
6. One begins by writing to the town hall.
7. Paul, see about preparing the drinks.

INFINITIVE (25–32)

11.
1. They watched him walk round the house.
2. Go down and tell her to stop making that noise.
3. We had to leave the house without waking the old grand-mother.
4. The greatest difficulty is to find enough paper.
5. We hope to find something to do this afternoon.
6. I have decided to have a house built in the country.
7. From here you can watch the cars coming across the bridge.
8. Send for the electrician.
9. He was somewhat surprised to find the luggage still upstairs.
10. Promise me to say nothing about it to my sister.

PRESENT PARTICIPLE (33–36)

12.
1. While looking for the photograph she had found some old letters.
2. Leaving the river bank the road climbs rapidly.
3. The cottage was charming, but there was no running water.
4. In the square there was a large crowd of people shouting and overturning cars.
5. The winners will receive the prizes later.
6. He earnt the money by working as a taxi-driver.
7. While wanting to help you, I have to think of the dangers.
8. On taking off his jacket he saw that there was blood on his shirt.

TRANSLATION OF VERB FORMS IN -*ING* (37)

13.
1. Sitting down all day is not good for the health.
2. Look left and right before crossing the road.
3. If you like listening to music, you may borrow my records.
4. They saw him waiting in the yard.
5. All night one heard the lorries passing on the main road.
6. The barometer is rising. We shall be having better weather.

PAST PARTICIPLE (38, 39, 43)

14.
1. Is this place occupied? No, no one is sitting there.
2. The injured woman was lying at the side of the road.
3. Surrounded by trees, the house was protected from the wind.
4. My sister is out, and Mother is not yet back.
5. The sum received is not yet known.

AGREEMENT OF PAST PARTICIPLE (40–42)

15. Re-write the following, making the Past Participle agree if necessary.
1. Elle est monté; elle a monté la valise.
2. Quelles nouvelles as-tu eu?
3. Les enfants s'étaient bien amusé.
4. Je leur en ai parlé.

5. Ils seront déçu.
6. Elle s'en est souvenu; elle se l'est rappelé.
7. On me les a rendu.
8. La maison a été démoli.
9. Elles se sont levé et sont descendu.
10. Nous nous sommes demandé la même chose.
11. Ces jolies fleurs que tu as apporté.
12. Nous n'avons aucune envie d'être écrasé.
13. Une idée qui m'est venu.
14. La situation a changé.
15. Elle s'est gravement blessé.

16.
1. All the girls have gone.
2. They had never met.
3. I have made them stay inside.
4. That woman has not told us the truth.
5. The road has been closed.
6. The storms which there have been.
7. What reasons have they given?
8. Has he heard us?
9. I have shown them the photo.
10. Some facts which she had not remembered.
11. The boys had disappeared without being noticed.
12. Have you looked for them?

SUBJUNCTIVE (44–49)

17. Is the Subjunctive necessary (or usual) in the following contexts? If it is, decide which verb would be in the Subjunctive and in what tense.

1. I am afraid of going out.
2. I am afraid you will have an accident.
3. He wanted them to help him.
4. He wanted to move his car.
5. It is possible that they have already gone.
6. It is certain they are not here.
7. They denied that they were involved.
8. They said that they were at home.

9. The last train of the day, which stopped at all stations.
10. The last passenger train which used this line.
11. I do not think he has got there.
12. Do you think he might be in difficulties?
13. It was a pity they had never seen it.
14. Let him get himself another!
15. I am ashamed to have forgotten it.
16. He ordered the coffee to be warmed up.
17. It is time they went.
18. It was not certain that it was lost.
19. There was no method which gave better results.
20. I did not think he was right.

18. Translate in full any *five* of the above sentences where you have decided the Subjunctive is necessary, and any *five* where it is not.

19. 1. One must wait until the train has passed.
2. It seemed that there was a third man.
3. It is true that they do not like each other.
4. May this never happen to us!
5. They prefer you to take dinner at the hotel.
6. It is important that we do not lose any time.
7. Mother is always afraid that we shall come home too late.
8. I am very glad that you have found it again.
9. I hope you are not too tired.
10. We must find a house which is farther away from the main road.
11. It was extraordinary that the car had not fallen into the river.
12. Did you know that there was someone else in the room?
13. He wanted his father to buy him a motor-bike.
14. There is no one who can do it better.
15. It was clear that the guests had already left.

VERB CONSTRUCTIONS (50, 54)

20. 1. Have you paid for the drinks? Have you paid for them?
2. I am looking for my best stockings. I am looking for them.

3. Don't listen to that man. Don't listen to him.
4. We saw the farmer open the gate. We saw him open it.
5. They made the driver wait. They made him wait.
6. I will make my father tell the truth. I will make him tell it.
7. Have you had your house repainted? Have you had it repainted?

VERB CONSTRUCTIONS (51–53, 55)

21.
1. That will please my uncle. That will please him.
2. I have not yet answered the letter. I have not yet answered it.
3. The owner offered the winners a free meal. He offered it them.
4. They borrowed clothes from the inhabitants. They borrowed clothes from them.
5. I have advised her to say nothing at present.
6. At Dover they ask everyone to open their luggage.
7. Do you allow your children to smoke? I have not forbidden it them.
8. Run to the policeman. Ask the policeman the way. Run to him. Ask him it.
9. The thought had come to her but she had paid no attention to it.
10. I have thought about it a long time. I can't give it up.

VERB CONSTRUCTIONS (56–58)

22.
1. They laughed a lot at my bad French. They laughed at it.
2. That depends on the depth of the water.
3. The children entered the building. They entered it.
4. Choose some fruit from the basket. Choose some fruit from it.
5. I would like to change this English money.
6. You must change trains at Rouen.
7. At the frontier they did not ask him for his passport.
8. She is really very nice but is sometimes lacking in tact.
9. I remembered that I had never paid for them.

10. They paid him well for his services.
11. She is always thinking of something else.
12. If you have no razor, you can use mine.

? **AVOIR** OR **ÊTRE** (59)

23. Complete by inserting the appropriate form of **avoir** or **être** to make the Perfect Tense, and make any necessary agreement of the Past Participle (see 40–42).
    1. Les enfants —— monté. Ils —— monté l'escalier.
    2. Elle —— né en 1881 et —— mort en 1952.
    3. Mes parents —— reparti et —— marché vers la gare.
    4. Deux valises —— resté en haut. Je les —— descendu.
    5. Notre ami —— resté deux mois chez nous. Maintenant il —— retourné en Suisse.

USE OF REFLEXIVE VERBS (60)

24. 1. Stop that man! Do the buses stop here?
    2. You must get up and dress.
    3. He felt ill and went to bed.
    4. I found myself in a large wood.
    5. They never meet. They never speak to each other.

PASSIVE (61)

25. Translate, using the Passive, or **on**, or a Reflexive, or some other means (see 61 (a) (iv)), as seems most appropriate.
    1. The boxes were brought down and placed in the hall.
    2. The door was opened by a disagreeable old woman.
    3. I was told that the post had been filled.
    4. The garage could not be opened because the key had been lost.
    5. The door was shut, but a light was seen at the window.
    6. The pond is completely frozen.
    7. The road was more used after the railway had been closed.
    8. I was asked for my ticket.
    9. This kind of cheese is only made in winter.
    10. The car was damaged, but no one was hurt.

313

AGREEMENT OF VERB AND SUBJECT (62)

26. Complete by putting the verb in the appropriate person of the Present Tense.

1. Philippe et moi (être) venus.
2. Vous, qui ne (dire) rien.
3. L'Assemblée (voter) le projet.
4. Combien de personnes (être) dedans?
5. Il y a très peu qui m'(intéresser).
6. Une foule de spectateurs (entourer) le Président.

MODAL VERBS

27. DEVOIR, FALLOIR (64, 65)

1. Tomorrow I shall have to buy the tickets.
2. It takes two and a half hours to get to the sea.
3. You ought not to smoke so many cigarettes.
4. Clearly we must stay at home this year.
5. This was to take place in the spring.
6. He should not have brought it.
7. They had to open their luggage.
8. He must have missed the train.

28. POUVOIR, SAVOIR (and CONNAÎTRE) (66, 67)

1. I could come next week.
2. Do you know who has written it?
3. The keys may be in your pocket.
4. I do not know this kind of wine.
5. He can drive very well.
6. That might be difficult.
7. May I borrow the matches?
8. My wife may have seen it.

29. VOULOIR (69)

1. I should like to drink something.
2. Will you wait a moment, please?
3. I went in, but they would not admit the dog.
4. We would have liked to stay longer.

MODAL VERBS (64–69)

30.
1. When I was younger I could walk all day.
2. It would be better to leave the car here.
3. If you don't want to do it, you should say so.
4. I knew that they might still be there.
5. It is the law. You must pay.
6. How much do I owe you?
7. There should be a better service than that.
8. My brother is to have the house and garden.
9. He knows trees extremely well.
10. The train may have left before time.
11. We might find a better hotel in the next town.
12. I ought not to have mentioned the perfume.
13. They had to fetch a tractor.
14. He cannot teach French by this new method.
15. Tomorrow may be too late.

ARTICLES (71–75)

31.
1. Wine is made from grapes.
2. Girls are not often interested in mathematics.
3. 1 fr. a litre; 2.50 frs. a metre; 8 frs. for 100 grammes; 1 fr. 80 a kilo.
4. 120 kilometres per hour; four times a year; once a day; two per person.
5. The farmer was carrying a big pole on his shoulder.
6. I have a pain in my knee.
7. They tied his hands behind his back.
8. He washed his feet in the stream.
9. She showed the doctor her swollen wrist.
10. This town is full of people with ugly faces.
11. She passed by me with her nose in the air.
12. Queen Elizabeth; President de Gaulle; Young Mozart, at Easter; on All Saints' Day.
13. Plan 4 is on page 112.
14. We are going to France, Spain, and Portugal.

15. After staying two years in the United States he returned to Africa.
16. We have offices in London, Moscow, and Cairo.

ARTICLES (76–79)

32.
1. They have a house like a museum.
2. Is there any cream? No, there isn't any cream.
3. Have you got a camera? Yes, but I haven't got any film.
4. I have brought you some melons. They haven't got any oranges.
5. It is quite good, but it is not real coffee.
6. I saw neither a car nor any tourists.
7. They offer only bread and cheese.
8. He never spoke about the war.
9. They have some fine animals.
10. Are there any rolls this morning?

ARTICLES (80–84)

33.
1. Man is always seeking happiness.
2. This tapestry is of great beauty.
3. She draws with intelligence.
4. I speak French but I have never learnt Spanish.
5. Lunch is at half past twelve.
6. He hurt his foot while playing tennis.
7. She laughs a lot, a sign of nervousness.
8. M. Tardieu, the owner of the restaurant, was imprisoned.
9. He only reads one thing in the paper, the sports news.
10. Jean-Claude is an intelligent boy.
11. My grandfather was an engineer.
12. Two businessmen were sharing a bottle of white wine.
13. We are short of bread, but there are some more biscuits.
14. Many of the beaches were covered with oil.
15. I need some help. It is a matter of urgency.

GENDER (88–92)

34. Add **le** or **la,** as appropriate (write **un** or **une** instead of **l'**)

raison	ménage	sentinelle
taureau	organisation	idéalisme
ornement	indépendance	lycée
spectacle	poule	réflexion
Espagnole	personne	bête

35. Translate (where there is no article in English, supply **le** or **la**).

an eighth	iron	China	memory
an oak-tree	Russian (language)	terror	a stove
Switzerland	happiness	a winter	a position (job)
chemistry	Sunday	a rose	a sum
a gramme	the south	painting	a tower

FEMININES (94–96)

36. Give the feminine form or equivalent.

vieux	un comte	vif	un monsieur
un élève	sec	un maître	doux
un Breton	un conducteur	un compagnon	un Russe
un époux	trompeur	long	inquiet
un neveu	un chien	neuf	un fermier

PLURALS (98–100)

37. Give plural form.

le travail	le monsieur	le passeport
le feu	un Bonaparte	l'oeil
la noix	le beau-père	faux
le journal	le chemin de fer	le pneu
nouveau	le lieu	la chambre-à-coucher

POSITION OF ADJECTIVES (104–8)

38.

the seventh day	a long road	a green, fertile valley
the French navy	an extremely high	the polished wooden
a small thing	wall	floor
an important reason	a very fine tree	an old toothbrush
a lost child	the poor little dog	an enormous vase of
	big dark clouds	flowers

317

AGREEMENT OF ADJECTIVES (110–13)

39. the woman found
    dead
  French industry and
    agriculture
  the old father and
    mother
  golden hair
  light green walls

the apple smells bad
a gas stove
the North Pole
copper wire
a master key

last year
next October
his own clothes
only the children
  knew it
the real position

FORMATION OF ADVERBS (114)

40. Form adverbs in **-ment.**
doux, large, sec, hardi, précis, évident, bon, heureux, tran-
quille, nouveau.

POSITION OF ADVERBS (115)

41. 1. They often meet the postman.
2. He thanked his host politely.
3. The boy had picked up an old tyre somewhere.
4. One can see everywhere recently demolished houses.
5. You should have come two days earlier.
6. I am taking five only.
7. Perhaps he has gone to the other station.

CERTAIN ADVERBS (117–21, 123, 125)

42. the front wheels
the underneath section
the top is square
to fall behind
a fairly large room
a little tired
there are very few restaur-
  ants
it is indeed important
tell me how to do it
how wide?

how much did you pay?
how many litres?
less noise, please
two metres more
I am very much annoyed
how are you?
as though dead
as if I were dreaming
as to though to reassure us
how kind you are!

EXERCISES

take another glass
it is not yet six o'clock
she works so fast
such little rooms
to wait so long

COMPARATIVES (127–33)

43. a better address
    not the least reason
    finer trees
    my oldest dress
    the most modern buildings

    the fastest train in the day
    three hundred metres higher
    the car is going better
    this is the least expensive
    the widest and highest door

    he has less money
    one more letter to write
    it is most encouraging
    a very disagreeable person
    wider and wider roads

44. 1. He works more than I. He works more than twelve hours a day.
    2. It costs less than four hundred francs. It costs less than the old model.
    3. In Australia there are more sheep than men.
    4. It is worse than you think.
    5. He has as much intelligence as the others.
    6. Write to me as often as possible.
    7. These holidays are not as long as the last.
    8. They have got a dog as big as a calf.
    9. It would be better to walk than to take the car.
    10. The more we thought of it, the less we wanted to do it.

NUMERALS (134–41)

45. Write the French form in full.

    16 19 21 48 73 81 95 100 101 512 780 1000 2191 10368 8m. frs.
    1st April, 21st July, Henry II, Francis I, in 1880.
    9th 21st 52nd 90th 100th 1000th $\frac{1}{3}$ $\frac{1}{4}$ $\frac{3}{4}$ $\frac{3}{8}$.

319

46. the first time
the last three days
a half-portion
one and a half bottles
a quarter of a metre
three quarters of the time

four fifths of the inhabitants
half hidden
one woman in three
thousands of flowers
a dozen eggs
thirdly

NUMERALS: TIME, DATES, &c. (142–52)

47. what time is it?
it is one o'clock
quarter to two
quarter past twelve (noon)
half past eight
exactly nine o'clock

at twenty to four
at ten past eleven
at three minutes to twelve (night)
about six o'clock
it is about ten o'clock
it was nearly nine

48. Write the French first in full (see 142 (a) (b) (d)), and then in figures and abbreviations, making use of 24-hour clock (see 142 (g)).

2 am. 10.50 am. 1.15 pm. 7.45 pm. 10.35 pm.

49. Half an hour, three hours and a half, a quarter of an hour, every two hours, he was ten minutes late, in the morning he felt better, every evening.

50. what is the date?
it is 18th February
on June 1st
Tuesday, 19th March
on 21st April in the morning
in January
it is Wednesday

tomorrow week
a fortnight ago
a month ago today
it is three years since he died
last month
last night on the television

I am leaving on Saturday
the shops are closed on Mondays
they are arriving on Friday
  evening
yesterday, the day before
tomorrow, the following day
yesterday evening
the following morning
how old is he?
I am twenty-four
a child of three
she is two years younger than I
in spring, in winter
in 1984

a bridge 600m long
the opening is 70cm wide
the maximum depth is 12m
the height of the mountain is
  3000m
a tube of 4cm diameter

the room is 3m long by 2m wide
the station is 2km from the town
three 80-centime stamps
I bought it for 400 frs
The tax is three per cent

PERSONAL PRONOUNS: CONJUNCTIVE (154–63, 167)

51. Re-write, substituting single pronouns for the words in italics.

1. *Ma chambre* se trouvait au troisième.
2. *Pierre* est un ancien collègue.
3. On n'avait pas trouvé *les clefs.*
4. Ouvrez *cette porte.*
5. Je crois *que la rivière est là-bas.*
6. Elle ressemblait *à sa femme.*
7. On ne pense plus *à cet événement.*
8. Demandez *à ces gens-là.*
9. Vous me retrouverez *à la gare.*
10. Elle n'est pas entrée *dans la maison.*
11. Impossible de s'asseoir *sur cette chaise.*
12. Il revient *de la ferme.*
13. Je me suis aperçu *du changement.*
14. Prenez *de ces pralines.*
15. J'ai pris cinq *billets.*
16. On parle *de construire une nouvelle route.*
17. N'as-tu jamais vu *notre prairie?*
18. Je voudrais emporter *les provisions.*
19. Voilà *le facteur.*
20. On va faire repeindre *la boiserie.*

52. Re-write, substituting single pronouns for each element of the phrases in italics.

1. Il a parlé *du projet à sa femme.*
2. Portez *ces paquets à la poste.*
3. Il volait *de l'argent à ses parents.*
4. Raconte *aux messieurs comment tu l'as trouvé.*

5. On n'avait rien dit *de tout cela à sa mère*.
6. Vas-tu laisser *la voiture dans cette rue*?
7. N'a-t-il pas dénoncé *ses camarades aux Allemands*?

PERSONAL PRONOUNS: CONJUNCTIVE AND DISJUNCTIVE (154–67)

53.
1. My dear daughter, you must be mad!
2. I am not buying any flowers. They are too dear.
3. They are people who do not encourage visitors.
4. I know him well. He is a man who came here after the war.
5. I have brought you a rose. Take it, please.
6. I have no intention of denying it.
7. Dinner is early tonight. Yes, I know.
8. The banks are closed on Saturdays. Why didn't you tell me?
9. There was a hole in the floor, and he put his foot in it.
10. I tried not to think of it any more.
11. My brother went to America but came back after two years.
12. She had forgotten the name of it.
13. It is delicious. Would you like some?
14. How many cups are there? There are seven.
15. Mother was not very pleased with it.

54.
1. Where are the scissors? Have you taken them?
2. Here it is! Keep it in your pocket.
3. Have you washed? Then get dressed quickly.
4. How can I describe it without having seen it?
5. It was impossible to make him work.
6. Show it me. I will give it you back.
7. Do they bring it to you in the bedroom?
8. Shall I introduce you to her?
9. I have not given them any.
10. If you trust him you should tell him the truth.

55.
1. There were at least ten customers in front of me.
2. It was a good idea, but they were not interested in it.
3. You can go if you like. I am staying here.
4. The farmer's wife herself was very kind to us.

5. It is he, the owner of the taxi.
6. You and I will have to do better than that.
7. It is an important matter for me and my parents.
8. He knows more about it than they.
9. She is keeping the best part for herself.
10. Sometimes one must think of oneself.
11. Go to him and tell him what I said.
12. If we pay no attention to them, they will not harm us.

DEMONSTRATIVES (171–73)

56. Insert **celui, celle**, &c., **ceci** or **cela**, as appropriate, adding **–ci** or **–là** where necessary.

1. Ne rigolez pas. Je n'aime pas ——.
2. Cette robe-ci ne me plaît pas. Je préfère ——.
3. Voila un hôtel! Est-ce —— dont tu parlais?
4. Il faut choisir entre les conseils du médecin et —— de ta tante Marie.
5. Il a été très aimable. —— est vrai.
6. Tous —— que j'avais vus portaient la même enseigne.
7. On lut ——: Fermé pour le mois d'août.
8. Il interrogea son médecin. —— hésita avant de répondre.
9. —— m'étonne que personne n'arrive.
10. —— est quelque chose de valeur.

DEMONSTRATIVES (174–76)

57. Insert **ce** or **il,** as appropriate.

1. —— est évident qu'il ne vient pas.
2. —— fera beau temps demain.
3. Tiens, —— est Papa qui revient!
4. On fera de son mieux, mais —— est presque impossible.
5. —— était important de le savoir au plus tôt.
6. Ce qui m'inquiète, —— est que la maison semble inoccupée.
7. Mon dieu, —— est déjà onze heures. —— est temps de faire le repas.
8. —— est au mois d'août qu'on prend ses vacances.
9. Il a triché. —— est clair à voir.
10. —— reste encore deux places.

DEMONSTRATIVES (168–76)

58. 1. This boy, this hero, this woman, those trees, these houses.
2. I shall never forget that day.
3. This material will last longer than that one.
4. These sheets are not those we sent to the laundry.
5. M. Bailhache was not the owner. We did not know this.
6. The Mayor was sitting beside the Prefect. The latter appeared half asleep.
7. If you have lost your passport you may not use your husband's.
8. That is a very bad reason.
9. It was freezing, and that made the roads dangerous.
10. It bores me to see nothing but museums.
11. What time is it? I did not know it was so late.
12. It was not easy to find the way.
13. It is very probable that they won't come at all.
14. What is it? It is a new model of Renault.
15. It is in spring that there is so much work in the garden.
16. Those who suffer most are the old and the sick.
17. It was fine yesterday and there was no wind.
18. She was a well-known artist.
19. All the same, it is a little discouraging.
20. It is a good idea to take both maps.

POSSESSIVES (178–83)

59. 1. His ticket, his suitcase, his idea, his wife, his other house, his high opinion.
2. Their house, your sister, her husband, my room and his, your family and theirs, my hat and coat.
3. One will lose one's money.
4. The signature is not his.
5. This land is ours, and we will not give it up.
6. At first I did not understand its importance.
7. The value of the house does not depend on its size.
8. A friend of his; a doctor friend of his.

RELATIVE PRONOUNS (185, 189–93, 196)

60. Complete with **qui** or **que** or **dont**.

Un cafe —— je connais	Les outils —— il me faut
Voila ton père —— arrive!	C'est ce —— j'ai dit
La femme à —— il pensait	Un employé —— nous avons vu
Les choses —— je parle	Tout ce —— m'intéresse
Des arbres —— sont en fleur	Un écolier, dans la serviette de ——

Une camarade avec —— je sors
Quelque chose —— j'ai besoin
Dis-moi ce —— il y a dedans
Moi, —— vous parle
Tous ceux —— assistaient.

RELATIVE PRONOUNS (185–97)

61. People whom we know

A door which is never open

You, who never want to go out

An event which astonishes me

The workers which there are at the factory

The tools with which he worked

A difficulty I was thinking of

The man beside whom he was sitting

The village in which we live

The day on which they arrived

Children whose mothers work

A path, at the end of which there was a gate

A matter of which he knew nothing

The man through whose carelessness this happened

Something on which I congratulate myself

What one doesn't know

All that he could see

That is what worries me

What you are thinking of

What I am grateful for

INTERROGATIVES (200–213) and QUESTIONS (243, 245)

62. In the first four sentences use both the short and the long form of the Interrogative Pronoun, e.g. **que** and **qu'est-ce que.**

1. Who told you that?
2. What have you done?
3. Whom did they arrest?
4. What is it?
5. Which kind do you prefer?
6. What reason has he given
7. What is making that smoke
8. What does one cut it with
9. Whose is that car?
10. Which of these roads is th shorter?

63.
1. I wonder who can have taken it.
2. What did you ask the policeman?
3. No one could tell us what had happened.
4. We knew very well what answer he would make.
5. What is there to do?
6. The wines are all good. Which shall we drink?
7. I don't ask whom she goes out with.
8. What was the title of that play?
9. It was impossible to know what he was talking about.
10. Whom did your brother invite?

INDEFINITE ADJECTIVES AND PRONOUNS
(215–23)

64.
1. We have no other friends.
2. Each evening the same thing happened.
3. Each of the designs was different.
4. At present there are certain difficulties.
5. The two gentlemen were supporting each other.
6. The houses had been built one beside the other.
7. There are two possibilities. Neither is pleasant.
8. The inhabitants themselves find it extraordinary.
9. He didn't even say good-bye.
10. I blame myself for the accident.

(224–30)

65. 1. They make one wait for ten or twelve days.
2. I have several purchases to make.
3. There was some difficulty at the customs.
4. We shall be going away for a few days.
5. Something unusual has happened.
6. Here is the pile of letters. Some are from abroad.
7. Such an event will have serious consequences.
8. I have had such a tiring day.

(231)

66. 1. All the night; every three days; the whole city; all foreigners; the whole of the beach.
2. All his papers; at any hour; of all kinds; in all directions; above all.
3. Everything was covered with dust.
4. The roses are all in the other garden.
5. Our grandmother lives all alone.
6. This collection is quite extraordinary.
7. Small though it is, it is extremely useful.
8. The gates were both shut.
9. We have received both replies.
10. Everybody has gone to the seaside.

PREPOSITIONS AND CONJUNCTIONS (237, 238)

67. 1. To the United States; from the north; because of her; without me; with what?
2. I will try to do it before leaving.
3. She remembered it after posting the letter.
4. That depends on the weight and size.
5. A well-situated house, which is not too dear.
6. So they will have to find another secretary.

CONJUNCTIONS (239, 240)

68. 1. Since it is so late, we had better put it off until tomorrow.
2. The cheese is kept in a cellar until it gets ripe.
3. They should arrive about 12.30, unless I have made a mistake.
4. You can look for a letter-box, while I get some petrol.
5. After they had examined our passports, we were able to go on.
6. Don't do anything before I come back.
7. Wait until they bring the bill.
8. This suitcase is too heavy for you to carry.
9. He had a boat ready, for fear that the water might rise higher.
10. We shall get there, provided the road is not too bad.
11. I used to walk a lot when I was younger and had more energy.
12. If it strikes twelve and we haven't arrived, don't wait.

PREPOSITIONS AND CONJUNCTIONS (241)

69. 1. I can do it without help.
I can do it without breaking the bottle.
I can do it without your telling me how.
2. You must buy it before six o'clock.
You must buy it before coming home.
You must buy it before the shops shut.
3. Read it while eating your breakfast.
Read it while I fetch the milk.
4. She never wears any jewels, for fear of losing them.
She never wears any jewels, for fear of someone stealing them.
5. We must put the butter in the box, so as to keep it fresh.
We must put the butter in the box, so that it does not melt.
6. There was no running water in the bedroom, so that one had to fetch it from the kitchen.
7. We lock the front door, so that the children do not go in the road.

QUESTIONS (242–43)

70. Translate first by using **est-ce que** and then by *inversion* (see 242, 243 (c) (d)).

1. Has he noticed it?
2. Did their friends help them?
3. Is the luggage ready?
4. Is it a good road?
5. Why has your father said that?
6. Where have those workmen put my brush?
7. Was the bus waiting at the station?
8. How much must one pay?
9. When does the new term begin?
10. Does the baker come every day?

QUESTIONS AND ANSWERS (244–47)

71.
1. I wonder if they are cheaper elsewhere.
2. Ask him whether the service is included.
3. Nobody knew when the museum was open.
   why the post had not arrived.
   where the information bureau was.
4. You have lost it, haven't you? No, I haven't.
5. Are we staying or aren't we?
6. He won't be there, will he? Yes, he will.
7. Is it raining? I think it is.

NEGATION (249–51)

72.
1. I have not brought them.
2. You will not find anyone there.
3. Don't buy anything too expensive.
4. Marcel has never been to England.
5. The central heating does not work either.
6. We have only seen the old part of the town.
7. Have you received any reply? No, none.
8. I told you to admit nobody.
9. We prefer not to stay too long.
10. The shops are only open for a few hours on Sundays.

11. I asked in my best French, but he only shrugged his shoulders.
12. Neither the hotel nor the bank would change our money.
13. Nothing new has happened.
14. None of these maps shows the new roads.
15. Nobody has come to see me.

73. 1. She no longer invites anyone.
2. These days I hardly go anywhere.
3. One could no longer see anything.
4. We never see any of our neighbours.
5. He never eats either meat or fish. (See also section 78.)
6. Have you ever tried to telephone in France? No, never.
7. We left without discovering anything.
8. It was impossible to warn anyone.
9. A vast plain. Not a tree to be seen. Nothing but fields.
10. I doubt if there is any possibility of repairing it.

APPENDIX C

ABOUT, AS, AT

74. 1. What are you thinking about?
2. I am about to start a new job.
3. A property of about three hectares.
4. The road goes as far as the next village.
5. Come back later, as we are very busy now.
6. The grass is as green as in spring.
7. She is still at the doctor's.
8. They were surprised at the result.

BE, BEFORE, BY

75. 1. It is hot, and I am thirsty.
2. The guide was to meet us at the foot of the big staircase.
3. I have never seen it before.
4. We shall meet before dinner.
5. It is a play by Sartre.
6. You will get there quicker by taking the other road.
7. The house was surrounded by woods.

EXERCISES

FOR, HOWEVER

76.
1. Thank you very much for this marvellous dinner.
2. The floods continued for three days.
3. We had been watching it for several minutes.
4. They had to turn back, for it was already dark.
5. I do not, however, want to spend too much.
6. However difficult it may be, you ought to make an effort.
7. However one looked at it, it was a curious thing.

IN, ON

77.
1. In prison; in this direction; in September; in London; in this way.
2. I am starting work in three weeks.
3. They hope to finish it in three weeks.
4. It is the oldest bridge in Paris.
5. Come back in the morning.
6. The next meeting takes place on 15th.
7. Turn right on leaving the building.

OUT OF, SO, SOON, THERE

78.
1. Please take my shoes out of the suitcase.
2. I apologise. I only did it out of ignorance.
3. There are no more trains, so we shall have to spend the night here.
4. Is it really so late?
5. The train has come too soon.
6. No sooner had we got home than the bell rang.
7. There will be an interval of ten minutes.
8. There is the street we were looking for.

THROUGH, TIME, NOT UNTIL

79.
1. One enters the castle through an ancient gate.
2. The water had come through my raincoat.
3. Several times; on time; supper-time; a long time; from time to time.
4. The next time we may be more fortunate.
5. At that time we were living in Algeria.

6. Could you tell me the time?
7. I have no time to see you.
8. The office does not open until nine o'clock.

WHATEVER, WHOEVER, WITH

80. 1. Whatever the answer may be, do not be discouraged.
2. They may do whatever they like.
3. Whatever they say in the papers, it is a dangerous situation.
4. The dog refuses to eat anything whatever.
5. Whoever you are, you are welcome.
6. Whoever left that gate open is no friend of mine.
7. You must not show this letter to anyone whatever.
8. The road was covered with broken glass.
9. He came back from school with his trousers torn.
10. That is the village with the modern church.